Global Re̶v̶i̶v̶a̶l̶

Worldwide Outpourings
Forty-Three Visitations of the Holy Spirit

THE GREAT COMMISSION

Revivals in Asia, Africa, Europe,
North and South America,
Australia and Oceania

Mathew Backholer

Global Revival – Worldwide Outpourings
Forty-Three Visitations of the Holy Spirit
The Great Commission – Revivals in Asia, Africa, Europe,
North and South America, Australia and Oceania

UK ISBN 978-1-907066-07-8

British Library Cataloguing In Publication Data
A Record of this Publication is available from the British Library

First Published in April 2007 under the title Revival and the Great Commission – Revised and updated, May 2010 by ByFaith Media.

- Jesus Christ is Lord -

Global Revival – Worldwide Outpourings
Forty-Three Visitations of the Holy Spirit
The Great Commission – Revivals in Asia, Africa,
Europe, North & South America, Australia and Oceania

'Lord, I have heard of Your fame; I stand in awe of Your
deeds, O Lord. Renew them in our day, in our time
make them known; in wrath remember mercy.'
Habakkuk 3:2 NIV.

'Give unto the Lord the glory due to His name; worship
the Lord in the beauty of holiness' Psalm 29:2.

- Mathew Backholer -

Contents

Content of Revivals and Awakenings

Continued over the page

Content of Revivals and Awakenings

Preface

'The works of the Lord are great, studied by all those who have pleasure in them' Psalm 111:2.

What is revival? When you want to explain what something is, it is often equally important to explain what it is not. This aids to eliminate any misunderstandings from the outset because the word 'revival' means different things to different people. It was the apostle Paul who wrote: 'If the trumpet gives an uncertain sound, who shall prepare himself for battle' (1 Corinthians 14:8), therefore, in section one; I explain what I mean and do not mean by use of the word revival (awakening and evangelism), as a way of introduction to set the scene. In the second section, there are forty-one historical accounts of revivals and awakenings (two accounts are in the appendices) and the third and final section, is the why and how of revival, our response, of how we can experience revival.

The apostle Paul declared in his letter to the Thessalonians '...always pursue what is good both for yourselves and for all' (1 Thessalonians 5:15b) and that is what revival is all about (as is the Good News being shared – part of the Great Commission). It is good for the reviving of Christians, and the Holy Spirit will in turn move hardened sinners to fall before the living God and to cry out for mercy and forgiveness, because whoever calls upon the name of the Lord (Jesus Christ) will be saved.

Out of revival, many good things happen, but one very important aspect is that Christians begin to take seriously the claims of the Great Commission and their individual and corporate responsibility towards it, at home and abroad.

Within this book, words of Scriptures that are in italics are the author's own emphasis, and unless otherwise stated, references to the word 'revival' means an outpouring of God's Spirit, a visitation, a true spiritual awakening. Though the Holy Spirit can still come down in renewal or during times of blessing such as the Toronto Blessing (1994) and Sunderland Outpouring (1994) which does not turn into revival, but the effect that it produces is instrumental in bringing refreshing to dry Christians, is glorifying to the Lord and edifying to the body of Christ. The Lakeland Outpouring (2008) was largely focussed on healings, and revealed the hunger within the body of Christ for the reality of the New Testament 'Book of Acts' now!

In times of revival there will always be a small minority who resist the Spirit of Grace and that includes those who are part of the Church; not everybody liked Jesus, some despised Him and all that He stood for, and that included many of the religious leaders of the day. See *Understanding Revival and Addressing the Issues it Provokes* by the author.

There is a danger in retelling history, (and Christian church history is no exception), to hype, exaggerate, distort or deny certain facts. As an avid revival historian with a keen eye for church history, I have endeavoured to be as accurate and as faithful to the true events as possible in researching, recording and collating another small portion of revival church history – and to God be the glory for the great things He has done.

The Proverbs declare, 'The heart of the righteous studies how to answer' (Proverbs 15:28a), and 'Diligence is man's precious possession' (Proverbs 12:27b) and it is to these two verses I have tried to exemplify in my writings to supremely lift up King Jesus to whom all honour and glory belongs and to pass on facts for future posterity.

'These things that you have heard from me among many witnesses, commit these to faithful men who will be able to teach others also' (2 Timothy 2:14).

Certain revivals in some Muslim populated countries, due to mass conversions, have upset the population (though any Muslim converting to Christianity is prone to persecution) and those in political power, resulting in persecution of individuals and sometimes harassment of the masses. For this reason, in the accounts of revival in El-Minya, Egypt, Eritrea and Malaysia, certain facts have to remain hazy, some names, dates and places are not given and my sources are not stated.

I gratefully acknowledge and appreciate those who have furnished me with factual accounts of revivals in which they were a part of and for those eyewitness who were present during times of revival. For those who have taken the time to correspond with me; have allowed me to interview them; who have informed and furnished me with their testimonies of revival, for aid in translation, and especially a big thank you for all those involved in the difficult, complex and labour intensive task of proofreading.

It is enjoyable to read about historical accounts of revivals, true spiritual awakenings, but let us not forget that our brothers and sisters are being persecuted around the world for their faith in Jesus Christ, the Son of God and Saviour of the world, many of whom were converted during times of revival. Please take a moment and lift them up in prayer and remember them during your quiet times.

- 'Remember the prisoners as if chained with them, and those who are mistreated, since you yourselves are in the body also' (Hebrews 13:3).
- 'Open your mouth for the speechless, in the cause of all who are appointed to die. Open your mouth, judge righteously, and plead the cause of the poor and needy' (Proverbs 31:8-9).

There is a present danger that by reading about the past, spiritual nostalgia can take over and we can become passive, this is not the aim of this book. I desire that we would become active in our prayers for revival, for our nation; (active in evangelism and world mission) whilst living up to the holy standard that God has set us – pleading His covenant promises so that the Spirit will be poured out on those who are thirsty, the Church will be revived and He will come and heal our land as floods are poured out on our dry and barren land. God will be glorified amongst the nations; Jesus will be lifted high (exalted in praise and adoration), drawing all men to Himself, the Holy Spirit will be given His rightful place within the Church and the desert will bloom once again and become fruitful.

The history of the Church has so many lessons to teach us today. It is not only foolish to neglect the lesson of the past, but ungracious not to pay tribute and honour, where honour is due to those who have gone before us and through whom many deep and precious truths can be learnt. I pray that through this book you will be able to discover some of these precious lessons and truths and be able to implement them in your own life on your own personal journey of renewal, revival and implementation of the Great Commission.

'One generation shall praise Your works to another, and shall declare Your mighty acts. Men shall speak of the might of Your awesome acts…they shall utter the memory of Your great goodness, and shall sing of Your righteousness' (Psalm 145:4, 6-7).

Section I

An Introduction to Revival

Chapter One

What is Revival?

'And it shall come to pass afterward that I will pour out My Spirit on all flesh. Your sons and your daughters shall prophesy, your old men shall dream dreams, your young men shall see visions; and also on My menservants and on My maidservants, I will pour out My Spirit in those days' Joel 2:28-29.

The Foundation in Understanding
In the eighteenth century, Britain saw its first Great Awakening (1739-1791), a nationwide revival under *John and Charles Wesley (*founder of the Methodists), and numerous other evangelical preachers including George Whitfield. A quarter of the population were converted, but the preachers, and especially Methodists were misunderstood and vilified by many. At the beginning of the Wesley's ministry the term 'Methodist' was vague and loosely thrown around. In Mr Vaughan's *Life of Robinson,* of Leicester, (a book from the eighteenth century) Robert's tutor and friend, Mr Postlethwaite, hearing that he was insistent on turning Methodist, with the kindest motives exhorted him to beware of them, 'to consider what mischief the Methodists were doing.' Robinson replied, "Sir, what do you mean by a Methodist? Explain, and I will ingenuously tell you whether I am one or not." This caused a puzzle and a pause!'

In around the year 1910, a Bible colporteur (an evangelist and seller of Bibles) arrived at the Rhenish Mission, Selindong on the Island of Sumatra where Dr. and Mrs Scriebner were working amongst the Battak villagers. The Battak's were former cannibals and head-hunters who had only received the Gospel in 1862. 'When Dr. Scriebner first operated on a native using chloroform, the report went around the country that he first killed the patient, then performed the operation, and afterwards brought him to life again.'[1] The Rhenish Mission Society was established in Barmen, Germany in 1828. Lutheran missionary, Ludwig Ingwer Nommensen, began working amongst the Battak people in Sumatra in 1862 and by 1880 entire tribes and villages began converting to Christianity. In 1871, Dutch Mennonites began working amongst the Battak people in

Sumatra which was the first Mennonite mission among non-Christians. The census of 2000 revealed that there were six million Battak inhabitants (in Indonesia and Malaysia) with 3.5 million Protestant Battak Christians so recorded the World Council of Churches (2009).

We can all have a little chuckle to ourselves upon reading the incidents of the ignorant Mr Postlethwaite or of the misinformed Battak people, but many Christians are just as ignorant of revivals from church history and misinformed about what revival is. To help reduce any misunderstandings of the word 'revival,' a foundation needs to be laid because Christian phraseology and verbiage can mean different things to different people and as doctrines can swing on a pendulum, clarity is needed.

The words: trinity, rapture, and soteriology (the doctrine of salvation) are all words that are not found in the Holy Bible, though their doctrines are. The majority of major Bible translations do not use the word 'revival' to describe a spiritual awakening; though by direct word of inspiration, in both the Old and the New Testament, 'revivals' are recorded by inspired inference and the concepts clearly laid out in the lives and events of many individuals and groups of people.

Five Revivals / Awakenings from Scripture
1. Those under King Hezekiah, who reopened the house of God (2 Chronicles chapters 29-31).
2. King Josiah, who acted on the Book of the Law which had been rediscovered (2 Kings chapters 22-23).
3. The city of Nineveh turning to the Lord under Jonah's reluctant repentance preaching (Jonah chapter 3).
4. Peter preaching at Pentecost when three thousand were instantly added to the Church (Acts 2).
5. Philip preaching in Samaria with miracles following as multitudes accepted Jesus Christ as their personal Lord and Saviour (Acts 8:5-8). See Appendix A for a complete list of revivals from the Holy Bible.

The Bible is full of spiritual principles and doctrines which are not as clearly laid out and defined as the Ten Commandments or the Beatitudes, but are nevertheless principles that have blessings for obedience and consequences for disobedience. If we obey the Scriptures we will get results, but if we violate them there will be consequences.

The laying down of the foundational truths of revival is exceptionally important as we all have differing views of what revival is. This is most clearly seen in books on revival and very evident between different fellowships in their prayer meetings for revival where some Christians are on a slightly different wavelength than others and some are very misguided in their praying.

The Word Revival

Out of five of the most popular versions of the Holy Bible, the Authorised Version (AV also known as the KJV), New King James Version (NKJV), New International Version (NIV), American Standard Version (ASV) and the New American Standard Bible (NASB); the word 'revival' is only found once. It is in the NKJV and has not been translated or interpreted to mean a heaven-sent revival or a spiritual awakening. It reads, '...give us a measure of revival in our bondage' (Ezra 9:8) which the NIV renders '...a little relief in our bondage.' The words 'revive' and 'revived' are found in all five of the above translations, from seven to twenty-seven times.

The word 'revival' first came into the English language in 1702; the standard definition being: an awakening in or of evangelical religion The word 'revival' comes from the Latin word 'revivere' meaning to live, to return to consciousness, to reawaken or a renewal of fervour, 'but strictly speaking' so wrote G. J. Morgan in *Cataracts Of Revival*, 'it means to bring to life again, to reanimate and has to do definitely with the Christian.' There can be no reviving of those who are dead in trespasses and sins; those who have never lived, cannot be reanimated. But wherever there is a reviving of Christians there will always be the conversion of sinners. Arthur Skevington in his book, *And With Fire* noted that 'revival [in the Holy Bible] is throughout associated with varying forms of the root hāyā, to live. The general sense of the verb usually (though not uniformly) translated 'to revive' is to quicken, to impart fresh life.'

Eighteenth century revivalist, Christmas Evans wrote: 'Revival is God bending down to the dying embers of a fire just about to go out and breathing into it until it bursts once again into flame.'

Revival Is

The word 'revival' means different things to different people, therefore a definition is in order to separate it from its adjuncts and accessories. Revival is essential for the life and well-being of the Church. Revival glorifies God, vindicates His name, uplifts Jesus, gives the Holy Spirit His rightful place in the Church, raises the high and holy standard of the body of Christ and saves sinners who become part of the Church. The term 'revival' also incorporates the definitions: an outpouring of the Holy Spirit, the Holy Spirit falling, the Spirit of God descending, God coming down, God visiting His people, a visitation, a spiritual awakening, days of heaven on earth and the presidency of the Holy Spirit in the Church.

Revival is the Church being saturated with God. Revival is primarily intended for the Church so that they can be revived into a true, proper and correct relationship with God. From this, revival, a spiritual awakening begins to affect those who are outside of the Church to a lesser or greater degree.

Revival is God rending the heavens and coming down, the hills melting like wax before His presence. It is water being poured out on the thirsty and floods on the dry ground. It is a turning from darkness to light, from the power of satan to God, a casting off of the works of darkness, the lights of the world becoming brighter and the city on the hill so illuminated that those who once sat in darkness can now see the light.

The word 'revival' is used to explain the amazing results of an outpouring of the Spirit of God, a spiritual awakening, when people are saved and communities are changed and become God-fearing. Firstly, the Church (God's people) gets on fire for God, as the Holy Spirit revives the body of Christ. Secondly, the Holy Spirit convicts non-Christians, (who become awakened) and shows them their sinfulness and their need of the Saviour, Jesus Christ. God is ultimately glorified, Jesus is exalted and the Holy Spirit is given His rightful place to move within the Church and work through the body of Christ.

Selwyn Hughes, founder of Crusade for World Revival (CWR) wrote: 'Revival is heaven overflowing its banks, producing in the Church such a sense of Divine majesty and power that it causes both Christians and non-Christians to stand in awe of the living God.'

Chapter Two

The Concept of Revival

'For I will pour water on him who is thirsty, and floods on the dry ground; I will pour My Spirit on your descendants, and My blessing on your offspring; they will spring up among the grass like willows by the watercourses' Isaiah 44:3-4.

The Word Revival

The word 'revival' is used to explain the amazing results of an outpouring of the Spirit of God, a visitation of the Holy Spirit, when Christians are revived, sinners are saved and communities are changed and become God-fearing. Firstly, the Church gets on fire for God, as the Holy Spirit revives the body of Christ. Secondly, the Holy Spirit convicts the souls of non-Christians, who become awakened and reveals to them their sinfulness and their need of the Saviour, Jesus Christ.

The term 'revival' also incorporates the definitions: an outpouring of the Holy Spirit, a visitation, a spiritual awakening, the Holy Spirit falling, the Spirit of God descending, God coming down, God visiting His people, a Pentecost, days of heaven on earth and the presidency of the Holy Spirit in the Church. A revival can come suddenly or gradually, accumulating in a spiritual climax and either run its course gradually or suddenly end.

The Order of Revival

Theologically and historically the river of revival is primarily inwardly intended for the reviving of the Church (the body of Christ), but it will naturally flow outwards and brings to life those who are dead in their trespasses and sins (non-Christians) because God has no pleasure in the death of the wicked. During times of revival, Christians always get revived before sinners get converted, because that is a spiritual law of revival. There is no point in God saving sinners if they are going to be placed in a church that is stale, stagnant and decaying because they will not grow or bear fruit, but will be stifled until the life is choked from them. On very rare occasions (the exception and not the norm), revival can be for those who are completely dead in their trespasses and sins. In these rare cases, it is a positive confirmation of Jesus' words which were spoken on the subject of lazy servants and hell, when He said, "I reap where I have not sown, and gather where I have not scattered seed" (Matthew 25:26). This is what happened in the case of the city of Nineveh who repented under Jonah's preaching, (the reluctant revivalist) who declared, "Yet forty days, and Nineveh shall be overthrown!" No seed was scattered, just a warning of judgment, but the people repented, responded and were gathered for the Kingdom. In a similar sense, it was like Jonah at Nineveh, when he preached to the Assyrians. They proclaimed a fast, turned to the Lord in repentance and changed their lifestyles (Jonah chapter 3). From revival church history, this concept is hard to discover because the likes of John Wesley, George Whitefield, Jonathan Edwards, Charles Finney, Dwight L. Moody, Duncan Campbell, Mary Morrison, Carlos Annacondia and Steve Hill etc. were preaching to both Christians and non-Christians, either in a church building or out in the open air to those who had congregated. Most, if not all of those present would have had a basic understanding of Christianity, with a church background in some form, even if they only went to a place of worship for christenings, weddings and funerals or during the festive seasons of Easter, harvest or Christmas. But this rare concept was demonstrated amongst the Angas tribe in Nigeria, (see appendix B).

Concepts of Revival

There are four main concepts (not definitions) of the word revival, they are:
1. A localised revival of a Church (the congregation) or community.
2. A national revival within towns, amongst a people group or across a nation.
3. An evangelistic campaign, (see chapter three).
4. A revival of religion – when people become interested in Christianity, (see appendices C and D).

The first two concepts of revival are heaven-sent, but they differ in degree, effect, manifestation and duration. The third is manmade, an organised event, and the final concept is a dictionary definition of a resurgence of – (Christianity or other).

Generally speaking, none of the four concepts are without the blessing of God on the preacher or evangelist, which results in rejoicing in heaven over sinners converted and lives transformed, though mass movements more often than not produce Christians in name only; as they have not been 'born again' and passed 'from death to life.'

With the first two concepts, the Holy Spirit comes in extreme convicting power (John 16:8) and there does not necessarily need to be a preacher or evangelist present at the inception of the revival, (though he or she will be highly anointed during it). During the Lewis Revival (1949-1952) seventy-five percent of the people were converted outside off the church building as the Holy Spirit simultaneously descended on the moorlands and the congregation who were at church.

During many great evangelistic campaigns, people outside of the Church can also be quickened to their sinful state and illuminated to their need of the Saviour, Jesus Christ.

Revival church history reveals that the correct terminology of the word 'revival' to distinguish it from other events which have usurped its name is: a localised revival (amongst a Church or community) or a national revival (within towns, people group or nation).

Eighteenth century preacher, theologian and revivalist, Jonathan Edwards, wrote: 'God hath had it much on His heart, from all eternity, to glorify His dear and only begotten Son; and there are some special seasons that He appoints to that end, wherein He comes forth with omnipotent power to fulfil His promise and oath to Him; and these times are times of remarkable pouring out of His Spirit, to advance His Kingdom; such a day is a day of His power.'

Local and National Revivals

A localised revival of a Church or community is a quickening from the Holy Spirit as Christians are revived. A national revival is where not only the Church becomes revived, but towns, a people group or nation gets transformed. A national revival is a visitation of the Holy Spirit on a people group, towns or nation. A national revival, is sometimes referred to as an awakening, but this does not mean that every village, town or city within the nation that experiences a national revival gets affected. Localised and national revivals differ in degree, effect, manifestation and duration. Whilst we can have a quickening of Christians without a visitation on towns, a people group or nation, we can never have a visitation without a quickening of the Christians. Arthur Wallis wrote: 'The quickening of the saints is the root, while the saving of sinners is the fruit.' The quickening, a reviving of Christians is 'floods being poured on the dry ground' (Isaiah 44:3) so that Christians get on fire for God and have renewed consecration and zeal – The Holy Spirit comes to refine, purify and to wash clean, to 'purge them as gold and silver that they may offer to the Lord an offering of righteousness' (Malachi 3:1-3). Only after the Christians have been quickened then a visitation of the Holy Spirit which is broader in effect (on towns, a people group or a nation) is possible and very probable as long as the Church keeps praying, seeking and pleading for the heavens to be rent and for God to come down – The Holy Spirit descends to 'convict the world of sin, and of righteousness and of judgment' (John 16:8).

A Localised Revival
1. Many individuals can share a common experience, but not multitudes.
2. It revives a Church or community.
3. The Church allows the Holy Spirit to move as He wants to within the church building, (whilst individuals in revival more frequently *fully* surrender themselves to God and are *filled* with the Holy Spirit).
4. It can be continuous for a few days, weeks, months or years, though the latter length is not so common.

A National Revival
1. Multitudes of people share a common experience.
2. It not only revives Christians, but can transform towns, a people group or a nation.
3. The Holy Spirit permeates the atmosphere, and the revival (which is often a collection of revivals over a geographical area) is accompanied with supernatural phenomena, frequently signs and wonders of biblical proportion. (Signs and wonder are not confined to times of revival – see 1 Corinthians 12 & 2 Corinthians 12:12).
4. It comes and passes, though the fruit abides, but the Church can still be revived and continue in a localised revival. This type of revival within towns, amongst a people group or across a nation, generally lasts for at least two years, but can continue for a decade or more in sporadic places across a nation.

Within this book, unless otherwise stated, all the accounts of revivals are either localised or national and the differences, though not stated can be clearly seen and are revealed through the forty-three visitations of the Holy Spirit.

The Word Awakening

The word 'awakening' first came into the English language in 1736, when Jonathan Edwards' published a letter referring to a 'general awakening' amongst his flock at Northampton, Massachusetts, New England, during 1734-1735 when virtually the whole town was converted. In the context of Edwards' letter, the definition of the word was: an awakening of conscience among the people.

The dictionary definition of an awakening in a religious sense is 'to become awake or conscious.' For Christians, they become awake or conscious to the greater need they have of making Jesus Christ their Lord and not just their Saviour. For non-Christians, they become awake or conscious that they are dead in their sins and trespasses and need Jesus as their personal Saviour (and Lord).

In 1929, Elmer T. Clark published *Psychology of Religious Awakening* that includes the listed data of 2,174 subjects from a religious questionnaire that was filled out by people at sixty different colleges in the USA. This data represented 50,000 entries of facts and was compiled and analysed in 1929. The book is the psychology behind Christian conversion (religious awakening). The author also compared data from the previous generation (1899) and come to some interesting conclusions. Whilst the book is more academic than spiritual, in some cases the terminology of Clark is more in line with evangelistic fervour rather than the Spirit of God being poured out in true heaven sent revival. But Clark does makes reference to revivalists (Wesley, Whitefield, Edwards, the Tennents and Billy Sunday) and various revivals (the Northampton Revival 1734-1735 revivals in Kentucky 1800+ & the wilderness, Great Awakening in the States and the Fulton Street Revival of 1858+). Clark states that there are three types of awakening – (in relation to individual conversion): crisis, emotional and gradual.

What Jonathan Edwards initially called a 'general awakening' (of a group of people) we would now call a revival because the word 'awakening' within revival church history has taken on a larger and more specific meaning. Though some people still refer to individual being awakened in the context of realising their sinfulness and surrendering their lives to the Saviour, and there is joy in heaven over every repentant sinner.

Concept of an Awakening

In a religious sense and in the context of a heaven-sent revival, the word 'awakening' is not as easy to define as the word 'revival,' but it is more distinguishable through the accounts of revival church history. The concept of an awakening is now best understood as a national revival that is deeper in its effect and longer in duration. As an analogy, an awakening is a collection of forest fires that consume and covers vast sways of tinder dry countryside. The flames can leap across roads, fields or rivers and ignite on the other side and are blown as the wind chooses, bypassing some villages or towns whilst engulfing others. However, whilst an awakening consists of many revival fires, they are united under the Divine conflagration for the glory of God. An awakening is more in depth than a national revival; they frequently carry on for years or decades and widely affect the moral makeup of society. If a four point criteria have been fulfilled, a national revival (in due time) can sometimes be referred to as an awakening.

Four Point Criteria – An Awakenings

Based on my research from revival church history, there is a four point criteria as to whether a national revival can be historically classified as an awakening or not. This criterion in no way decries any national revival, or any move of God but is purely intended as a historical reference for future researchers and classification of an awakening (of a nation).

This four point criteria is:

1. Simultaneous revivals breaking out in a complete geographical area such as an island, county, state, nation or within a people group, (whom may live both sides of manmade boundary, even straddling international borders).
2. The duration of the revival has to exceed a minimum period of four years.
3. A minimum of fifteen percent of its population must repent of their sins and give their lives to Jesus Christ, being "born again" as Jesus said.
4. It must affect the moral makeup of the island, county, state, nation or people group. There must be a notable change within society in general – social transformation.

The best examples of awakenings from revival church history, due to the duration of simultaneous revivals in a geographical location and the percentage of conversion per population is the American Great Awakening (1735-1760) and the British Great Awakening (1739-1791). From my research of noting more than one thousand revivals and awakenings, I have come to a conservative conclusion that on average, for every one hundred revivals in church history there is one awakening, but that is merely an observation, not a pretext for a formulae! For more information about awakenings see appendix E.

Global Awakenings

There is also the concept of a global awakening when simultaneous revivals break forth at the same time or when one revival ignites revival fires in different countries and on different continents and reverberates around the globe (encouraging Christians to pray for revival for their own church, town or nation). Global awakenings generally occur every fifty years or so – a Jubilee, but is more of a general observation, not a guaranteed outcome. Global awakenings are most clearly demonstrated during the years 1857-1860 (which was birthed from the Fulton Street Prayer Meeting Revival, see page 74) and the years 1904-1910 which was birthed from the Welsh Revival (1904-1905) leading to other revivals, (though some are unrelated as revivals are continually igniting as the Holy Spirit descends), the Mukti Revival (1905-1906), Khasi Hills Revival (1905-1906), Korean Revival Movement (1903-1906), revival in China and Manchuria (1906-1909), Azusa Street Revival (1906-1909), Pyongyang Great Revival, Korea (1907-1910), Fukuoka Revival (1906 and 1907, at a holiness convention and crusade in Japan), Norway (1907), India (1908), Arima, Japan (1909) and Osaka Girls School, Japan (1910).

Personal Revival

What all disciples of Jesus Christ should be doing is to seek God's face for their own personal revival (when this happens amongst a group it can also be known as a renewal), a quickening of ones personal life. Seeking God and praying, not only for a localised revival within their Church, but a national revival for their nation. It has been said that the greatest enemy to each individual is self – self that has not surrendered to God. We have not offered our bodies as 'living sacrifices' which is merely our reasonable service (Romans 12:1), nor taken up our cross daily and followed the Master (Matthew 16:24). As the Scriptures declare, Jesus 'died for all, that those who live should live no longer for themselves, but for Him who died for them and rose again' (2 Corinthians 5:15). All too often it is not Thy will be done, but *my will* be done. Self must be crucified and dethroned. If we truly desire to see our lives changed in personal revival – which always precedes local or national revival, then we must die to self. See also Galatians 2:20.

Oh, God, "Send revival, and start the work in me" should be our cry to our heavenly Father, whose will should be done on earth, as it is in heaven. "I must decrease and He must increase" should also be our declaration, repeating the words of John the Baptist – the revivalist (John 3:30).

Kevin Adams in his book, *A Diary of Revival* wrote: 'Evan [Roberts of the Welsh Revival 1904-1905] was convinced that the way to national revival was through the Church, and the way to revive the Church was through the individual.'

- C.T. Studd founded the Worldwide Evangelisation Crusade (WEC) in 1914. His motto, which became the motto of WEC is: 'If Jesus Christ be God and died for me, then no sacrifice can be too great for me to make for Him.'
- During the World Wars, the Chinese of China had a Five Year Plan of advancement with the motto commended to every member: 'Lord, revive Thy Church, beginning with Me.' See Psalm 139:23-24.
- Dr. Joe Church was a medical missionary to East Africa in the 1940s who was a leader of the East Africa Revival (1930s-1950s). His motto card was: 'Not I, but Christ' on which the 'C' of Christ was shown as a bent 'I'.

Revival is for the glory of God, because as Peter, in his first epistle wrote: 'Gentiles...glorify God in the day of visitation' (1 Peter 2:12). Jesus is exalted and the Holy Spirit is welcomed to move in the Church. Christians get revived because God said, "I will pour water on him who is thirsty, and floods on the dry ground" (Isaiah 44:3), and sinners get converted because Jesus said, "When He [the Holy Spirit] comes, He will convict the world of sin, and of righteousness and of judgment" (John 16:8). Backsliders are also drawn back into the fold of God and communities can be transformed.

Chapter Three

Evangelism Verses Revival

Thus says the Lord, "Rain down, you heavens, from above, and let the skies pour down righteousness; let the earth open, let them bring forth salvation, and let righteousness spring up together. I the Lord have created it" Isaiah 45:8.

Evangelism verses Revival

In around the mid-1860s in North America, the word 'revival' began to be linked to evangelistic campaigns; man-planned events rather than Divinely God-orchestrated. As an example, evangelist, Reuben A. Torrey (who saw revival on some of his campaigns) edited *How To Promote And Conduct A Successful Revival with Suggestive Outlines* (1901) which was written as a guide to evangelists on motivating the believers. By the 1920s, revival and evangelism were glued to this concept and became known as revivalism. This distorted meaning of the word 'revival' is in many places now considered an organised and controlled event so that you can have a "revival" without changed lives, repentance or conversions! One church can have revival meetings every Friday and Saturday evening, whilst another has them every evening except Friday and Saturday! Evangelistic events and campaigns are great, but there is a gigantic difference between effective evangelism (man-planed) and revival (heaven-sent), though out of an evangelistic campaign a revival can break forth. Revival cannot be put together, manufactured or produced. If it can be planned, orchestrated and be turned on or off then it cannot be revival. Revival cannot be worked up, but it needs to come down as the Spirit of God is poured forth from on high.

In evangelism, the focus is on the evangelist or preacher, and many who profess Christ soon fall by the wayside. But, in revival the focus is on God, and the vast majority of those who profess Christ stay true to Him as abiding fruit. The exceptions can be when new Christians are not discipled (and therefore they can easily fall prey to false teachers, false prophets etc.) and / or if they are illiterate or do not have the word of God in their own language so they cannot fully distinguish between the clean and the unclean, the holy and the unholy and thus being ignorant of the precepts of God are unable to live by them; and they will be judged by the light they have received.

In effective evangelism, God may bless the work and people will respond to the call of repentance and give themselves to Jesus. However, in revival there is an overpowering presence and move of the Holy Spirit regardless of the anointed evangelist or minister's exhortation for people to repent. The people will be moved by God's Spirit to repent, often breaking down and will pour out their hearts to the Almighty, which can lead to the transformation of a church, town, community, people group or country.

Selwyn Hughes wrote: 'Evangelism is the expression of the Church; revival is an experience of the Church. Evangelism is the work we do for God; revival is the work God does for us.'

Twentieth century evangelist, revivalist and revival historian, J. Edwin Orr expressed it well, when he said, "In times of evangelism, the evangelist seeks the sinner, in times of revival the sinners comes chasing after the Lord."

Sam H. Hadley of Water Street Mission, New York, led more than thirty-five thousand drunkards to Christ, but this in itself does not constitute revival and does not make Hadley a revivalist, but a man with an intense anointing from God, a supreme soul-winner. Gideon L. Powell wrote: 'He was a personal soul-winner, Spirit-filled, Spirit-anointed, Spirit-baptised Christian, seeking by personal effort to win others for Christ!...It is not learning, nor rhetoric, nor logic, nor oratory, nor social prestige – although, God can use all of these, But it is the Holy Spirit that is the great dynamic of evangelism.'[2]

Revival and Evangelistic Campaigns

Revival is not an organised event, though out of an organised event, such as an evangelistic campaign or during effective evangelism, revival can break forth. This has happened during William Booth in Hayle, Cornwall, England (1860-1861), D. L. Moody's Campaign in Great Britain (1875), *Stephen Jeffreys in Cwmtwrtch, South Wales (1913), Billy Graham's Boston Campaign in America (1950) and under Tommy Hicks in Buenos Aires, Argentina (1954). *Stephen's younger brother, George Jeffreys saw his first revival in 1915 and Edward Jeffreys (son of Stephen) saw revival in the Liverpool Crusade of 1934 whilst all three were known as healing evangelists, who all saw revival. Geoffrey R. Green in *Revivals in Merseyside* (2007) wrote about a century of Merseyside's Revivals (1840-1940) all of which took place under evangelists / revivalists such as James Caughey, William Lockhart, Moody and Sankey, Torrey and Alexander, Evan Roberts and Edward Jeffreys.

George Jeffreys held massive evangelistic and healing campaigns across Briton for seventeen years (up to 1932) and saw ten of thousand of converts and thousands of miracles. He knew that whilst it was prudent to book large premises for his evangelistic campaigns; without the Spirit of God, it would all be in vain. Many of his campaigns broke forth into revival as people were saved and healed. Jesus was exalted, the Holy Spirit brought conviction of sin, and people saw the cross and called upon the name of the Lord who is mighty to save!

In 1932, George Jeffreys wrote: 'How true it is that when the Church compromises with the world and diverts from the pathway of holiness, the power of God is withdrawn. It has been so from the beginning. The Creator withdrew from the first man because of transgression, the glory of God was withdrawn from the Temple in the land because of the backsliding people. Today the community of the Church that mixes with the world and does not stand for separation from it, need not expect an outpouring of the Holy Ghost.'[3]

Selwyn Hughes wrote: 'Revival is big and beautiful, awesome and majestic, revolutionary and powerful, engulfing and overwhelming, staggering and stunning. Let us not call anything a 'revival' that does not fully accord with all those descriptions.'

Colin C. Kerr in a broadcast for the BBC from St. Paul's Church, London, England, in October 1942 said, "Missions are the result of great consecrated human activity: publicity drives – great choirs – well-known evangelists – carefully organised plans, and so on. Revival is exactly opposite. The revival creates the activity. Because God has in this special way visited the people, all that is needed just happens. The movement is its own advertisement, produces its own speakers, singers, halls, churches, finances, everything. Even Evan Roberts [from the Welsh Revival 1904-1905] was more the child of the revival than its parent. It even developed its own technique, and ever changing at that. Seldom were meetings organised. There were few chairmen. Not often were speakers known to be coming, yet whether in halls or upon the hills, you found this strange phenomena, a sense of awe which feared almost to break the silence, mingled with the most unfettered freedom in song and prayer. Nearly always there was order in those order-less meetings!"[4]

Twentieth century revivalist, Rev. Duncan Campbell wrote: 'I would like to state what I mean by revival as witnessed in the Hebrides [1949-1952]. I do not mean a time of religious entertainment, with crowds gathering to enjoy an evening of bright Gospel singing; I do not mean sensational or spectacular advertising – in a God-sent revival you do not need to spend money on advertising. I do not mean high-pressure methods to get men to an inquiry room – in revival every service is an enquiry room; the road and hillside become sacred spots to many when the winds of God blow. Revival is a going of God amongst His people, and an awareness of God laying hold of the community. Here we see the difference between a successful campaign and revival...'[5]

Twentieth century evangelist and revivalist, Steve Hill preached five nights a week during the Brownsville Revival (1995-2000) in Pensacola, America, and after each sermon gave an altar call. Some people would say that this was not revival because of the altar call; however, challenging the people to make a response (or application to what has been preached) is a Scriptural process. Many revivalists from revival church history have been noted for their altar calls, enquiry rooms or after meetings – Moses came down from Mount Sinai and saw the Israelites unrestrained and declared, "Whoever is on the Lord's side, let him come to me" (Exodus 32:26). Joshua declared, "Choose this day whom you will serve..." (Joshua 24:15). Elijah challenged the people, "How long will you falter between two opinions? If the Lord is God, follow Him; but if Baal, then follow him" (1 Kings 18:21). On the other hand, people crying out under conviction of sin is also a Scriptural response – Peter preached at Pentecost and the people cried, "What shall we do [to be saved]" (Acts 2:37). After the supernatural earthquake, the Philippian jailor came trembling and fell before Paul and Silas and said, "Sirs, what must I do to be saved?" (Acts 16:30).

When I visited the Brownsville Revival in 1997, I knew that God was in the Sanctuary. It was an awful, yet exhilarating experience to behold. Who can stand before a holy God or see Him and live? – Night after night, I saw hundreds of people run to the front and weep and wail under deep conviction of sin.

Sometimes during the preaching, teenagers would come up and put items on the platform such as pot-pipes or cigarettes. One night, one man ran into the car park under conviction of sin, got out his pornographic magazines and made a bonfire in the parking lot!

When Claudio Freidzon held an evangelistic campaign in Guayaquil, Ecuador in the mid 1990s, the football stadium of 160,000 was filled to capacity under the motto: 'Holy Spirit, Glorify Christ.'

The Distinguishing Features

Sometimes there can be a blurred line between a successful evangelistic campaign (or a people group coming to Christ, see appendix C) and a heaven-sent revival, though they are all wonderful blessings from the Lord and there is always rejoicing over just one converted sinner; as well as a newly consecrated saint, revived and renewed Christians.

Paget Wilkes, founder of the Japan Evangelistic Band (JEB), was no stranger to revival, yet in October 1911, he visited a Mission School for girls and wrote: 'I hesitate to write more, lest I should appear to exaggerate; but as far as I can judge, God seems to have visited the school in somewhat of revival power.' He went on to write about the deep spirit of prayer amongst the girls who held meetings; confession of sin, conversions and 'the joy in many of them is unbounded.'

The distinguishing features, which separate revival from a successful evangelistic campaign are: weeping over sin, people being broken before the Lord (producing a contrite heart), confession of sin (to the Lord, to another Christian or to the one who has been wronged, privately or publicly), requests for forgiveness, restitutions and reparation where necessary. These are true signs of revival, because when the Holy Spirit descends, He comes to 'convict the world of sin, and of righteousness and of judgment' (John 16:8); to refine, purify and to wash clean, to 'purge them as gold and silver that they may offer to the Lord an offering of righteousness' (Mal. 3:1-3).

Another interesting gauge to revival is whether the secular press report on it (unless it is a localised revival) though sometimes governments suppress Christian news as has happened in China during the last five-six decades whilst the El-Minya Revival in Egypt (1991) was not reported. During the Welsh Revival (1904-1905), columns were written in the tabloids following the progress of the revival, whilst the Shillong Revival (2006-2007) in India received favourable reports in tabloids and on international news websites.

Revivals are Controversial

Revivals can be highly controversial. With many saying, "It's from God" and some believing it's of the devil! While others will say, "It's merely mass hysteria." In Jesus' day there was much murmuring among the people concerning Himself. Some said, "He is good" others said, "No, on the contrary He deceives the people" (John 7:12). Even Jesus' own people thought He was "out of His mind" (Mark 3:21). Now, if they said that about Jesus and His ministry, how much more controversial will revivals, awakenings and those that are involved appear?

In any revival there will be physical phenomena, bodily movements as the Holy Spirit touches a person in convicting power as well as other supernatural events which affect a person bodily. The devil will try to influence people, Christian and non-Christians as he is an infiltrator and imitator, and the kingdom of darkness and the Kingdom of Light inevitably clash.

It is wrong to say that everything you see in revival is from God, because it's not, there will always be opportunists and exhibitionists. The issue is not to focus on the excesses, but to focus on God and to give glory to Him for the great things He has done and is doing. The Pharisees looked for the negative, even when the miraculous was performed before their eyes. They watched Jesus closely to see whether He would heal on the Sabbath, just so that they might accuse Him! (Mark 3:1-5). This was not a sign of maturity but of immaturity. They went with the wrong attitude and were so blinded in the process that they were unable to see the wood from the trees.

My book *Understanding Revival & Addressing the Issues it Provokes* (2009) covers this in detail so that we can intelligently cooperate with the Holy Spirit during times of revivals and awakenings and not reject His workings due to religious affections, physical phenomena or manifestations and that we may not be caught unaware of the tactics of the enemy.

It is also wrong to believe everything negative you are told or read about another (especially during times of revival), because even the apostle Paul was slanderously reported as saying, "Let us do evil that good may come" (Romans 3:8). Yet we all know that after his dramatic conversion he led a morally upright life and strived to keep a clear conscience before God and man.

Chapter Four

How did the Revivalist see Revival?

The Lord said, "If My people who are called by My name will humble themselves, and pray and seek My face, and turn from their wicked ways, then I will hear from heaven, and will forgive their sin and heal their land" 2 Chronicles 7:14.

How does God Work in Revival?

G. J. Morgan in his book, *Cataracts Of Revival* wrote: 'As He is an unconventional God, He is not tied down to one method of working; like nature He has diversities of aspects attached to revivals.' There are differing views as to how revivals issue forth, though all concerned know that it is the Holy Spirit coming down that affects people, but the difference is in the degree that man has to play towards seeing a revival. Naturally speaking, if we only know about some of the more famous revivals such as the Fulton Street Revival (1857-1859), the Welsh Revival (1904-1905) or the Lewis Revival (1949-1952) then our perception of revival, how it comes about, the effect it can produce and other factors are incorrectly narrowed into the funnel of revival church history, resulting in a limited and constricted concept of understanding.

Dr. Michael Brown said, "Once you read about revival it has a holy addicting force to it..." Having read more than two-hundred books on the subject and studied the history of revivals through the ages for more than a decade and a half, I have distinctly seen that there are three prevailing views, with interesting fourth and fifth observations, which can be observed in the spectrum of revival, producing a breadth of understanding with different shades of colour:

1. It is totally a sovereign work of God, whilst man makes application of God's promises. Jonathan Edwards, Rev. Duncan Campbell and Dr. Martyn Lloyd-Jones held this view and they saw revival.

2. Anybody can have revival at any time as long as the conditions and promises have been appropriated. Charles Finney, Jonathan Goforth and J. Edwin Orr held this view and they saw revival.

3. Just preach the pure Gospel. George Whitefield a Calvinist, John Wesley an Arminianist (both of opposite theological persuasion), Howell Harris and James A. Stewart held this view and they saw revival.
4. There are those who had such an anointing on their life that in many places, regardless of the countries or towns visited, they saw revival. Charles Finney, J. Edwin Orr, George Whitefield, John Wesley and Rev. Douglas Brown (at least for a time) saw this in their ministries.
5. Some preachers specifically aim at seeing revival amongst the Christians. They preach the word of the Lord; denounce sin and challenge the brethren to respond in repentance and confession of sin which leads to contrition, humbling and brokenness before the Lord. This leads to a reviving of Christians which in turn flows into a community and soon souls are saved. Paget Wilkes, Jonathan Goforth and J. Edwin Orr (for the first few years of his world tour at least) aimed their teaching at Christians (as can be clearly seen in their writings and biographies) and they all saw localised revivals which transformed the brethren and out-flowed into the community.

God's Revival Pendulum

My understanding of revivals based from the first three prevailing views, is that they are all part of the same swing of God's revival pendulum; it just depends at which end you are viewing the marvellous work of God! It is the same Holy Spirit that comes down and touches people's lives from different countries in different centuries from varying cultures. God is no respecter of denominations or the countries or continents that He works in. The educational ability, age, social and political background or gender of the revivalist is immaterial, though ninety-five percent of revivalists are male, though many wives compliment their husbands ministries. Revival church history does reveal that older revivalists are generally able to handle contention better than their younger counterpart, though he or she might not be able to keep up with the pace of youth.

The common feature amongst all revivalists is that Jesus was at the very centre of their lives, they had fully surrendered their lives to God. They had a deep encounter with the Holy Spirit and lived exceptional lives of piety, having crucified the flesh with its passions and desires, though many were flawed in areas and had weak spots, (just like us). Most had an off day (or more) where they said something or responded in an incorrect manner or got overexcited and stumbled from the Spirit into the flesh, whilst some had a greater anointing on their lives than the character of Christ formed in them. All preached the pure uncompromising Gospel, the cross, the atonement, the blood and law and grace (the wrath and mercy of God) and they all desired that God be glorified in their midst and amongst the graceless. Whilst some prominently emphasised doctrines which were very real in their own lives: holiness, sanctification (victory over sin), baptism in the Holy Spirit, healing, deliverance, discipleship, evangelism / soul winning etc.

G. J. Morgan in his book, *Cataracts Of Revival* wrote: 'In the hidden ledger of God there is a specific law where every revival works accordingly, and every law runs back to the source of all things, even the wise Lawgiver who planned, the Mind that thought, the Heart that felt – the God that purposed everything in the end to reach the goal of perfection.'

P. V. Jenness wrote: 'Revivals are supernatural demonstrations of God's power. When will we learn to let God work in His own way? When will we spend more time in seeking to know what His way is than we do in devising human plans and methods which only bring us a sense of failure and loss? We need a revival. The Church needs a revival. The world – hungry, restless, sin-cursed, dying – needs a revival. God wants us to have it. Let us make every effort to meet the Divine conditions and let us expect Him to answer by fire.'

An Assurance of Revival

On occasions certain prayer warriors or leaders have had an assurance by the Spirit of God that revival will come, (though David Brainerd was the exact opposite). This is always after a process of intense intercession (Holy Spirit led prayer) which includes identification, agonising (which incorporates: weeping, travail, crying out and groaning) which results in the assurance (spiritual authority), so that they know without a shadow of doubt that the victory has been won in the heavenlies and will soon be manifested in the physical realm on earth, in their Church, town or nation.

William Burns, referring to the Kilsyth Revival (1839) in Scotland, UK, on the 23 July 1839 wrote: 'Some of the people of God who had been longing and wrestling for a time of refreshing from the Lord's presence, and who had during much of the previous night, been travailing in birth for souls, came to the meeting, not only with the hope, but with well-nigh anticipation of God's glorious appearing.'

Charles Finney, from the nineteenth century wrote: 'There was a woman in New Jersey who was very positive there was going to be another revival.' She spoke to the minister and elders to hold conference meetings but they ignored her request. So convinced was she that God was going to move that she employed a carpenter to make extra seats so that she could hold meetings in her home. 'She had scarcely opened her doors for meetings, before the Spirit of God came down with great power. And these sleepy church members found themselves surrounded all at once with convicted sinners...'

A few months prior to the Lewis Revival (1949-1952), two sisters in their eighties who had been persistently praying for revival into the early hours for months knew that their prayers had been answered when one of them received a vision of a packed church in their community of Barvas. The parish minister was informed and for at least three months, prayer meetings for revival were held twice a week in a thatched cottage with church deacons and elders in attendance, whilst the sisters prayed at home. Rev. Duncan Campbell arrived in late 1949, after his first meeting, as the people were dispersing the deacon told him not to be discouraged, "God is hovering over; He is going to break through...He is coming. I hear already the rumbling of heavens chariots wheels." About thirty people went into a cottage to pray and at 3am God came down and swept in which set the community ablaze for three years!

The Rev. David Davies and his wife Ann were used in the Congo Revival of the 1950s. In July 1953 they brought a native evangelist, Tomu from Lubutu, N. E. Belgian Congo (the place where revival first broke out in February) to their large mission station at Wamba. On Thursday the sixteenth; the evangelist spoke from Exodus 19:11 'Let them be ready for the *third day*. For on the *third day* the Lord will come...' and on Sunday the *nineteenth*, God came and revival continued for four years!

Steve Hill, a visiting evangelist to Brownsville AOG Church, Pensacola, told the congregation on Father's Day, June 1995 that God was going to do something special and within an hour, He did. The man who came with just five sermons ended up staying for five years, preaching four nights a week!

Chapter Five

Revival – The Divine-human Partnership

"Thus saith the Lord, the Holy One of Israel, and his Maker, ask Me of things to come concerning My sons, and concerning the work of My hands command ye Me" Isaiah 45:11, AV.

God's Sovereignty and Mans Responsibility

Christianity spread into all parts of the world because Jesus told the disciples about the Great Commission saying, "Go into all the world and preach the Gospel to every creature" (Mark 16:15), and "Go therefore and make disciples of all the nations..." (Matthew 28:19). God sent His chosen vessels to proclaim the Good News; the truth and the Holy Spirit revealed it to fallen mankind, thus it became a Divine-human partnership.

Historically, there have been seven distinct waves of mission within Christendom, which I first published In *How to Plan, Prepare and Successfully Complete Your Short-Term Mission* (2010). The first was after the ascension of the Lord Jesus Christ; at Pentecost when the Holy Spirit was outpoured and those present in the Upper Room received power from on high for works of service (Acts 1:8-14 and Acts 2:1-4). The disciples and the apostles went and proclaimed the Good News; they made disciples and planted churches. The second wave was during the third to the sixth century when much of Europe received the Good News, whilst in key locations there sprang up mission sending centres with dedicated missionary monks.

The third wave of missions was during the Middle Ages when from 1100 to 1300, hundreds of Franciscans and Dominican monks went to evangelise the Muslims in North Africa, which had been a centre of Christianity in the second and third centuries. The Franciscan Revival (c.1209-1220) in Italy, gave extras impetus to the work, though in the span of two hundred years, two hundred monks from both the Franciscans and Dominican lost their lives in this missionary advance; many were martyred.

The fourth wave of missions came out of the Moravian Revival (1727) when in 1731, the Moravian Mission was founded and the small church at Herrnhut (in modern day Germany) sent more missionaries in twenty years than Protestant Christians had done in the past two centuries!

The fifth wave of missions sprang out of the Evangelical Revival (1739-1791) at the end of the eighteenth century and rolled into the twentieth century. Missionaries sailed to the farthest part of the world; largely to the colonies of European nations, but also to the unevangelised around the Pacific Islands and Darkest Africa. The Baptist Missionary Society was birthed in 1792. The non-denominational London Missionary Society was founded in 1795. The Anglican Church Missionary Society began in 1799 and the British and Foreign Bible Society was formed in 1804 though its beginnings were birthed in 1787. In America, the American Board of Commissioners for Foreign Missions (1810) was the direct outcome of the Haystack Revival of 1806, which broke out at Williams College in America.

John Wesley of England, a former missionary to the American Indians (1735-1737) had encouraged missions all his life. Wesley's right-hand man, Dr. Thomas Coke, officially inaugurated Methodist Missions in 1787 and became known as the Missionary Bishop of Methodism. He crossed the Atlantic to America eighteen times whilst the Wesleyan Missionary Society began its work in 1817.

The sixth wave of missions began in the late 1920s, the native missionary movement, when Andrew Gih was touched by the Shanghai Revival (1925) and (inspired by Mary Stone and Miss Jenny Hughes, founders of Bethel Mission, China) began the Bethel Worldwide Evangelistic Band, where Chinese Christians formed teams and began mass evangelism, first in China, then across Asia, alongside Dr. John Sung. However, during the Pyongyang Great Revival (1907-1910) Koreans began mass evangelism campaigns such as the 'Movement of Saving One Million Souls for Christ' which began in the autumn of 1909. The Oriental Missionary Society (OMS) was founded in 1902 and in 1912, the 'Great Village Campaign' began where all 10.3 million homes in Japan were given a gospel booklet and was completed by 1918! By 1923, the Tokyo Bible Training Institute had trained no less than one thousand national preachers and by 1925, OMS had 201 mission stations and an equal number of itinerary points had been opened. Out of China in the 1920s came the vision of 'Back to Jerusalem;' Chinese Christians evangelising along the old Silk Road (which lies along the 10/40 window – the least evangelised countries of the world situated at the 10-40 latitude) which was re-birthed in the 1980s. Since the 1980s, the native missionary movement from developing countries within the continents of Asia and Africa have mobilised to take the Good News to the nations along the 10/40 window of which Gospel for Asia (GFA) is very prominent.

The seventh wave of missions began in the late 1950s / early 60s when lay personnel took time out from work and went on Short-term Missions (STMs), originally known as Short Terms Abroad or Short Service Missionaries. STMs increased in strength as new mission agencies such as Youth With a Mission (YWAM), Campus Crusade for Christ (CCFC) and Operation Mobilisation (OM) were birthed giving the opportunity for a layperson to "Go" even, if just for a few weeks.[1]

God and Us – Cooperation and Assistance

The working of revival is similar to the Great Commission, God needs our cooperation and assistance as much as we need His (though the work of the Divine is far greater!). This is not in any way belittling God, because He is the Creator of the universe, and we are but dust, but this is the way He works – He uses human vessels to accomplish His purposes for His glory. God had mercy on the inhabitants of Nineveh, but He could not have sent revival without Jonah's preaching, even though he was very reluctant. Humans are the vessels on earth through which God works through – and He *only* use them in proportion to the measure of their surrender and obedience unto Him. The Gospel spread from Jerusalem, Judea, Samaria and to the ends of the earth because Christians took the commands of Christ seriously. They understood their duties and responsibilities in the eyes of a covenant-keeping God as they offered their bodies as 'living sacrifices' (Romans 12:1) because Jesus 'died for all, that those who live should no longer for themselves, but for Him who died for them and rose again' (2 Corinthians 5:15). Hence, why they went into all the world, preaching the Good News, made disciples & planted churches.

Rev. Duncan Campbell wrote: 'God is sovereign and will act according to His sovereign purposes – but ever keeping in mind that, while God is sovereign in the affairs of men, His sovereignty does not relieve men of responsibility.'

Human Responsibility

Whilst God does not need us to do anything, He has always placed His followers in positions to do things on His behalf. God gave the tabernacle plans to Moses, but he had to organise the people to bring in the materials and oversee the construction of it. God spoke to Moses and said, "I have put wisdom in the hearts of all who are gifted artisans, that they may make all I have commanded you" (Exodus 31:6), with two highly anointed workers, Bezaleel the son of Uri from the tribe of Judah and Aholiab the son of Ahisamach from the tribe of Dan (Exodus 31:1, 6). In a similar manner the plans for the building of the temple were given to King David by Divine design and the human partnership was practically worked out by stockpiling the building materials for his son Solomon, who constructed God's house. David had been promised the throne of Israel by Divine command, everybody knew it including King Saul who habitually pursued David and tried to kill him. Eventually David becomes King of Judah, while Ishbosheth (Saul's son) is king over Israel. Abner, the commander of Saul's army has a major bust-up over Saul's concubine and declares in fierce anger, "May God do so to Abner, and more also, if I do not do for David as the Lord has sworn to him" (2 Samuel 3:9). Abner makes a covenant with David, though he soon gets killed by Joab, the commander of David's army who had a score to settle and the chain reaction (after the murder of Ishbosheth) led to David being anointed to reign over Israel.

Throughout the Bible, especially in the books of First and Second Kings and First and Second Chronicles there are accounts of different kings and persons fulfilling the words which had been uttered from a prophet, such as Elijah or Elisha. The human instruments are aware of these prophecies and bring them to fulfillment under the Divine-human partnership, often by the execution of those under Divine judgment for their sins, or the sins of their forefathers, see, 2 Kings 9:1-13 and 25-26, and 2 Kings 10:10-17.

At a more common level if a married woman wants a child, whilst she can pray to God to help her conceive, without her husbands assistance she will never conceive, this was the case of Hannah with Elkanah (1 Samuel 1:5-20).

God told Abram to leave Ur of the Chaldeans which was the pre-birth, in preparation for the nation of Israel. He asked Moses to lead the Israelites out of Egypt. He called Samuel to watch over the nation of Israel. He called Saul to be the first king of Israel. He called Isaiah, Jeremiah, Ezekiel and the twelve Minor Prophets to speak to the nations of Judah, Israel and beyond. He called John the Baptist to prepare the way of the Lord. Jesus' disciples were commanded to go into all the world and spread the Good News. William Carey was called to go to India. Henry Martyn was called to Persia. Robert Moffat was called to Africa. George Müller was called to help the orphans of Bristol in England. Hudson Taylor was called to China. William Booth was called to serve the down and outs of London and beyond. Rees Howells and his team of intercessors were called to intercede for Britain during the darkest days of World War II, and multitudes of other Christians have been obedient to their heavenly calling.

The Divine-human Partnership Quotes

- John George Govan, founder of The Faith Mission (Edinburgh, Scotland) who partook of several revivals at the end of the nineteenth century said, "Without God we cannot, without man He will not."
- V. Ellenberger wrote *A Century of Mission work in Basutoland 1833-1933*. In reference to the Qalo Awakening (c.1912) in Basutoland (modern day Lesotho), she wrote: '…The awakening of a whole district under the guidance of a missionary who had joined the mission rather late in life, is a veritable miracle of the power of God in conjunction with the faithful service of man.'
- Rev. Duncan Campbell, in his book, *God's Answers, Revival Sermons* wrote: 'Let me say what I frequently say – that the God I believe in is a covenant-keeping God who is true to His engagements. 'If you will keep My commandments and execute My judgments, then will I *do it*!" (1 Kings 6:12).
- Norman Grubb, in the foreword to *Floods on Dry Ground* which documented the Imbai Revivals (1935) and (1935-1936), in the N. E. Belgian Congo wrote: 'It clearly demonstrates that revival is not an act of Divine sovereignty apart from human co-operation, but the legitimate outcome of man's compliance with Divine conditions for revival.'
- Eva Stuart Watt's, in her book, *Thirsting for God* wrote: 'Let us realise that revival is not a miracle, but like other events, is brought about by fulfilling God's requirements for revival and paying His price.'
- Arthur Wallis, in his book, *In the Day of Thy Power* wrote: 'The word of God presents to us side by side the two foundation stones of every revival [Acts 1:4, 11, the

brethren were united and in prayer] – the sovereignty of God and the preparedness of man. Because we cannot understand how they harmonise is no reason for emphasising one at the expense of the other.'

- Michael Howard, a Rhodesian intercessor, who has seen at least six revivals in various African countries during the 1980s-90s, in his book, *Tales of an African Intercessor* wrote: 'No move of God or mighty revival is His sovereign act. God works and moves by the distinct cry of His people or is prevented by the distinct lack of their cry.'

Rev. C Perren, in his book, *Revival Sermons In Outline* wrote: 'Who can question the importance of human instrumentality in the salvation of men, when the word of God so plainly declares, 'he that wins souls is wise'? [Proverbs 11:30] 'They that turn many to righteousness shall shine as the stars forever and ever.' [Daniel 12:3] 'Let him know that he which converts the sinner from his error of his way shall save a soul from death and shall hide a multitude of sins' [James 5:20].

'While human agency is thus very plainly declared, we should ever remember that all man's work, however zealous and untiring; all his words, however eloquent; all combined forces of the professed people of God, apart from Divine sanction and aid, shall be powerless in bringing one soul to Christ or reinvigorating the Church. Such results are 'not by might, nor by power, but by My Spirit says the Lord of hosts.' To attain success we must be 'labourers together with God,' labourers not idlers, labourers together with God, not equal with, but under and belonging to Him, in subordination to God as instruments in His hand.'

'Great was the success of [Charles] Finney in revivals, and of his preaching it was said, "He preached God's word clear through and without flinching, never muffling the sword of the Spirit, he made it cut to the very marrow." These words may with equal force be applied to Jacob Knapp and Elder Swan, whose labours were blessed to thousands. Thus, in God giving the word, and in man preaching it, there is a union of Divine and human agency, and without the knowledge of God's word there can be no revival.

'Divine and human agency in revivals is markedly seen in the efficacy of personal and united prayer. The history of revivals amply proves prayer to be the right arm of every great awakening. To quote Scripture in proof of the necessity and potency of such work would be to transcribe a great portion of the sacred word.'[2]

Covenant-Keeping God

God is a covenant-keeping God, because Scripture declares, 'know that the Lord your God, He is God, the faithful God *who keeps covenant and mercy* for a thousand generations with those who love Him and keep His commandments' (Deuteronomy 7:9), and 'God of heaven, O great and awesome God, *You who keep your covenant* and mercy with those who love You and observe Your commandments' (Nehemiah 1:5). There is a covenant of blessing for obedience and curses and consequences for disobedience (Ex. 20:5-6 & Deut ch. 27-28)!

God is not obligated to send revival if we have negated our responsibilities and this focuses on holiness, right living before God and man (see Psalm 15, 24:3-6, Isaiah 58, Hosea 10:12 and Matthew 5:1-12), but as long as we do not fail to fulfill our part, then He will not fail to fulfill His. This is not trying to twist the arm of God or being presumptuously arrogant, but our covenant-keeping God has declared, "*If My people* who are called by My name will humble themselves and pray and seek My face and turn from their wicked ways, *then I will hear* from heaven, and will forgive their sin *and heal their land*" (2 Chronicles 7:14). 'God is not a man that He should lie...has He said, and will He not do it? Or has He spoken, and will He not make it good?' (Numbers 23:19).

Arthur Wallis in *The Day of Thy Power,* relating Nehemiah's intercession for Jerusalem wrote: 'Nehemiah was able to prevail in prayer because he held God to be faithful and pleaded His promises. He reminded Him of what He had covenanted to do [Nehemiah 1:4-11] and pressed Him to fulfill it. This is a spiritual lever that never fails to move the hand that moves the world.' Praying for revival is taking God's promises as revealed in the written word, the Holy Bible and presenting His own words to Him and seeking the fulfillment of those Scriptures because He has promised – but it is foolhardy to pray these Scriptures whilst neglecting those which need to be lived out daily, e.g. "Be holy because I am holy" (1 Peter 1:16).

The Fullness of Time

Revival is accomplished through God's sovereignty and mans fulfilled responsibility, (the Divine-human partnership) which is revealed in the fullness of time. All things are decreed in heaven (Psalm 119:89), but they have to be outworked on earth. If we do not fail to fulfill our responsibility then God will not fail to fulfill His. It was Lewis A. Drummond who wrote: 'Prayer opens the door to the fullness of time.' The fullness of time is a series of synchronised events coming together as one which unlocks and releases all that God has for that particular situation. It was the accumulation of Divine orchestrated events that fulfilled the prophecies of the Messiah: the conception of the forerunner, John the Baptist, the census which resulted in Joseph returning to his home town of Bethlehem, the Virgin Birth, the flight to Egypt and the death of Herod which enabled Mary, Joseph and baby Jesus to live in Nazareth because 'when the fullness of time had come, God sent forth His Son...'

The fullness of time, waiting upon God (Jeremiah 14:22b) is revealed when we have prevailed in prayer like the persistent widow because prayer is the prevailing key to answer. But we also have to be living a consecrated life with a pliable, contrite and broken heart; pliable to the Master. Whilst we have to wait on God, 'the Lord God does nothing, unless He reveals His secrets to His servants the prophets' (Amos 3:7), hence the reason why many revivalists and prayer warriors have that assurance that God will move in a specific time frame. If we have not done our part, then we cannot expect God to do His. But if we have done our part, then we can expect God to do His; though the timing and the method maybe different than what we expect (Isaiah 55:8), but those of us who wait upon God will not be ashamed (Isaiah 49:23). We should all pray and not lose heart (Luke 18:1). Therefore, 'be patient, brethren, until the coming of the Lord. See how the farmer waits for the precious fruit of the earth, waiting patiently for it until he receives the early and the latter rain' (James 5:7).

Rev. John Smith, from the early nineteenth century wrote: 'The *mode* of the Divine working is dictated by sovereign wisdom; but the *degree* depends on the faith of the Church. God Himself determines whether He will descend as the dew upon Israel or as the burning flame; but it is for His people to decide whether He shall come upon the single fleece while the rest of the floor is dry, or whether the whole of the camp shall be surrounded and gladdened by the scatterings of angel food...'[3]

'Let us not grow weary while doing good, *for in due season we shall reap* if we do not lose heart' (Galatians 6:9).

Chapter Six

How Revivals are Birthed

'Bow down Your heavens, O Lord, and come down; touch the mountains and they shall smoke' Psalm 144:5.

There are many stimulating factors which effect, birth and encourage people to pray for revival. This can bring about the heaven-sent blessing, revival, as God comes down, the hills melt like wax before His presence, the thirsty are quenched and the floods are poured on the dry and barren ground which results in the desert blooming and becoming fertile once again.

There are three primary reasons as to why revivals are birthed:

1. There are those who just want revival, to see God glorified and the Church revived. They may be a successful evangelist or missionary or have a successful church, but they are just not satisfied, it is a godly discontentment for the "greater things" as Jesus promised (John 14:12-14), and a longing for God to be vindicated and glorified in their sphere of work (Leviticus 10:3 and Isaiah 48:11). Seasoned Canadian missionary to China, Jonathan Goforth, began to be restless and dissatisfied by the results of his work under the North Honan Mission, though humanly speaking it was very successful, but Goforth called it, "just touching the fringes" of the multitudes without Christ. He longed to see in his ministry the "greater works" and saw revival in China and Manchuria during the years 1906-1909 and 1915.

Pastor John Kilpatrick was dissatisfied with his role at the large, successful Assembly of God church at Brownsville, Pensacola, America, and knew there was more. One night in the early hours, whilst alone, he went into the church, placed his keys on the platform, and cried out to God, "God, I want to see You move. If You are not going to send revival here, please send me to a place where You are. I don't care if it's a small congregation in the middle of nowhere with just twenty-five people. Just take me where You're going to move." Within a few years the Brownsville Revival (1995-2000) began.

2. There are those who want to see Christian's revived. Knowing that revival is primarily for the reviving of Christians

they are encouraged by what can be, yet discouraged by what they see, therefore they pray for a spiritual awakening amongst their congregation or mission community or compound. C. T. Studd entered into central Africa in 1913 and a year later a pioneering work was begun at Ibambi (also spelt Imbai), Belgian Congo. By 1925, in a letter, C. T. (as he was referred to) wrote about an undercurrent of opposition to his leadership, and how the natives had begun to backslide. This drove C. T. and other missionaries to seek God's face for a move of His Spirit so that they would all be united as one. One evening, eight missionaries made a vow before God, 'I won't care what happens to me, life or death, aye, or hell, so long as my Lord Jesus Christ is glorified' and revival fire swept through their mission station and beyond!

Jonathan Goforth desired the Christians of Manchuria to be revived and so held three special conferences for Christians in February 1908. He held around forty meetings, taught on the Holy Spirit and He came and dealt with the Christians! In the spring and for the next few years he held week long revival missions across China amongst different denominations with amazing results and became China's greatest evangelist.

3. There are those who hear about revival in one locality and are encouraged to pray for and seek the blessing within their own church, community, town or country. This was evident in the: Kilsyth Revival (1742) who were encouraged after hearing about the Cambuslang Revival (1742) which was just twelve miles away. The Fulton Street Revival (1857-1859) in America affected four men in Kells, Ireland to see the same blessing in their community which led to the Irish Revival (1859-1860) which encouraged others, that in turn spread and affected Scotland, Wales and England to pray and believe for revival which in turn went around the world resulting in a global awakening. After hearing about the Welsh Revival (1904-1905) various countries such as India and Korea were encouraged to pray for revival and they received according to their faith.

God has certain towns or countries designated as the geographical apples of His eye, because in these locations revivals just thrive and across the decades or centuries keep re-birthing as the tidal surge of the Holy Spirit ebbs and flows as Christians cry out to God. We know that God is no respecter of person and that He has no favourites, but He does have intimates (those who are close to Him e.g. Abraham was God's friend, Isaiah 41:8) and He did choose the people of Israel (His chosen ones), and Jerusalem, as a special place of His habitation and praise. Whilst Jerusalem got ransacked, burnt with fire and destroyed, it got rebuilt again and again; Israel was re-birthed as a nation in 1948, Jerusalem was retaken in 1967 and it is the place where Jesus will return to when He descends on the Mount of Olives. Some of these spiritual hotspots as recorded by revival church history are: Northampton, America, Great Britain (especially Ulster, Ireland; Kilsyth, Scotland; Sunderland, England and the nation of Wales – 'the land of revivals'), Tinnevelli, India; Imbai, Congo; China, Korea, Nagaland and Argentina to name but some of them.

Rev. Gordon I. Thomas, in the foreword to *The Lewis Awakening* wrote: 'Let us now cry to God with that confidence Mr Campbell found in the people of Barvas right at the beginning [of the Lewis Revival]. I believe such a confidence is born only of prayer and of sacrifice – much prayer and deep sacrifice. Whilst God alone can send revival and we cannot work it up, yet it may be that we can help to prepare the way by prayer...'Wilt Thou not revive us *again,* that Thy people may rejoice in Thee?' (Psalm 85:6). 'Oh, Lord revive Thy work...in the midst of the years make known; in wrath remember mercy' (Habakkuk 3:2). Oh, Lord revive me!'[1]

Miss Eva Stuart Watt, Home Secretary of the Sudan United Mission wrote: 'When He [God] finds Holy Ghost men willing to use Holy Ghost methods, things happen beyond the range of human effort or understanding. The Spirit of truth is come to guide us into all truth and, if we are willing, [He] will teach us the truth about this mighty challenge.'[2]

Evangelist, John R. Rice, preaching in Dallas, Texas in 1936 said, "Of the ten virgins [Matthew 25:1-13] five were wise (they were saved), and five were foolish (they were unsaved). Yet, they all slumbered and slept. But I am sure the Bridegroom was more concerned and more embarrassed about the wise who had the oil and yet went to sleep than about the unsaved. It is powerless Christians, not wicked unbelievers alone, who curse a country and block revivals."[3]

Revival and the World
It is my personal belief that since the resurrection of Jesus Christ, virtually every country in the world has seen a revival,

even if only a localised revival in a church. Many of the countries where Christianity flourished such as in North Africa, where Tertullan and Augustine came from have long since been overrun by the invading forces of Islam and its sword. They have tried to extinguish those who follow in the footsteps of the One who came in the sandals of the Gospel of peace. Therefore most of the Arab nations and the Middle East saw revival before the sixth century, before Islam was conceived, though less than two decades ago, El-Minya in Egypt witnessed a revival when 20,000 Coptic Christians were saved in a few months under the watchful eye of Father Daniel, but this was unsurprisingly heavily suppressed by the Muslims and the local authorities. Also, Egypt saw the Shebin-el-Kanâter Revival (c.1928) under Pastor Marcus of the Evangelical Church of Egypt (Presbyterian) who assisted the Egyptian General Mission.

It is the sincere understanding of many godly persons that revival has never come to their country or to their surrounding countries (whilst they have had the Good News for more than a century), but I would suggest that with careful and diligent research from revival church history they would happily be able to alter their views.

Many years ago I was in the Netherlands (commonly referred to as Holland, though that is their best known province) where after the service the gracious Pentecostal pastor informed me that Holland has never had a revival and so for many years this is what I was led to believe. This incorrect view was also confirmed to me by another Dutch pastor who, when asked, "Why have the Netherlands never had a revival?" Stated that the Dutch have a saying which is laced with pride, "God made the world, but the Dutch made Holland!"

It was six years later that I jubilantly read that Rev. James Robe who factually recorded the Kilsyth and Cambuslang Revivals (1742) referred to revivals in the Netherlands and Holland: 'At Niewkerk, [also spelt Nieuwkerk] Putten etc., in the Duchy of Guelderland, about the later end of 1749; and of its continuance since which spread into Juliers etc.'[4] John Wesley in 1757 when visiting Everton, England, writing about physical phenomena under John Berridge's preaching wrote: 'I have often observed more or less of these outward symptoms to attend the beginning of a general work of God. So it was in New England, Scotland, Holland, Ireland and many parts of England...'[5] The following year, I obtained John Gillies'

Historical Collections of Accounts of Revival (1754, revised and enlarged in 1845) where quoting minister's letters it records the Dutch Revivals of 1749-1754 which began at Nieuwkerk and 'spread itself through many other places...The plentiful outpouring of the Holy Spirit in several congregations in the Velurve, one of the quarters of the Dutchy of Guelderland.' By 1751, there was a revival at 'Rheid, in the Dutchy of Juliers and several other places throughout the country.'[6]

In 1984, Paul Yonggi Cho was the senior pastor of the Yoido Full Gospel Church, Seoul, South Korea; the largest church in the world – which is now led by Young-Hoon Lee. Cho in his book, *Prayer: Key To Revival* (1984) with R. Whitney Manzano stated that his church is committed to pray for Japan (praise God) but incorrectly wrote: 'Many don't realise it, but Japan has never had a revival' (*page 17). Japan has had at least ten revivals in a span of just over thirty years bridging the nineteenth and twentieth century and in the 1600s was thirty percent Christian until extreme persecution arose.

- A circular letter was sent from Peking, China, in June 1885, signed by twenty-five people from six different mission organisations, including the Inspector-General of I.M. Customs, Peking, which states: '...The present revival in Japan began with a daily prayer meeting....'
- Rev. Barclay Buxton, the leader of a missionary group, saw a revival which sprang from Matsuye in 1899 and was 'influencing the whole of Japan.'
- Paget Wilkes wrote about a revival amongst the Japanese on the Pacific coast of the USA in 1892. One of the converts from this revival was much used amongst his own people in America, but some years later was appointed an English teacher in a large Mission school in Japan where 'almost at once a revival followed; both teacher and students were convicted of sin in no ordinary degree. Many were converted and saved of the Lord.'
- A Japanese worker in an undated letter, which was referring to a revival sometime between the years 1890-1900, wrote: '...What was the beginning of the great movement in Japan. It seems to date from Mr [Barclay F.] Buxton first convention in Kobe, when Mr Hudson Taylor [founder of the China Inland Mission] joined him; for it was

at this time that the Lord began to pour out His Spirit abundantly.'

- A revival also broke out in a convention in Osaka sometime between the years 1902-1905, Barclay Buxton, referring to fervent prayer wrote: 'No wonder the Holy Spirit broke forth and the melting fire descended.'
- Paget Wilkes, founder of the Japan Evangelistic Band partook of a localised revival at a convention at Arima in September 1910.
- The Mukti Revival (1905-1906) under Pandita Ramabai of India and their prayer bands led to 'a great revival...started in a school in Japan' sometime between 1905 and 1907 as wrote Basil Miller. Godfrey Buxton wrote: 'A very remarkable work of the Spirit of God was seen in Miss Tristram's school of two hundred Japanese girls, when almost every girl, and later through them each teacher, received Christ, and a wholly new spirit pervaded the school.' This was in 1905 and is probably the same as referred to by Pandita Ramabai.
- Paget Wilkes wrote about the Fukuoka Revival of 1906 and 1907 and the revival at the CMS Girl's School in Osaka in October 1910.[7]

R. Arthur Matthews in *Born for Battle* wrote: '...Disciples need to pray. "Thy will be done on earth as it is in heaven." The obvious [implication] is that God has limited certain of His activities to responding to the prayers of His people. Unless they pray, He will not act. Heaven may will something to happen, but heaven waits and encourages earth's initiative to desire that will and then to pray that it happens. The will of God is not done on earth...by overriding or ignoring the will of people on earth. On the contrary, God has willed that His hand be held back while He seeks for a person, an intercessor, to plead, "Thy will be done on earth," in this or that specific situation...'[8]

Rev. T. Gear Willet of the China Inland Mission said, "The revival that we pray for must be deep and as abiding at the eternal word of God. It must be based upon the promises of God."[9]

Chapter Seven

Revival and the Great Commission

"Ask of Me, and I will give You the nations for Your inheritance, and the end of the earth for your possession" Psalm 2:8.

Missionaries and Revivals

God does not work without the cooperation of His Church; without the willing vessels of the members of the body of Christ. Whilst He does not need us He has always chosen to use us. Leonard C. J. Moules of the Worldwide Evangelization Crusade noted that in the Bible there are three incidences where: 'God has linked His sovereignty to the pace of man. First, the Ark [of the Covenant] waiting in the river bed of the Jordan (Joshua 3:17). Second, the preaching of the Gospel, "And then shall the end come" (Matthew 24:14). Finally, waiting for those who are to give their lives unto death [Christian martyrs]... 'White robes were given unto everyone of them; and it was said unto them that they should rest yet for a little season, until their fellow servants also and their brethren, that should be killed as they were, should be fulfilled' (Revelation 6:11).'[1]

Revival can only come to a nation when disciples of the Lord Jesus have entered a geographical location and began to evangelise that nation and persistently call upon God to pour out His Spirit from on high. Rev. Duncan Campbell said, "God is the God of revival but man is the human agent through whom revival is possible."

If there is no Christian present then generally speaking, a revival cannot break out – though God being all powerful can pour out His Spirit on the heathen and they can call upon the Most High as the One true God, but in practical reality and human responsibility, they need to be evangelised, discipled and to have the Holy Bible in their mother tongue. At present there are 6,912 known spoken languages of the world, 2,479 with some books of the Bible or the entire Bible completed; with 1,300 in progress and the remainder (3,133) needing translation work! This represents 300 million people without access to ANY portion of the Holy Bible out of a world population of 6.9 billion.[2]

There are numerous accounts and written records of revivals across Africa from the time of the pioneer missionaries in the south, and from east to west, notably in the nineteenth and twentieth centuries as God's word and power was demonstrated to the natives. In 1894, the Gospel arrived at the Solomon Islands (in the Pacific, to the east of Papua New Guinea) which brought to an end the beginning of evangelisation of every country in the world and Tahiti, (French Polynesia) being the ends of the earth from Jerusalem. Though there are still people groups and tongues (different tribal groups with different dialects) within these countries (and some yet undiscovered, so some Amazon Jungles explorers and anthropologists have put forth – some "stone age" tribes which have been photographed from the air) who have not yet heard the Good News and until then, Jesus cannot return. Even this century, a graduate of the Brownsville School of Ministry (now under Tommy Tenny's leadership) found an unevangelised people group amongst the 13,000 islands of Indonesia!

Fulfilment of the Great Commission

The Bible clearly states that in heaven there will be people 'out of every tribe and tongue and people and nation' standing before the throne of God (Revelation 5:9 and Revelation 7:9). That is why we (you and me) are called *and* commanded to 'Go into all the world and to preach the Gospel to every creature' (Mark 16:15 and Matthew 28:19) to 'hasten the coming of the day of God' (2 Peter 3:12), because unless the Gospel is preached in all the world 'as a witness to all the nations' then the end cannot come (Matthew 24:14). That is unless the 'angel flying in the midst of heaven, having the everlasting Gospel to preach to those who dwell on the earth – to every nation, tribe, tongue, and people' (Revelation 14:6) has to finish the job because of our lack of obedience and concern for those whom have never heard. As Romans chapter ten declares: 'How shall they call on Him in whom they have not believed? And how shall they believe in Him of whom they have not heard? And how shall they hear without a preacher? And how shall they preach unless they are sent? (Romans 10:14-15). Let us not forget that 'faith comes by hearing, and hearing the word of God' (Romans 10:17).

Hudson Taylor, founder of the China Inland Mission (CIM), sixteen years before his death, issued a pamphlet entitled: *To Every Creature*, part of which read: 'The Masters words are 'to every creature,' how far are we fulfilling them...How are we going to treat the Lord Jesus Christ in reference to this command? Shall we definitely drop the title Lord as applied to Him?'

Jesus should be at our very core, the power plant and fuel of our very existence, if we do not want to please Him, then who are we trying to please? It was Henry David Thoreau who said, "It is not enough to be busy, so are the ants. The question is, what are we busy about?"

My first book, *Mission Preparation Training* covers the various aspects of implementing the will of God, mission work; notably short-term mission (which is often in preparation for a longer commitment) because 'as cold water to a weary soul, so is good news from a far country' (Proverbs 25:25). My second mission book, *How to Plan, Prepare and Successfully Complete Your Short-term Mission – For Volunteers, Churches, Independent STM Teams and Mission Organisations* is the why, where, and when of STMs and reveals how to successfully complete your STM at the right time, with the right people to the glory of God.[3]

Missionary Pioneers and Revivals

The evangelisation of the world in this generation; the evangelisation of this generation, and the decade of evangelism have all been mottos in past centuries and decades. However, the work of the Great Commission is so large that the Church needs extra impetus, a tidal surge of the Holy Spirit (with signs following, see Romans 15:16-20), a spiritual awakening and that only comes in times of revival.

Charles Finney wrote: 'It is altogether improbable that religion will ever make progress among heathen nations, except through the influence of revivals. The attempt is now to do it by education and other cautious and gradual improvements. But as long as the laws of the mind remain what they are, it cannot be done in this way. There must be excitement sufficient to wake up the dormant moral powers and roll back the tide of degradation and sin.'[4]

Revivals – a Thrust to Evangelism and World Missions

Revivals have always given a thrust to evangelism and world missions. This was certainly true of the Moravian Revival (1727) which led to the one hundred year prayer meeting and gave the impetus to the Moravian Missions which began in 1731. Jonathan Goforth, missionary to China, in his book, *By My*

Spirit, referring to the Moravian Revival wrote: '[It] transformed them into what has been the mightiest evangelising force in the world for the past two centuries [and] was born in prayer.'

There is also a link between pioneering missionaries and many revivals, because many of the missionary pioneers saw revival. I. R. Govan Stewart (the daughter of John George Govan, the revivalist, who founded The Faith Mission, in Glasgow; now in Edinburgh, Scotland), writing more than fifty years ago wrote: 'Every new movement which counts for God seems to be born in revival.'

Before any of the following pioneer missionaries (some of whom saw revival), and for some of them, before they arrived in their field of labour, they had to make huge sacrifices. They all lived holy lives, though were ongoing works of grace. Hudson Taylor was betrothed to a lady who point-blank refused to go to China, so he had no choice but to break off the relationship. William Carey's wife refused to go to India, but God had called him to go, so he left without her – a storm delayed the sailing of the ship, and she eventually changed her mind, but being maladjusted in her mind, she was more of a burden than a blessing. Many of the missionaries saw their children and wives slip into eternity in a foreign land. If you were to read their diaries, journals or biographies you will often hear the pages declaring their inadequacy, but the Holy Spirit's sufficiency in opening the hearts and minds of the heathen (unevangelised people). Frequently they prayed for an outpouring of the Spirit of God to bring that much needed extra impetus to the work and desired and sought their own enduement of power from on high. Someone once said, "More people are converted in times of revival than fifty years without one."

The reason why so many missionary pioneers saw revival is because they were fully committed and surrendered to the will of the Master; Jesus was central to them, they were willing to spend and be spent for Him. They knew the Holy Spirit as a Person and had a deep intimate communion with the Father through His Son Jesus Christ. They were men and women of prayer, hardened prayer warriors, many of whom had been inspired by the revivals of the past and had a hope for the future. They did not limit God and knew His all sufficiency, His all powerful compassionate nature, the One who is only too willing to quench him who is thirsty and to pour out His Spirit on a dry and thirsty land, because He has no pleasure in the death of the wicked and has stated that He will pour out His Spirit on all flesh. Some missionary pioneers paved the way for future revivals by their toil, intercession and blood, through martyrdom by the natives, death by disease or deprivation in the Master's service. Their graves became steeping stones as they gave their all, even their very lives (see Revelations 12:11).

Some of these pioneers who became revivalists were: David Brainerd and his love for the American Indians, John Beck who went to the frozen wasteland of Greenland, Robert Moffat in Kuruman, Africa, Adoniram Judson who laboured in Burma (modern day Myanmar), Thomas Birch Freeman along the Gold Coast of West Africa, John Geddie from Novia Scotia in the evangelisations of the islands of the Pacific, John G. Paton for the New Hebrides, Jonathan Goforth of China and Manchuria who 'tapped a mine of infinite possibilities' after reading the works of Charles Finney; and C. T. Studd of central Africa (Belgian Congo) who declared the objective of his mission organisation was to accomplish the evangelisation of the un-evangelised with the utmost urgency, with the motto: 'If Jesus Christ be God and died for me, then no sacrifice can be too great for me to make for Him.' See appendix I. There were other great missionaries, like Mary Slessor, 'the White Queen of Calabar' (Nigeria) who whilst she did not see revival, planted dozens of churches in hundreds of square miles of uncharted jungle and saw hundreds, if not thousands of converts.

Pioneering Works

The link between missionary pioneers and many revivals also extends to certain God-ordained pioneering works (or actions). George Whitefield and John and Charles Wesley began open-air preaching to the masses of the un-churched and the British Great Awakening (1739-1791), also known as the Evangelical Revival, of the eighteenth century began. It was John Wesley who encouraged William Wilberforce to keep battling on over the abolition of slavery and wrote in his very last letter: '...Go on, in the name of God and in the power of His might, till even American slavery, the vilest that ever saw the sun, shall vanish before it...' Within eights days, John Wesley was dead.

William Carey read Jonathan Edwards pamphlet, *A Humble Attempt To promote Explicit Agreement and Visible Union of God's People in Extraordinary Prayer for the Revival of Religion* and *the Advancement of Christ's Kingdom on Earth* (1747) which led to the ministers of the Northamptonshire Association holding a monthly prayer meeting for the unreached people of the earth. Carey then read Andrew Fuller's pamphlet, *The Gospel Worthy of all Acceptation* (1785) and came to the conclusion that, "If it be the whole duty of all men, where the Gospel comes to believe unto salvation, then it is the duty of those who are entrusted with the Gospel to endeavour to make it known among all nations for the obedience of faith." Out of this, the Baptist Missionary Society was formed (1792). Carey became known as the 'Father of Modern Missions' and laboured in India for thirty-eight years under the motto: 'Expect great things from God, attempt great things for God.' Carey wished to improve the social conditions for the natives of India and his social reforms included the prohibition of child sacrifice held at the Ganges River (the festival at Gunga Saugor) where the river meets the sea, child sacrifice were made to the water. Suttee was also outlawed where widows were burned (or buried) alive on the funeral pyre of their deceased husbands, believing it to be a great act of holiness. Carey's social work also included starting schools, a college and hospitals.

It was the sixteen-year-old Mary Jones who having saved for six years (walked twenty-five miles, barefoot over the rugged Welsh mountains to Bala) to buy a Welsh Bible in 1800, which led to the founding of the British and Foreign Bible Society (1804). Thomas Charles of Bala retold the story of Mary Jones to a group of ministers, proposing to start a society to print Welsh Bibles. Rev. Joseph Hughes response was, "I say if for Wales, then why not for the world?"

George Müller and his Bristol orphanages in England (which at their peak supported two thousand children and two hundred missionaries from the China Inland Mission (CIM) were maintained by a life of faith) inspired four men to meet in Kells, Ireland, to pray for revival. Soon they began to see more conversions and in 1859, the heavenly fire fell!

It was Hudson Taylor who said, "Man's extremities is God's opportunities." In China, a new convert asked Hudson, "How long have you had the Glad Tidings in England?" Ashamed Hudson vaguely replied that it was several hundred years. "What exclaimed Nyi in astonishment, "Several hundreds of years! Is it possible that you have known about Jesus so long, and only now have come to tell us! My father sought the truth for more than twenty years," he continued sadly "and died without finding it. Oh why did you not come sooner?" Hudson founded the CIM in 1865 and before his death, had opened up every Province in China, with 1,000+ CIM missionaries!

David Livingstone read *The Life of Rev. Henry Martyn* (1831), a missionary to India, Persia and Arabia and an *Appeal to the Churches of Britain and America on behalf of China* (c.1836) by Dr. Charles Gutzlaff, a medical missionary and former Interpreter in Hong Kong to the British Government, and said, "It is my desire to show my attachment to the cause of Him who died for me by devoting my life to His service." He became the missionary explorer who opened up Africa, which led the way for trade, commerce and more importantly, Christianity, stating, "The end of the exploration is the beginning of enterprise."

William Booth had a vision of a black and dark stormy sea of the perishing lost, which profoundly changed his life forever. He founded The East London Christian Mission which in 1878 was renamed the Salvation Army, with its social concern linked to spiritual matters. General Booth said, "You cannot talk to a man about heavenly glories if he hasn't eaten for two days." Their message and concern spread from London across the entire globe, because, as General Booth wrote (in King Edward VII autograph album): '…my ambition is the souls of men.'

In two thousand years no group of people have done as much as Christians to help humanity[5] by serving people as the outflow of God's love toward mankind. Christians have had the initiative in bringing about the following changes, founding or implementing: Abolition of slavery, child work laws, public education, trade unions, orphanages, prison reforms, the development of hospitals and much more! – See *How Christianity Made the Modern World* by Paul Backholer.[6]

A month before I visited the Brownsville Revival in July 1997, a hurricane had just passed through Florida causing storm damage along the miles of beach front. At the same time, there was a youth conference which broke away for one day to assist in shovelling the sand off the sea front. Driving into the Brownsville car park on a Monday, (a day on which no services were held) I was greeted by a team of older youth members who were preparing to visit the citizens of their neighbourhood. Going from door to door they offered assistance to those in need, such as, help with their shopping, baby sitting, doing the gardening etc. as a practical expression of love in Christ because revival always imparts a heightened awareness of social concern. This can be expressed in many practical ways and is an outworking of the Scriptures of loving ones neighbours as ourselves which is pure and undefiled religion (Mark 12:31 and James 1:27).

Section II

Accounts of Revivals

Chapter Eight

From Darkness to Light

'I will give thanks to You, O Lord, among the Heathen, and sing praises to Your name. He is the tower of salvation...' 2 Samuel 22:50-51a, AV.

Moravian Revival 1727

Count Nikolaus Ludwig von Zinzendorf was born in Dresden and grew up in a Prussian pietistic family. Zinzendorf's passion was "to live for the One who had given His life for him, and to lead others to Jesus."

The Moravians were originally from Bohemia, the native Czechs who had a Reformation in the late fourteenth century under various Bohemian preachers and in the early fifteenth century under John Hus. They were also influenced by the writings of John Wycliff of England and had suffered persecution in Bohemia and Moravia for their Christian beliefs for two centuries until they decided to move. In 1747 and 1749, England passed Acts of Parliament recognising the Moravian fraternity as an ancient Protestant Episcopal Church, and granted it civil and religious privileges at home and in British colonies.

In June 1722, when Zinzendorf was just twenty-two years old, displaced persecuted Moravian Christians (under the leadership of Christian David) began to gather on his estate, a mile outside of Berthelsdorf, Saxony, at a place called Hutberg or Watch-Hill which would later become known as Herrnhut. As the years passed, word got out that Herrnhut was a Protestant refuge and all sorts of malcontents arrived pushing their particular pet doctrines and ideas, soon there were six hundred people. After 1724, the community found it hard to live together in peace, especially when the outwardly godly, yet inwardly religious crank Krüger turned up and denounced the Lutheran Church. He called Zinzendorf "The Beast" and John Andrew Rothe (the pastor of the local church), "The False Prophet;" and even Christian David came under his spell and was led astray for a time. Up until 1727, Zinzendorf got on with his own life but he then began to try to settle the differences amongst his community. He was ordained a Lutheran minister in 1727 whilst Krüger eventually went out of his mind and was committed to an asylum in Berlin. On the 12 May 1727, the community resolved to bury their disputes forever after Zinzendorf summoned them to the Great House on the Hutberg and taught them for three hours of the sin of schism and stated some community rules for the benefit of all. They resolved to settle their differences and gave of themselves afresh to God. Zinzendorf, from this time onward lived in the Herrnhut community to help teach the brethren.

A. Bost, in *History of the Moravians* wrote: 'From that time on there was a wonderful effusion of the Spirit on this happy church, until August the 13th when the measure of Divine grace seemed absolutely overflowing.' It was at this time that little groups of Christians, two or three persons 'met together privately, to converse on their spiritual state, to exhort, and reprove, and pray for each other.' Zinzendorf visited these groups which were later called 'bands.'

On the 22 July 1727, some brethren agreed to meet at a regular time on a hill near Herrnhut 'in order to pour out their souls to God in prayer and singing.' On this same day, Zinzendorf set out for Silesia, a neighbouring estate, but before his departure 'several of the brethren engaged to devote themselves to the advancement of the revival.' The first epistle of John was read and there was great blessing.

At about noon on the 10 August 1727, 'while Pastor Rothe was holding the meeting at Herrnhut, he felt himself overwhelmed by a wonderful and irresistible power of the Lord and sank down in the dust before God, and with him sank down the whole assembled congregation, in an ecstasy of feeling. In this frame of mind they continued till midnight, engaged in praying and singing, weeping and supplication.'

A communion service was held on the 13 August 1727; the whole community united as one, amidst tears and sobs they sung, 'My soul before Thee prostrates lies.' Within a few days 'a remarkable revival took place amongst the children at Herrnhut and Bertholdsdorf. On the 18 August 1727, all the children of the boarding school were seized with an extraordinary impulse of the Spirit, and passed the whole night in prayer.' The work amongst the children carried on for some time.[1]

Between the 25 and 27 August 1727, the community began a 24 hour prayer meeting which lasted for one hundred years! It was based on the fact that in the Temple, the fire on the altar was to perpetually burn, and that as the Church is now the Temple of God, Christians ought to ascend prayers continually.

Zinzendorf, looking back on the four months of revival during the summer of 1727 said, "The whole place represented a visible tabernacle of God amongst men." Zinzendorf held meetings every day and the church at Berthelsdorf was crowded out.

Jonathan Goforth quotes Bishop Hasse who wrote: 'Was there ever in the whole of church history such an astonishing prayer meeting as that which, beginning in 1727 went on one hundred years? It is something absolutely unique. It was known as the 'Hourly Intercession,' and it meant that by relays of [24] brethren and [24] sisters, prayer without ceasing was made to God for all the works and wants of His Church. Prayer of that kind always leads to action. In this case it kindled a burning desire to make Christ's salvation known to the heathen. It led to the beginning of modern foreign missions. From that one small village community more than one hundred missionaries went out in twenty-five years...'

In January 1728, the Herrnhut church held their first missionary meeting. They studied different portions of Holy Scripture, participated in fervent prayer; 'in the midst of which the church experienced a remarkable enjoyment of the presence of the Spirit.' The Moravian Missions began in 1731; work was commenced in the West Indies in 1732. David Nitschmann (an elder) had accompanied Zinzendorf to Denmark for the coronation of King Christian VI, where they met a converted Negro called Anthony (who had a Danish master) from St. Thomas Island who told them that the West Indies needed saving. David Nitschmann and Leonard Dober were willing to sell themselves into slavery to reach the Negroes, because the West Indian Company's ships refused them board, which was eventually paid for by the Danish Royal family, they arrived at St. Thomas in December 1732.[2]

In 1733, two brothers, Matthew and Christian Stack followed in the footsteps of Han Egde, (of Norway) to become missionaries to Greenland and were accompanied by Christian David to see them settled in their mission field. Han Egde had arrived with his family in the summer of 1721 (seventy-one years before the Baptist Missionary Society was founded under William Carey and his associates!). In 1733, small-pox killed between 2,000 to 3,000 Greenlanders and Egde's wife died. By 1736, Egde's had seen no fruit and by invitation of the King of Norway he returned home and used his remaining years to drum-up support for Greenland and others would see the souls that he laboured for. He died in 1758 and the mission which Egde had begun was eventually handed over to the Moravians. By the end of the nineteenth century the Greenlanders along the West coast 'had generally accepted Christianity.'[3]

German historian of Protestant Missions, Dr. Warneck wrote: 'This small church in twenty years called into being more missions than the whole Evangelical Church had done in two centuries.' By 1757, Moravian missionaries were ministering in nearly every country in Europe and they went into Asia, South Africa, Australia and North and South America.[4]

North American Indians 1745-1746 (David Brainerd)

David Brainerd was born in April 1718, in Haddan, New England, and was descended from one of the Pilgrim Fathers who emigrated to America nearly a hundred years earlier. He was converted in his early twenties after deciding to train for the ministry. He became known as a man of prayer whose heart was for the lost which eventually led him to be a missionary to the North American Indians. Brainerd wrote: 'God enabled me to so agonise in prayer that I was quite wet with perspiration, though in the shade and the cool wind. My soul was drawn out very much from the world, for multitudes of souls.'[5]

In April 1743, Brainerd began his ministry amongst the Indians at Kaunaymeek, in the province of New York, in woods, about twenty miles from Stockbridge. Most of his communications were through an Indian interpreter who had been trained at a mission school in Stockbridge. Within a year, Brainerd was ordained; he refused to take up a pastorate in East Hampton, Long Island, amongst his own people, but accepted a post amongst the Indians of Delaware River in Pennsylvania.

In May 1744, after a dangerous journey of one hundred miles through a thinly populated and wild and dreary country he arrived. The principle chief was favourably disposed towards Brainerd's work and he travelled hundreds of miles over mountains and along the banks of the Susqueannah River holding services with natives and Europeans settlers wherever he could gather them.

The film *Dances with Wolves* staring Kevin Coster as Lieutenant John Dunbar was set more than a century later than the revival under David Brainerd, but showed Lieutenant Dunbar trying to make friends with the Sioux Indians. In this film

I caught a small glimpse of what it must have been like for David Brainerd. Brainerd, who travelled with his interpreter, became greatly discouraged as he entered some Indian settlements after long days of travel. Sometimes the Indians would be participating in their heathen dances and revels, highly excited after drinking the white mans 'fire water' and would not be in a fit state to hear the Good News.

On the 9 June 1745, David Brainerd preached on Isaiah 53:10, 'Yet it pleased the Lord to bruise Him' and 'the word was attended with resistless power; many hundreds in that great assembly, consisting of three or four thousand, were much affected so that there was a very great mourning, like the mourning of Hadadrimmon' (see Zechariah 12:11) – this greatly encouraged Brainerd, but he still had to face many disappointments.[6]

Soon Brainerd settled at Crossweeksung (near the sea), on the border of New Jersey, which was more than eighty miles from his principle station and home at the Forks of Delaware. The native Indians were very receptive, by August 1745, the small Indian settlement had grown and it was not long until revival broke out. It was a good job too, because Brainerd was so discouraged just a few days before the revival that he 'began to entertain serious thoughts of giving up...' and quitting as a missionary. On the 2 August 1745, he wrote: 'My rising hopes, respecting the conversion of the Indians have been so often dashed, that my spirit is as it were broken, and courage wasted and I hardly dare hope.'[7]

On the morning of the 6 August 1745, after giving a sermon, Brainerd recorded in his diary: 'Many of them were tenderly affected, so that a few words about their souls would cause the tears to flow freely, and produce many sobs and groans.' In the afternoon, he preached again, but nothing happened until near the end of the sermon, 'All seemed in an agony to obtain an interest in Christ. It was surprising to see how their hearts seemed to be pierced with the tender and melting invitations of the Gospel, when there was not a word of terror spoken to them.'[8]

Two days later, on the eighth, Brainerd was preaching to sixty-five Indians, men, women and children and wrote: 'There was much concern among them while I was discoursing publicly; but afterwards, when I spoke to one and another more particularly, the power of God seemed to descend upon the assembly, like a mighty rushing wind, and with an astonished energy bore them all before it.' Brainerd stood amazed as the Holy Spirit swept down as 'a mighty torrent that bears down and sweeps before it whatever is in its way.'

Old men and women who had been drunkards for many years were converted and delivered. Children and those in old age also came under conviction of sin. 'The most stubborn hearts were obliged to bow. One man who had been a murderer, 'a powow' or witch-doctor and a notorious drunkard, was also brought to cry out for mercy with many tears. Indeed the people were almost universally praying and crying for mercy in every part of the house, and many out of doors.' Some of the white people came to investigate and 'were much awakened, and appeared to be wounded with a view of their perishing state. I never saw any thing like it in any respects' wrote Brainerd. 'It was a day in which the Lord did much to destroy the kingdom of darkness among the people.'

Out of this revival, an American Indian Christian village was formed on a tract of land at Crossweeksung and was called Bethel. The land was cultivated and a thriving community arose which included teaching the Indians several trades, a school was founded, for children and adults alike and a teacher was employed.

On the 10 October 1747, after years of battling consumption, David Brainerd passed into glory, aged just twenty-nine at the house of Jonathan Edwards at Northampton, Massachusetts, New England. Edwards had seen revival in his parish at Northampton (1734-1735) which was the precursor to the American Great Awakening (1735-1760). Edwards' daughter, Jerusha, and David Brainerd had a close relationship, which grew as she nursed him for four months until he passed into glory. She was twelve years his junior and is buried beside him, having died four months later of the same disease. On Brainerd's tomb was etched: 'Sacred to the Memory of the Rev. David Brainerd, A Faithful Missionary to the Stockbridge, Delaware, and Susquehannah Indians; who died in this town October 10, 1747 – Æт. 32.'[9]

His age at death was incorrectly engraved; he was just 29 and is buried at Bridge Street Cemetery, Northampton, America.

Chapter Nine

To Give Light to Those who Sit in Darkness

'To give knowledge of salvation to His people by the remission of their sins, through the tender mercy of our God, with which the Dayspring from on high has visited us' Luke 1:77-78.

Tinnevelli, India 1802

In 1726, Christian Fredrick Schwartz was born at Sonnenburg, in the Prussian province of Brandenburg. In 1746, he began his studies at the University of Halle where he was influenced by two men; Schultz (a former missionary to India) and Herman Francke, (a professor who was interested in mission work). Halle University had begun printing the Tamil Bible and Schwartz along with another student was asked to learn the Tamil language which took eighteen months of study.

Prior to his graduation, Francke suggested to Schwartz that he should become a missionary to India. He was ordained at Copenhagen, and sailed from London in January 1750 and reached Tranquebar in July. This was forty-three years before the 'Father of Modern Missions' William Carey arrived in India! In November he was able to preach his first sermon in Tamil and his work became successful.

In 1760, he visited Ceylon (modern day Sri Lanka). In 1762 he trekked to the south of India, to Trichinopoly (Tiruchchirappalli) – 150 miles from Madras (Chennai) and Tanjore (Thanjavur) which became the chief centres of his work, being just over fifteen miles apart. At Trichinopoly he was asked by the Governor to become chaplain to the English soldiers. He gained great influence over the garrison and a stone church, Christ's Church was built accommodating 1,500 people, which was opened in May 1766. At Tanjore he was even allowed to preach at the rajah's palace, though the rajah himself could not be seen in person as he was shielded by a hung veil.

In 1766, Schwartz came under the Society for Promoting Christian Knowledge (SPCK), and he returned to Trichinopoly. In 1773, Tanjore was captured and the church which he used to preach in was destroyed. In 1776, the East India Company restored the rajah and Tanjore became his base for missions.

In 1778, Schwartz left his base and travelled south, 110 miles to Tinnevelli, at the base of India, three hundred miles from Madras and began preaching. By this time, Schwartz had become a very influential missionary by all concerned because of his character, purity of heart and the consistency of his life. In the early 1780s, twice Tanjore was in famine and men were dying in the streets, the rajah was powerless to help, but Schwartz was not. On one occasion he wrote letters to the native Christians asking for them to bring in food to Tanjore which he would pay for, within a few days he received over a thousand bullocks and eighty thousand kalams of grain, thus the prince and his people were saved from starvation.

In 1787, at the court at Tanjore, the rajah adopted a ten year old boy who he named Serfojee Rahaj. He was to be the successor to the throne, the rajah asked Schwartz to be his guardian stating, "This is not my son, but yours; into your hands I deliver him." Schwartz replied, "May this child become a child of God." The rajah retired with the excuse of a bad cough. The next day Schwartz had to decline the offer, declaring that due to the animosities within the kingdom he would not be able to protect him, but offered to visit him once or twice a month to instruct him.

In 1790, Schwartz revisited Tinnevelli and ordained an Indian catechist (one who prepares people for baptism, teaching them the principles of Christianity) and left the work in his capable hands. In February 1798, Christian Fredrick Schwartz passed into glory having laboured forty-eight years in India. Serfojee Rahaj, (who was now an adult) shed a flood of tears over him and covered his body with a gold cloth.

In 1802, this unknown Indian catechist (who had been ordained by Schwartz twelve years previously) baptised 5,000 Hindus in three months, but with no missionary in charge many fell away for a time. This does in no way decry the work of God as for many of us in the West we 'live in ease in Zion' and have no conceptual understanding of the cost of following Christ, of changing ones religion, nor of breaking caste (see the following page). A convert from Hinduism can suffer the wrath and retribution of family, friends and those within the same village. For a Hindu to convert to Christianity, breaking away from his old gods is confirmed by baptism, the outward sign of an inward faith. After 1820, when the missionary Rhenius began work in earnest, there was a steady growth in the church.

Some people find it hard to believe that mass movements are possible (see appendix F), but does the Lord find it easier, and prefer to save singly rather than enmasse? – Is there anything too hard for God? At Pentecost, were not 3,000 won to the Lord in a day? In August 1885, Dwight L Moody, with several hundred delegates attended a ten day convention in Northfield, America, where they discussed and prayed for world revival. At the end of the conference a circular letter was prepared and sent to all believers throughout the world calling upon all disciples everywhere to unite in prayer for an infusion of the Spirit upon the whole habitable globe. One portion of the letter as way of encouragement stated: 'Even Pentecost is surpassed by the ingathering of 10,000 converts in one station in India within sixty days in the year 1868...' During the Northampton Revival (1734-1735) under Jonathan Edwards, virtually the whole parish which consisted of 220 families was converted. 620 persons were able to prove their conversion; (including almost all the adults) therefore they were permitted to partake around the Lord's Table.

Missionary to India, Sherwood Eddy, in 1910 wrote: 'During the last century multitudes have come over to Christianity. Since *caste conditions all Indian life, and has for centuries crushed out individually, and punished all efforts at independence and progress, men have been compelled to act together. Minds move in mass in India. We have to take the people as they come.' Is that not what Jesus has done for us, taken us how we are and cleaned us? – Over time our understanding of Jesus and Christianity has grown, we are ongoing works of grace with much to learn.

*Caste may be defined as a collection of families holding a common title or name, claiming descent from a common ancestor, originally professing to follow the same calling, and unified into a single community by a tradition of fixed rules and customs. Those from different castes are not permitted to intermarry or eat with each other; those from the lowest caste are worth less than the price of an animal (see appendices G and H).[1]

Student Revival 1816-1819 – Geneva, Switzerland

In 1816, Robert Haldane, was strongly moved to visit the Continent of Europe. The journey was meant to take six weeks, but took three years! At the end of the year, he set out accompanied by his wife, both of whom longed to see Europe revived, where once much light had shone during the Reformation.

In Paris, France, he sensed a spiritual gloom that could be felt and after diligent search he could not find a single copy of the Scriptures. In vain he sought for an opening for the Gospel, but with none, he headed onto Geneva, Switzerland. As he passed through its ancient gates he fervently prayed for Divine leadings as he knew not one person within it. Robert was on the point of departure when an old pastor, due to sickness was unable to go with Robert on a short excursion beyond the walls and so in his place he sent a young student of Divinity. Robert, ever eager to share the Gospel did so, and the student returned to his lodging where they continued in discussion till late at night.

Geneva had long since disregarded the faith of her fathers and a deep darkness shrouded the once 'Fount of Evangelical Truth.' Geneva's noble school of theology had long since lost is nobility and had rapidly declined since the days of John Calvin, the great Reformer of Geneva. It was corrupted by Unitarianism, thus denying Jesus Christ's deity and magnified the goodness of man. The Bible was entirely set aside as a textbook; Plato and Seneca taking the place of Christ and Paul. During the four-year theology course, the only time the Bible was used was for the teaching of Hebrew, when a few Psalms and chapters were read!

On the following day, the Divinity student appeared with a friend. So astonished were these two by what they had heard that they told their fellows. The students were intrigued by a man of one book, and this book the Bible, was indeed a great book, well worth the perusal of Divinity students! The students stated, "He knew the Bible like Calvin!" and was "a living concordance." They were amazed to find that the problems which had vexed them for so long were easily solved as Robert turned to various passages of Scripture.

Soon Robert was besieged with enquirers, so many students sought out his knowledge that he started his famous Home Bible College. About thirty attended, three times a week for two hours of evening Bible study. The home (and college) was located at 19 Promenade St. Antoine – a suite of apartments. The students were seated around a long table where copies of the Bible in French, German, English, Greek, Hebrew and other languages were placed. The students fired off many questions, to which the Scriptures were turned to, he spent no time in argument, but pointed to the relevant text and said, "Look here -

how readest thou? What thinketh thou?" Soon the students after having their concerns answered from the truth of God's word were prepared for the essential truths of salvation.

Robert commenced a systematic study of the epistle to the Romans, where the students were told of man's depravity and their need for a Divine Saviour. Soon intellectual knowledge burst forth into deep spiritual concern. One by one they surrendered their lives to Jesus Christ – and this became known as the Student Revival, where the theological class, became a class of anxious enquirers. Robert knew that by winning one student of Divinity to Christ it could lead to a chain of grace that could affect thousands who would later come under their influence. Bitter persecution soon followed from professors and clergy alike as a living Church arose and this work of God became known as 'Geneva's Second Reformation.'

When Robert left to preach the Gospel at Montauban, God sent another teacher to continue the work, Henry Drummond, a talented and wealthy Englishman, who was devoted to Jesus Christ. He was on a voyage to the Holy Land, when a storm compelled his ship to seek refuge in Genoa. Here he heard of the Student Revival, changed his plans and came to Geneva, arriving just two days before Robert's departure, the Lord's timing is always perfect!

The persecution eventually encouraged the students to scatter across Europe; many in time were to become in themselves famous for their work for the Lord. Just as Robert had foreseen as a spiritual strategist, they influenced thousands for Christ Jesus, as preachers, authors and missionaries across Europe and beyond.[2]

Two of these pupils were Madame Feller and Pastor Louis Roussy; they went to French Canada and began a work in a log cabin near St. John's Quebec Province. They founded the Grande Ligne Mission and its school, the Feller Institute which was 'born in prayer, continued in prayer, and has grown by prayer.' As they began evangelising their province the school grew. Roussy died in 1880, a dozen years after the saintly Madame Feller had passed into glory, and was succeeded by Rev. Alphonose de L. Therrin, a former Mission student whose ministry was marked by many blessed revivals.[3]

In 2006, I visited Geneva on a short-term mission where I saw the Reformation monuments and the site on which John Calvin's house once stood. No doubt, Robert Haldane and his students would have been inspired by many of the Reformation characters and because of the smallness of Geneva, (which is like a bowl surrounded by mountains) their presence must have made quite an impact on the community.

Alleghany Tract Revival c.1835

The following revival came from *Narrative of Remarkable Conversion and Revival Incidents* (1859) and is undated. I put the year as c.1835 as it is the central date between the 1820s and 1850s, which is the general dates of most of the revival incidents contained within the book I am quoting from.

'An agent in New York says, a young man in L------, being about to remove to Alleghany County (in America) called at the [Tract] Depository in Utica, and obtained about one thousand tracts. These he caused to be faithfully distributed in the town where he had fixed his abode. Their distribution was soon followed by a general revival of religion. Between fifty and sixty professed converts to Jesus Christ were the first fruits of this revival; and nearly thirty of them traced their first serious impression to the tracts which had been put into their hands.'[4]

Hawaii Awakening 1836-1840

In 1801, Titus Coan was born in Killingworth, Middlesex, Connecticut, New England. He was a son of a farmer, though well educated and became a teacher until he was enlisted in the army. After a handful of years he reverted back to his old profession and was converted when he was about twenty-seven years old. He led 200 people to Christ at Auburn State Prison School. In 1831, he attended Bible College and by 1835, after he had been ordained, he was accepted by the American Board of Commissioners for Foreign Missions.

In late 1835, Titus Coan and his wife, Fidelia landed on the shore belt of Hawaii and were stationed at Hilo. Within three months he had mastered the language and preached his first sermon. He ministered in the districts of Hilo, Puna and parts of Kau; a hundred mile coastline, with between 15,000-16,000 inhabitants and went on three or four preaching trips annually. These trips were from ten to twenty days in duration and for the first few years had to be done on foot; there were no horses, roads or bridges and crossing rivers in certain seasons was very dangerous. Schools had already been established by earlier missionaries, most of whom had not settled permanently except Mr and Mrs Lyman. There was a little over twenty natives Christians when he arrived, and much superstition, ignorance and vices abounded amongst the natives.

Knowing a little about medicine he helped the natives with his chest full of medicines and even performed surgery. He was more than a missionary, but a pastor, preacher, peacemaker and magistrate, and immediately the hearts of the natives were warmed to him. On his first tour, in December 1836, multitudes flocked to hear him at the western boundaries of Puna, so much so that he had scarcely time to eat and would preach up to five times a day. On one occasion he preached three times, at three different villages, a half a mile apart before he was able to eat his breakfast at 10am. Often he would be preaching till ten or until midnight and then again when the cock crowed. Many were converted including the pagan High Priest of the volcano; a man of influence, though he was an idolater, drunkard, murderer and an adulterer, and 'became penitent and seemed earnest in seeking the Lord.'

In late 1837, the fires of revival peaked when nearly the whole population became an audience. He was ministering to 15,000 people and for two years he held a camp meeting where the people flocked to hear him preach Jesus and Him crucified. They built little huts and planted food, whilst others fished. There was not an hour of the day or night when an audience from two to six thousand would not rally to the signal of the bell. His church was only 200 feet long by 85 feet wide and was crowded to suffocation, so the natives decided to build a second church which could accommodate 2,000 people.

There was trembling, weeping, sobbing, and loud cries for mercy, in hundreds of cases his hearers fell to the floor 'in a swoon.' On many occasions he had to stop preaching because the cries of the penitents drowned him out. Some would cry out, "The two edged sword is cutting me to pieces." The wicked scoffer who came to mock fell to the floor and cried out, "God has struck me!" Once whilst preaching in the open field to two thousand people, a man cried out, "What must I do to be saved?" and prayed the publican's prayer, (God have mercy on me a sinner), and the entire congregation took up the cry for mercy. For thirty minutes Titus Coan had to hold back his address, stood still and watched the Holy Spirit at work.

Quarrels were made up, sins of a lifetime were renounced, drunkards reclaimed, adulterers converted, murders revealed and pardoned, whilst thieves returned stolen property. In one year, 5,244 joined the church. In June 1837, on one Sunday,

1,705 were baptised and 2,400 partook of communion around the Lord's Table. During times of mass baptism, Titus Coan had to sprinkle water on a brush and walk up and down the rows of converts in scores or hundreds repeating the sacred rite of, "In the name of the Father, the Son and the Holy Spirit."

During 1839-1840 more than 7,000 joined the church at Hilo and 12,000 were baptised and his church became the largest Protestant church in the world! When Titus Coan and his wife left for America, after thirty-five years of service, he had personally received and baptised 11,960 people – but in 1871, they returned to the mission field of Hawaii.[5]

In *Incidents of Missionary Enterprise* (1841), a former missionary to Hawaii, a Mr Stewart visited Hido, Hawaii and recounted some of his impressions. Four years ago, he noted, you could scarcely get 100 people assembled for a church service, yet as he made his way towards the worshiping assembly in a 9,000 square foot church under Mr Goodrich, he said, "What a change! What a happy change!" Stewart recounted that he had 'listened with delightful attention to some of the highest eloquence' from the pulpit of America and England until 'all who heard were wrapt into an enthusiasm of high-toned feelings... I have seen tears of conviction and penitence flow freely as if to the breaking of the heart...but it was here at a worshipping assembly at Hido, the most obscure corner of these distant islands, to excite, the liveliest emotions ever experienced, and leave the deepest impression of the extent and un-searchable riches of the Gospel which I have known. Emotions and impressions derived simply from an ocular demonstration of the power of God on untutored man, which is without parallel in existing events, if not in the records of history.'

Stewart went on to describe the congregation of thousands, dressed in native "clothing" as he stood next to Goodrich (the preacher) and looked out over the vast congregation. He wrote: 'The depth of the impression arose from the irresistible conviction that the Spirit of God was there; it could have been nothing else.' In the evening, he spoke to some of the missionaries that confirmed his own conclusion that 'an entire moral reformation has taken place in the vicinity of this station' whilst 'Instruction of every kind is eagerly and universally sought... The mansion house is daily crowded with earnest inquirers in every way; evil customs and atrocious vices are abandoned [&] a strict outward conformity to morals observed.'[6]

Chapter Ten

Knowledge of Salvation

Jesus said, "The Spirit of the Lord is upon Me, because He has anointed Me to preach the Gospel to the poor. He has sent Me to heal the broken hearted, to preach deliverance to the captives and recovery of sight to the blind, to set at liberty those who are oppressed, to preach the acceptable year of the Lord" Luke 4:18-19.

Jamaican Awakening 1838-1845

Christopher Columbus discovered Jamaica during his voyage from 1493-1496, and the country became a British colony in 1655 after Britain went to war with Spain and won.

William Knibb was born in Kettering, England, in 1802 and is best known for his work for the emancipation of slaves amongst the West Indies. What most people do not know (including the documentary I watched on national television) was that four years after the Emancipation Day, (after the 'free' slaves had served a four year apprenticeship) a spiritual awakening broke out across the entire country of Jamaica and lasted for seven years. His story is told in *William Knibb: Missionary in Jamaica, A Memoir* by Mrs John James Smith (1896).

After Knibb's conversion in England, he became a street preacher and through his care and visitations amongst the poorest parts of Bristol, many people were converted.

In 1824, as a Baptist missionary, he arrived in Kingston, Jamaica, with his wife Mary, to take the place of his deceased brother and became the schoolmaster. On his arrival, he found that he was one of only seven missionaries amongst a vast slave population who worked the sugar plantations. By 1826, the plantation owners, who hated the missionaries (Dissenters / Nonconformists, Baptists, Methodists, Moravians etc.) wanted the British Government to pass anti-missionary laws and so accused them of stirring up the slaves by preaching on equality and human rights. Other false charges were levied against them. Due to the Baptist Society policy, Knibb did not incite the slaves to desire their own freedom, but he always told the slaves to obey their masters as the apostle Paul had written.

In 1829, several of the missionaries were summoned before the hostile House Assembly of the Jamaican colonial authorities. The Consolidated Slave Law of 1810-1814 had been re-enacted which prohibited the meeting of slaves during daylight hours, taxed the churches and banned the taking of offerings from slaves for Nonconformist work. Many slave owners forbade their slaves to attend church and made them sell their wares in the markets on the Sabbath which was illegal (in Jamaica and in Britain), though overlooked by the Jamaican authorities who were slave and plantation owners!

Knibb wrote: 'Notwithstanding all opposition, the work is proceeding gloriously. Thousands are flocking to hear the word of the God, and great numbers are joining themselves to the Lord. We are persecuted, but not in despair.'

In 1830, Knibb became the pastor of a six hundred strong Baptist Church at Falmouth. In 1831, the slaves heard a rumour that King William was to free all slaves because a motion was brought before the British House of Commons for the gradual abolition of slavery in the British colonies. Some Jamaican planters threatened to kill their slaves rather than have to pay them! In October, some slaves asked Knibb whether their freedom was to be granted. He replied in the negative.

On the 27 of December 1831, there was a slave revolt. They burnt their masters' sugar plantations and martial law was imposed. A colonial army was enlisted by force to fight; Knibb was one of them, who tried to suppress the revolt, but he was soon arrested as an accomplice and was on bail for seven weeks before being cleared of all charges. The authorities killed many of the slaves, including some from Knibb's own congregation that was 885 strong; others were flogged even though none of his congregation were involved in the revolt, but yet they still suffered retribution.

During this revolt, an Anglican clergyman called Bridges formed a Colonial Church Union, which called for the expulsion of all Nonconformist missionaries, destroyed their churches and opposed all anti-slavery sentiment. Many of the planters set out to kill Knibb. On one occasion, the planters tried to tar and feather him, and for three successive nights, fifty white planters stoned his rented home.

In 1832, Knibb visited England and Scotland where virtually every evening he spoke at public meetings informing the people about the conditions of the Baptist slaves in Jamaica. He even stood before both Houses of Parliament who were inquiring into the state of the colonies in the West Indies and told it how it was; which was a shock to those who heard.

In August 1833, the British government passed the Abolition of Slavery Act, which was to be enacted on the 1 August 1834. The 'free' slaves were then to serve a six year apprenticeship, but this was later reduced to four years. Emancipation Day was on the last day of July 1834 where an hour before midnight the slaves at Falmouth passed the last hour in worship at church.

Knibb returned to Jamaica before Emancipation Day and everywhere he went, the slaves greeted him. He held many packed services, beginning at one place at 6am and then another at 10am! The British government had given Knibb a sum of money to rebuild his church and prior to his return, the congregation was more than 1,600. In 1837, his congregation was 1,800 strong. After the opening of the new chapel at Falmouth, freed slaves belonging to Knibb's church, who owned apprentice slaves, set them free at a public meeting. Opposition towards Knibb did not cease and he was vilified constantly.

After August 1838, when all slaves were free – free to attend church, they flocked to churches across the island and the Jamaican Awakening began, which lasted for seven years. Knibb wrote: 'Today I baptised 75 persons and 1,300 sat down at the Lord's Supper. It was one of the happiest days of my life.'

Peter Masters wrote: 'Vast numbers were moved to repentance and faith...The seven years following 1838 – the dawn of *full* freedom – proved to be years of quite astonishing harvest...Baptists, Methodists, Moravians and Presbyterians were all mightily instrumental, but the Baptist missionaries and chapels were the most numerous, and they undoubtedly saw the greatest fruit of this glorious fire of the Lord. Baptists, with all their Calvinistic care and concern to see a real work of God in hearts, did not receive new members easily, and yet the people came, wept, and clung to Christ, repenting and believing with all their hearts.'

In 1833, in Westmoreland there were not any couples who were legally married. Yet during the years 1842-1844, registered marriages for the whole of Jamaica was more than 28,300! This awakening not only saved souls, but as all true awakenings, it affected the moral climate of the country.

Knibb wrote: 'In the midst of these scenes the work of mercy extended so that in those seven years, through the labour of about twenty missionaries, 22,000 people were baptised upon their profession of faith in Jesus Christ.'

Since 1831, forty-seven new chapels were built along with many school rooms and many of the churches were self supporting. In Falmouth, Knibb's own church had planted six churches and more than 3,000 people had been baptised before he visited England in early 1845.[1]

In 1840, Knibb's second visited to England, he met the Baptist Committee and pleaded the cause of an African Missionary Society (more missionaries to Jamaica and for their Fatherland) and on the 3 June, the West Africa Mission was commenced.[2]

When Knibb returned to Jamaica in August 1845, he was greeted by a procession, at Granville, which was more than a mile long. On Sunday the ninth of November 1845, Knibb baptised 42 people. Six days later he died of yellow fever, aged forty-three. Eight thousand people attended his funeral service at Falmouth and he was buried outside his church.

New Hebrides Revival 1852-1854

On the 20 November 1839, John Williams, the apostolic pioneer of the South Seas Mission and his young missionary companion James Harris came ashore on the island of Erromanga, New Hebrides, South Pacific, (part of the island nation of modern day Vanuatu) and within a few minutes were martyred, cooked and then eaten by the native savages! 170 years later, in November 2009, descendants of John Williams travelled to Erromanga to accept the apologies of descendants of the cannibals in a ceremony of repentance and reconciliation. The President of Vanuatu, Iolo Johnson Abbil said. "Since we claim to be a Christian country it is very important that we have a reconciliation like this," he said. "Erromango needs it very much. People always look upon them that they killed a missionary, they think that it has sort of a curse on Erromango and that's why it's very important for them to have this reconciliation."

Three generation of Williams were present, Charles Milner-Williams, the great, great, great grandson of John Williams headed up the family alongside seventeen other members (6th and 7th generations) from England, Canada and Africa. To mark the occasion, Dillons Bay was renamed Williams Bay and the Williams family agreed to take on responsibility for the education of a seven-year-old girl who was ceremonially handed over to them in exchange for the loss of John Williams.[3]

Incited by the martyrdom of John Williams in 1839, the Rev. John Geddie, a young Presbyterian minister of Scottish birth, in

Nova Scotia, Canada, began to arouse interest in the evangelisation of the cannibal infested islands of the Pacific. Eventually, and by only a majority of one, he succeeded in persuading the Synod to appoint a foreign missionary. Rev. Geddie offered himself for the post and was duly accepted.

In March 1846, Rev. Geddie and his family sailed to Boston, America. After a wait of two months they boarded a ship which took six months just to get round the dreaded Cape Horn. They eventually arrived at Honolulu, in the Sandwich Islands, but had to wait seven weeks for a ship to Samoa. On his arrival he found that he could not arrive at his intended destination as no ships were sailing for at least six months. At Samoa he studied the methods of mission until in July 1848 he embarked with the Rev. Thomas Powell of the London Missionary Society for the New Hebrides and arrived at Aneityum, the most southerly of the islands. Rev. Powell stayed for about one year, to advise as to his settlement and to assist in opening up the work.

Dr. Steel of Sydney, in the late nineteenth century, wrote: 'The Geddies had to pass through a hard and trying experience in dealing with a people so low and savage. Their property was stolen, their house threatened with fire, and their very lives imperilled. Meanwhile the horrid custom of strangling widows on the death of their husbands continued. Intertribal fighting was chronic, and people were afraid to go from one side of the island to the other, for fear of being killed, cooked and eaten.'

In 1852, the Bishop of New Zealand, assisted the Rev. John Inglis (and his wife) of the Reformed Church in Scotland to a new station on the opposite side of the island.

Approximately from 1852-1854 a revival broke out across the entire island. John G. Patton, missionary to the New Hebrides on the island of Tanna (the nearest island to Aneityum) wrote: 'Marvellous as it may seem, the natives on Aneityum showed interest in the missionaries from the very first, and listened to their teachings; so that in a few years Dr. Inglis and Dr. Geddie saw about 3,500 savages throwing away their idols, renouncing their heathen customs and avowing themselves to be worshippers of the true Jehovah God. Slowly, yet progressively they unlearned their heathenism; surely and hopefully they learned Christianity and civilisation.' Soon, a simple form of family worship was introduced and observed by every household on the island; God's blessing was asked over every meal; 'peace and public order was restored and property was perfectly safe under the sanctifying and civilising Gospel of Christ.'

Dr. Steel wrote: 'Young people were all taught to read and write, congregations were organised with elders and deacons, fifty day-schools established and over 2,000 persons admitted into the visible Church by baptism. The whole people were evangelised. It was a marvellous change in a degraded and cannibal people.'

The missionaries along with Rev. Joseph Copeland eventually translated the entire Bible into the native language. Prior to this no written page or book had ever been translated into their tongue. During this time, the Aneitumese, planted and prepared arrowroot which was set apart to the Lord and sent to Australia and Scotland where it was sold by friends. After fifteen years the finances raised was £1,200 so that the British and Foreign Bible Society could published this Bible.

In 1863, Rev. Geddie made a brief visit to Nova Scotia when he was given an honorary degree. He returned to the place of his earlier triumphs and within a few years he retired in Geelong where in 1872 he passed away. In the wall of the stone church which he had erected at Anelgauhat, Aneityum, a wooden tablet was placed and inscribed in the native tongue to the memory of John Geddie: 'When he landed here in 1848 there were no Christians, and when he left here in 1872 there were no heathen.'

The church at Aneityum was the first of the Papuan race to be welcomed into the Kingdom of Christ on earth and subsequently stood forth as the pioneer bearer of the Gospel to the scattered sea-girt islands of the New Hebrides.[4]

Canada 1857-1858

In 1857, Canada witnessed revival as part of a worldwide religious awakening – a revival which swept the globe which had its beginnings in New York, America, during the Fulton Street Revival (1857-1859) which began in September 1857. The revival fires spread and virtually simultaneously burst forth in Kells, Ireland and then touched Wales, Scotland and England during the years 1858-1860. In 1858, Sweden saw 200,000 conversions as revival touched them for two years. The heaven-sent blessing circled the globe as the news spread of this great awakening. In late 1859, revival broke out across India in what became known as the India Awakening, though the broadest work was seen in the South of India. 1859 was the beginning of the evangelisation of Brazil, though Protestant had arrived in 1555 and settled in Rio, whilst David Livingstone (en route to Africa) met a missionary there in 1840! In 1860, revival also broke out in Jamaica, in various towns and areas across the Cape Colony of South Africa (especially among the Dutch Reformed Church) and in Shanghai, China.[5]

This Canadian revival began in Hamilton, Ontario which is known as Canada West. It began when Holiness Methodist preachers, Dr. Walter C. Palmer and his wife, Phoebe, took their responsibility seriously for the Great Commission and held evangelistic campaigns in early October 1857.

Its small beginning began in one service when twenty-one people got converted, and as the Scriptures declare: 'Do not despise the day of small things.' Within a few weeks 300-400 hundred people had surrendered their lives to Jesus Christ. The conversions steadily grew, a score here, to forty-five daily. One hundred converts were recorded the Sunday prior to the following report. The front page headline for the Methodist *Christian Advocate and Journal* of New York, dated the 5 November 1857 was *Revival Extraordinary*. The reporter wrote: 'The work is taking within its range persons of all classes, men of low degree, and men of high estate for wealth and position; old men and maidens, and even little children, are seen humbly kneeling together pleading for grace. The mayors of the city, with other persons of like position, are not ashamed to be seen bowed at the altar of prayer beside the humble servant....'

This localised revival under the Palmer's soon spread as if by Divine conflagration under spontaneous combustible circumstances and birthed other localised revivals. These localised puddles of blessing soon became various streams for the glory of God in different states. J. Edwin Orr, noting the press coverage wrote: 'steadily [the press wrote] increasing number of paragraphs,' a few in November 'increasing in December, and a veritable flood in the late winter and spring of 1858.'

The teaching of the preaching Palmers was a message of holiness and full surrender; a full consecration to God, of ones money, spouse, children, reputation etc. and Phoebe's emphasis to the women was the willingness to preach!

The Palmers went to the United Kingdom in the late summer of 1859 where they held evangelistic campaigns for four / five years and saw a reported 25,000 conversions during that period. The revival in Britain was still going strong and the Palmers anointing did not diminish.

In Sunderland, England, over 3,400 joined the local Wesleyan Societies in 1859. In the spring of 1862, the Palmers held a month campaign in Cardiff, Wales, where according to an Anglican Councillor, crime cases began to dwindle and a police detective stated that Cardiff had become a different place.[6]

Zululand 1874

In February 1869, the missionary magazine, *The Net Cast In Many Waters* published an article on Zululand which read: 'The most sorrowful part of the mission work in Zululand hitherto had been, while the truth was freely and fully preached, the people have not been free to accept it. In individual cases, when the converts' hearts burned with the conviction that what they believed in their hearts they must confess with their mouths, application was made, and special permission given by their chiefs, that they might be baptised. But there were many, who although they believed, shrank from persecution, and of all states for a man or woman to be in, that is the most dangerous, to know the truth and to be afraid to profess it...Mr Robertson...[gave] details...[that] in our last number, that a general permission has been given [on the 16 August 1868] by King Panda [King of the Zulus] that his subjects may become Christians when they like...'[7]

B. K. Hazell, writing about Methodism in Zululand and Maputaland wrote: 'That [the] Methodist entry into Zululand was so long delayed does not mean that there was no missionary zeal [there]...On the contrary, so far as Natal was concerned, this was a time of remarkable fervour. In 1874 there had been a significant revival at a place called Jonono's Kop in which the agents were African laymen.

'This revival was accompanied by a strong desire among African Christians to seek the salvation of the 'heathen beyond.' As a result special arrangements were made to send evangelists into areas yet unevangelised, and to contribute the money required for this purpose. That this movement of the Holy Spirit did not have greater influence upon the work in Zululand may be attributed to the troubled times through which that territory was passing and the fact that the door of Missions was for some time closed to all accept the Lutheran group.'[8]

Chapter Eleven

Forgiveness of Sins

Jesus said, "The time is fulfilled and the Kingdom of God is at hand. Repent and believe in the Gospel" Mark 1:15.

Telugu People 1878 (Lone Star Revival) – India

The Telugu country, is just north of Madras (modern day Chennai), along the southern east coast of India. At the end of the nineteenth century, nearly ten thousand people were converted in one year! Here in 1840, the pioneer missionary, Samuel Day began to labour at Nellore, fifty miles from Madras, for His Lord and Saviour Jesus Christ. After eight years of hard and faithful labour there were such discouraging results that as the annual American Baptist Missionary Union (which was later called the American Baptist Foreign Mission Society) met in Boston, they raised the question of abandoning the field. Instead, another labourer, Dr. Jewett was sent out and ploughed a lonely furrow, seed sowing for nine years with no sign of harvest.

In 1857, the annual meeting was held and the question was posed again, "Shall the mission be discontinued?" One of those present, turned to the map, pointed to Nellore and called it the "Lone Star Mission." Dr. S. F. Smith caught on those words and that night composed some prophetic lines which were read out the following day and when the words struck home, many wept:

'Shine on, Lone Star; in grief and tears, and sad reverses oft baptised; shine on till earth redeemed, in dust shall bid it idols fall; and thousands where Thy radiance beamed, shall crown the Saviour Lord of all.'

They unanimously voted to reinforce the mission. But in 1868, after twenty years of labour they urged Dr. Jewett to give up the field, he declined and stated that if the Missionary Union would not aid him, he would go back alone to live and die amongst his own people. The Missionary Union stood by him and sent out young Clough "to bury Jewett," as one of the missionaries put it.

During the great famine of 1877, Dr. Clough took a contract to cut a portion of the Buckingham Canal (for irrigation); he could employ the locals and thus save thousands from starvation. His native preachers were placed over the work, and during periods of rest they gathered the people together and preached to the captive audience. Fearing their motives, the missionaries allowed no one to receive baptism during the famine which was followed by Cholera. Dr. Clough tried to hold back the converts but 'they thronged in upon him from distant villages.' They said, "We don't want money. We have lived by our work. The blisters on our hands will prove it, but we want you to baptise us."

On the third of July 1878, 2,222 people were baptised and before the end of the year, 9,606 converts had been received into the church![1]

James A. Stewart in *Opened Windows – The Church and Revival* wrote: 'The lonely labourers [of the Lone Star Mission] definitely claimed and believed on the authority of the word of God, that a mighty movement of the Spirit was coming. Before long their prayers were answered, and the good news flashed back to the thousands of praying saints in North America that God had performed a miracle.'[2]

At the dawning of the twentieth century, missionary, Sherwood Eddy wrote: 'As I stood there at Ongole [one hundred miles from Madras] with Dr. Clough, white haired, a missionary Napoleon; as I looked out over the great buildings, colleges, churches, schools, and manifold institutions; as I looked beyond the crowded villages with their thousands of Christians, I was deeply moved...this Telugu mission now numbers over 150,000 persons in the entire Christian community.'[3]

Rothesay Revival 1888-1889 – Scotland

In October 1888, in the town of Rothesay on the island of Bute, Scotland, UK, a true heaven-sent revival broke forth as God's Spirit visited the people at the West End Halls when two 'un-assuming young women' as the papers called them began to preach and sing of the wonders of Jesus Christ. Two Pilgrims, workers of The Faith Mission, Pilgrim Martin and Pilgrim Mitchell, held the mission. The evangelistic mission was due to end in November but went on till March 1889 with glorious results. In all, ten Pilgrims assisted in the work along with the founder of The Faith Mission, the Chief, John George Govan, his three brothers (Williams, James and Horace), Pilgrim (Jim) Morrison and a few other labouring friends.

J. G. Govan was able to differentiate between 'good missions' and what God means by 'revival.' He wrote: 'True revival is *from* God *and* of God. Anyone who has been in a revival knows what a difference it makes when 'the Spirit is poured upon us from on high' (Isaiah 32:15). Human powers cannot make mountains flow at Thy presence (Isaiah 64:1).' Govan continued: 'The outpouring of the Spirit of God changes the whole atmosphere of places, and the interests, feelings and conversations of populations; making the truths of the Bible and of eternity stand out in bold relief and in the strong light that will show them to be of first importance; and, on the other hand, making people feel how little are the things of time in comparison. A revival that is of God will be deep and thorough in its results...'

The mission began on the 20 October 1888 with meetings attended by just a handful of Christians and some children. Within ten days they were having 'glorious meetings' with four hundred people in attendance and rising. It all began when the Pilgrims spoke on the gifts of the Spirit which was followed by a prayer meeting that continued for many hours. *The Christians were transformed and the next day the town's people could see it! I. R. Govan, the daughter of the Chief who chronicled the history of her dad's life and the story of The Faith Mission wrote: *'They were transformed – radiant, full of joy, seeing the things of eternity in a clearer light than they had ever seen them before, and speaking to all they met about them. And so the "fire" was kindled.'

When the Chief and Pilgrim Morrison came, 'the blessing deepened and spread until the whole town was filled with the Spirit of Revival' and within two weeks of their arrival there were about two hundreds converts. Whilst a mission was in continuance, revival broke out as God came down and various meetings were held throughout the days and weeks, with three services on Sunday, with up to 1,500 filling the hall for the salvation meeting. J. G. Govan, in a letter wrote: '[The] last two nights the large hall was well-filled below, probably six or seven hundred present. Powerful times and about thirty or forty adults at the Penitent Form altogether...' The Missions were closed at no scheduled times because the Chief's instructions to his fellow labourers was, "Keep yourselves free to be led by the Spirit."

The work of God affected all types of people; many drunkards were to be seen kneeling at the Penitent Form (the space at the front of a traditional church where you kneel) along with poor folk, business men and wealthy ladies wearing their fur coats. The work began open-air marches which soon encouraged the new converts to march out for Jesus; their singing echoed over the town. The crime rate dropped and the chief magistrate attributed it to the work of the Mission. Prayer meetings at churches and the YMCAs were crowded. The Pilgrims used song tunes for hymns, sang solos and used musical instruments which for many a Scot was outside of their Christian tradition – many God loving Scots, had (and some still hold) the view that musical instruments and songs were of the devil. They only sing the Psalms, unaccompanied, by the lead of a presenter.

There was opposition by the traditional clergy who tried to assassinate the characters and work of the Mission and called into question their teaching and methods; even a pamphlet was written against them entitled *Perfectionism* in which the Pilgrims were charged with erroneous teaching on the life of holiness. Negative comments started appearing in the local papers, which spread further afield, but by this, the work of The Faith Mission became widely known 'and true friends rallied to its defence.' The Chief, via a letter was asked to publicly answer seven questions, but after prayer, felt led not to be drawn into or to respond to such arguments and replied as such in an acknowledgment of the letter: '...We seek souls, and the Kingdom, and desire to keep as clear of controversy as possible' ending in the words of Nehemiah: 'I am doing a great work, I cannot come down to you!' (Nehemiah 4:3). Though his brothers, William and James felt it right to make a written statement regarding Scriptural holiness which brought the Mission new friends.

There were also complaints about the use of the Penitent Form, for many a Scot it was considered presumptuous to admit that you were saved, while in one district, they believed that unless you had been under a 'proper state of conviction for six weeks' it was impossible to be saved! As the Chief's daughter wrote about her dad's conversion sixteen years previously: 'Testimony was neither enjoined nor practised in those days, when religion was more awe-full than joy-full.'

The methods that the Pilgrims used were not unscriptural, just contrary to tradition, but the fruit spoke for itself, souls were saved, bad debts were paid, the drunks became sober, the frivolous and careless became serious minded and the rich used their means to assist the poor. Whilst there is no specific recorded opposition about women workers during this revival, undoubtedly there was, as it was an incredibly rare sight to see women evangelists, even more so, women leading and preaching in a meeting. Women Pilgrims first joined The Faith Mission in 1887. As I. R. Govan (daughter of the Chief) wrote: 'Scotland was not accustomed to women evangelists, and there was much criticism.' Nearly seventy years later when revival broke out in North Uist (1957-1958), Outer Hebrides, Scotland, under four Pilgrim women in their twenties, there was much opposition from the clergy due to their gender. I liked what Rheinard Bonnke, (founder of Christ For All Nations CFAN) said when asked about his opinion on women evangelists, live on African television, he replied, "If I am drowning, I don't care who saves me!"[4]

Matsuye 1899 – Japan

Paget Wilkes was converted in March 1892, aged twenty-one and within a week sensed a call to the mission field. A few weeks later, he was invited to a convention at Colwyn Bay, North Wales, where he met several outstanding men. One of them was John George Govan, founder of The Faith Mission who was used in the Rothesay Revival (1888-1889) and who witnessed revival in Cellardyke and Whitburn (1890). Paget was greatly inspired and challenged by his preaching on a life of separation unto God. One night he came forward to the Penitent Form where he unreservedly gave his life to God knowing that he needed power in his life to live for God and to witness to others.

During his time at Oxford University (October 1892 – June 1897) he became a successful open-air preacher and in the summer he worked for the Children's Special Service Mission (CSSM). In July 1897 he married Gertrude Barthorpe, a month later they sailed for Japan and arrived in October, having been invited to Matsuye by Rev. Barclay Buxton (a revivalist and the future son-in-law of C.T. Studd).

Matsuye is on the west coast of Japan and is situated between two lakes ringed with mountains. It was here that 'Paget found himself in the midst of a remarkable work of God which was influencing the whole of Japan' under the leadership of Buxton who was 'a copybook of a holy life,' who taught his disciples the way to victory alongside his team of indigenous workers, Takeda San, Mimaki San and Sawamura San, all of whom were all filled with the Holy Spirit. There was between twenty-four to thirty Japanese businessmen, pastors and evangelists who were attending Buxton's Bible studies when Paget arrived, who would become 'outstanding leaders of the Church of Christ in

Japan.' Paget wrote: '...Oh, how they [the Japanese] put us to shame – men who think nothing of spending a whole night in prayer on the mountain; men who are daily gaining the victory over the keenest temptation...men filled with the Holy Ghost...'

On another occasion, Paget wrote about a gathering during a week of prayer: 'Mr Buxton was in the chair, but he let Mr Mitani take the whole meeting. God's power came down indeed, and from 9am till 6pm without the slightest intermission the meeting went on. Everyone was searched and humbled before God...The following days were days of blessing. Often we were up until three and four in the morning. While the blessing was most marked in the country districts, the churches as a whole have been wonderfully quickened...'

I. R. Govan Stewart (daughter of J. G. Govan) wrote: 'Here was a "fire" which seemed to burn out self-esteem and self-concern and self-indulgence, and fill the heart with the love of God.'

A gathering of missionaries was arranged at Mount Heizan and God was there in power! In one of these services Paget received his own "Pentecost" when the church was full and he was the only European present. The Japanese preacher spoke on God's provision for 'full salvation for fallen humanity – of the cleansing of the innermost desires by the blood, the purifying of hidden motives by the Spirit, the exalting of Christ and Christ only in the life.' Paget felt prompted to go to the front when the invitation was given for this deeper blessing, but was inwardly struggling as he believed he had already received it and had told others he had! He humbly went to the front and knelt with the others and God met with him. Paget's steps of obedience 'was the birthplace of a movement which was to bless Japan and the world beyond' as he founded the Japan Evangelistic Band (JEB) in 1904.[5]

Portions of Paget Wilkes journal are recorded in *Missionary Joys in Japan* (1913); he also wrote *Dynamic in Service* (1925) whilst his life story is told in *Ablaze For God* by his sister, Mary W. Dunn Pattison (1936).

Mukti Revival 1901-1902 – India

In 1898, Pandita Ramabai, in returning from America visited the Keswick Convention in England, an annual holiness conference. Ramabai had the opportunity to speak to those present for five minutes. She wrote about it later: 'My heart was filled with joy to see nearly four thousand people seeking and finding the deep things of God. At that time the Lord led me to those present to pray for an outpouring of the Holy Ghost on all Indian Christians.' She requested those present to pray with her that God would raise up indigenous evangelists, 100,000 men and 100,000 women to reach the whole of India. Ramabai's testimony was: 'The blessings of God are sufficient for India's needs' and her motto to all new converts was, 'Saved to serve.'

Back in India, Pandita Ramabai carried on her duties for the emancipation of the high caste child widows of India (see appendix H) and at Mukti started a rescue home for those who had fallen into temple prostitution. She was assisted by Miss Edmonds who was already involved in this type of ministry in the north of India. Six girls soon increased to twenty and by 1901 there were three hundred who had been taken out of immorality.

The Mukti Mission was constantly expanding; the land covered one hundred acres on two adjoining sites. There was from eighty to one hundred and twenty workers employed at a time on building projects (classrooms, store rooms, hospital, printing rooms, carpenter and blacksmith's shop etc.) for nine hours a day. The last hour of each work day was given over to worship, where one of the missionaries or Ramabai would preach to the workers. A number of the labourers were converted at this time.

At Christmas 1898, Miss Abrams, a missionary at the Mukti Mission challenged the girls to the need of their nation. She spoke about the Student Volunteer Movement in America and England and suggested they form a mission band at Mukti and thirty-five of the girls volunteered for this evangelistic training. At noon, they met for an hour of extra Bible training and within a few months, joined other Bible women in visiting the villages. Throughout the years hundreds of these Bible women have been trained, for evangelism and the selling of the Scriptures.

During the famine of 1900, workers went throughout India and brought back 1,350 children and women. One day nearly two hundred starving people arrived at Mukti. The fruit trees were dying, the grass was dead, the wells began to dry up and the cattle produced so little milk that there was not enough to feed the babies. Ramabai's faith in the living God did not waver and each day the Lord provided for the 1,900 people and one hundred cattle, often $500 was needed each day and the money came in just as it was needed, one day at a time. Soon the work at Sharada Sadan was moved to Mukti and a day school, for boys and girls was added for the village children.

In 1899, the Rev. W. W. Bruere furloughed in America and in replacement the Rev. W. E. Robbins was prayerfully asked to teach at the mission every other week. During this time the girls and women became very generous with their giving to world missions as Rev. Robbins spoke of the Gospel work in other lands.

For the next two months, beginning in December 1901, the Holy Spirit began to move and 1,200 girls were baptised. Dr. Basil Miller wrote: 'Times of spiritual harvest were enjoyed, for carefully, throughout the two preceding years, she [Ramabai] laid the foundation for a revival...' All of those who had been baptised during this time 'had been taught the Christian way. Many of them had been genuinely born again. Some had accepted the doctrines of Christianity, but they did not know the power of the new birth.' Helen Dyer wrote: 'The workers felt the need of a much deeper work of grace to be manifested in the lives of the converts and continued to cry to the Lord.'

In July 1902 many were saved, and for nearly three weeks this spiritual revival continued; meetings were held daily which increased in size until about six hundred had been led to the Lord.[6]

Within three years, revival once again broke out at Mukti (1905-1906) under Pandita Ramabai, which swept across India and affected every state of India and lit some fires of revival in a handful of places around the world, including 'a great revival' which 'started in a school in Japan.'

The first president of Youth for Christ International, Dr. Robert A. Cook, published a little tract, *Revival, the Beating Heart of Youth for Christ*. He wrote: 'And there went with him [David] a band of men whose heart God had touched' (1 Samuel 10:26). Every great religious movement starts with a man [or woman] on fire. Strange how seldom we realise this truth, and really count on it!....Ye (not methods) shall receive power after that the Holy Ghost (not better connections) has come upon you (not better committees) and ye (not elaborate organisations) shall be witnesses (not glittering meetings) unto Me (a pre-eminent Saviour, not prominent speaker) unto the uttermost part of the world.'[7]

Chapter Twelve

Compel them to Come

Jesus said, "All authority has been given to Me in heaven and on earth. Go therefore and make disciples of all the nations, baptising them in the name of the Father and of the Son and of the Holy Spirit, teaching them to observe all things that I have commanded you; and lo, I am with you always, even to the end of the age" Matthew 28:18-20.

Australian and New Zealand Revivals 1902-1903

In 1902, evangelist Reuben Archer Torrey began his worldwide evangelistic campaigns. After having spent time in China and Japan he began a six month campaign in Australia, New Zealand and Tasmania where phenomenal results were seen. The revival was traced to three or four ministers who met weekly to prayer for revival, which encouraged others. These prayer circles grew until 40,000 people were daily praying for revival within 2,000 prayer circles!

From April to May 1902, R. A. Torrey preached in Melbourne, Australia and for the first two weeks, he was part of the Simultaneous Missions in which fifty meetings were held by fifty different evangelists or ministers in fifty locations across the city. Melbourne attendances totalled 250,000 a week when the population of Victoria was just one million! It was in Melbourne that R. A. Torrey teamed up with the singer, Charles Alexander and for many years they toured. Their evangelistic ministry became known as the Torrey-Alexander Campaigns. Their stories are told in *Torrey and Alexander – The Story of their Lives* by J. Kennedy MacLean (1906) and *Charles M. Alexander – A Romance of Song and Soul Winning* by Helen C. Alexander and J. Kennedy MacLean (1920). Torrey wrote many books, including *How to Win Men to Christ* (1903) and *Revival Addresses* (1908), both of which reveal what he taught (in evangelism principles) and preached (evangelistic messages).

From 1902-1903 there was a tent crusade throughout two hundred country towns of New South Wales where it was reported that 25,000 made enquires about the state of their souls. Those who wished to know more about the work of Jesus

Christ were asked to stay behind after each meeting for further discussion and explanations. After ministering for six months R. A. Torrey left for India on route to England. In India, he spoke in Calcutta on prayer and greatly influenced two lady missionaries from the Khassia Mission. When they returned to their home in the Khassia Hills (also spelt Khasi) their one theme was prayer and they were part of the Khasi Hills Revival (1905-1906) where they saw 8,200 baptisms.

Pandita Ramabai, of the Mukti Mission Station, Kedgaon, India, also heard of the Australian Revival (1902) which inspired her to form prayer circles and prayer bands for revival resulting in the Mukti Revival (1905-1906) which affected every state of India, though she had already seen revival at Mukti (1901-1902) which lasted for just two months.

From 1903-1906, R. A. Torrey (with Alexander) revisited many of the countries and cities he had visited in 1902 on his second world tour, which also saw phenomenal results. By 1904 there were 30,000 people praying for revival. In January 1904, they began their 31-day crusade in Birmingham, England, where 7,000 were converted. From July to August they were back in America. In September 1904, 3,600 were converted in Bolton, England. From there they went to Cardiff, Wales, just prior to the outbreak of the Welsh Revival (1904-1905) and 3,750 were saved. From Cardiff they went to Liverpool and held a nine week campaign, where there was the largest evangelistic choir to date of more than 3,600 persons and 7,000 were saved. From February to June 1905, Torrey and Alexander held the London Crusade in three locations. There were more than 1.1 million total attendances and 15,000 professed conversion.

Pyongyang Great Revival 1907-1910 – Korea

In 2010, more than twenty-five percent of South Koreas 48 million inhabitants are Christian, but a census a few years ago revealed a 144,000 decrease in Protestants, which, while fractional, is the thin end of a dangerous wedge. Korea has 50,000 churches with 12 million members (approximately 13 million Christians) and is the second largest missionary sending nation in the world with 13,000 missionaries in 160 countries. They have a vision for 48,501 missionaries by the year 2030. There are 76 million Koreans in total, six million of whom live outside of South and North Korea.[1]

The Korean Church was founded in 1885 and the following year the first Korean was baptised. In September 1866,

Welshman, Rev. Robert Jermain Thomas soaked the land in his own blood and became known at the first Protestant missionary and martyr to Korea when he was stabbed, beaten and finally beheaded at Pyongyang (now the capital of North Korea, see page 91).

Korea saw its first revival in 1903; known as the Wonsan Revival Movement (1903-1906), but by the middle of 1906, after 30,000 new converts in that year alone, it had waned and died out. The second Korean Revival is known as the Pyongyang Great Revival (1907-1910). Pyongyang in 1907 was known as a city of wine, women and song. It was a dark city in the early twentieth century with sin abounding and it even had its own Gisaeng (Korean geisha) training school. At the beginning of the Japanese Russian War of 1904, American missionaries were initially confined to Pyongyang by government order. In the autumn of 1906, the threat of Russian invasion had passed, but the Japanese did not withdraw. This caused anxiety amongst Korea's oppressed people who were constantly being fought over by Japan or China. William Newton Blair, a missionary at Pyongyang wrote: 'With the Japanese occupation accomplished, patriotism was born in Korea.' At the same time a number of young Korean Christian 'big heads' returned from America and caused problems with their personal ambition and true stories of American corruption. Also, America, following Britain's example 'hastened to recognise Japan's control' which caused an anti-American sentiment to sweep over the land.

In 1907, the Korean Church (Presbyterian) was to become independent of its American Board of Foreign Mission which had been 'practically self-supporting for several years' but things did not look good. In August 1906, the Pyongyang missionaries met for a week of Bible study and prayer. They invited Dr. R. A. Hardie, (William Newton Blair spells his name Hardy) to lead them, whose public confession and repentance in Wonsan in 1903 was the beginning of the Wonsan Revival Movement (1903-1906).

Their text book for the meeting was the First Epistle of John. Blair wrote that the message became personal and living: 'We had reached a place where we dared not go forward without God's presence.' The missionaries poured out their hearts before Him, and searched their own hearts whilst seeking to meet the conditions. Before the meeting had ended the Spirit showed those present that 'the way of victory' is the way of, 'confession, of broken hearts and bitter tears.' They decided to pray for 'a great blessing' a revival amongst their Korean Brethren and especially amongst the Pyongyang Bible-study classes for men which would take place in January 1907. They left those August meetings 'realising as never before that nothing but the baptism of God's Spirit in mighty power could fit us and our Korean brethren for the trying days ahead.' They knew that the Korean Church needed to repent of hating the Japanese and needed 'a clearer vision of all sin against God' because many had professed Christ as their Saviour 'without great sorrow for sin because of its familiarity.'[2]

In September 1906, Dr. Howard Agnew Johnston, of New York, whilst in Seoul, informed a group of missionaries (and Korean Christians) about the 1905-1906 Khasi Hills Revival in India. Jonathan Goforth, missionary to China, wrote that because of this more than twenty missionaries from Pyongyang Presbyterian and Methodist missions resolved to meet together to pray daily for 'greater blessings.' Over the Christmas period the Pyongyang Christians instead of their usual social celebrations met each evening for prayer. The evening prayer ceased at the start of the Pyongyang General Class but continued at noon for those who could attend.

A Bible colporteur from Kan Kai Church (along the Yalu) of 250 believers, who was also in Seoul, heard Dr. Johnston and encouraged his church to meet for prayer at 5am through the autumn and winter of 1906-1907. For six months they prayed until the Holy Spirit 'came as a flood.'[3]

The Pyongyang General Class of one thousand began on the 2 January 1907, it would last for two weeks and representatives came from as far away as one hundred miles. The evening meetings began on the Saturday the sixth and 1,500 attended. Blair preached on 1 Corinthians 12:27, members of the body of Christ, and exhorted those present to get right with one another, 'as discord in the Church was like sickness in the body.' After the sermon 'a number with sorrow confessed their lack of love for others, especially for the Japanese' and 'many testified to a new realisation of what sin was.'

The Sunday evening meeting had no life in it and they were 'conscious that the devil had been present, apparently victorious.' The next day the missionaries met 'and cried out to God in earnest,' they were 'bound in spirit and refused to let go till He blessed' them. As the people (and only some of the missionaries) entered the church at 7pm God's presence was felt. After a short sermon, missionary Graham Lee led the meeting in prayer and soon, 'the whole audience began to pray out loud together.' It was 'a vast harmony of sound and spirit, a mingling together of souls moved by an irresistible impulse to prayer.'[4]

Jonathan Goforth in his brief account of the revival (he visited in June 1907) wrote that Elder Keel, (also spelt Kil and later known as the Rev. Sun Joo Kil) of the Central Presbyterian Church, confessed his sin of 'Achan' (see Joshua 7:1, 20-21) in front of 1,500 people and thus the revival began. He had promised a dying man to look after his estate because his wife was unable to, but in the process he had taken one hundred dollars for himself. The next day he gave the money back.[5]

Soon the prayer turned to weeping. Graham Lee wrote: 'Man after man would rise, confess his sins, break down and weep, and then throw himself to the floor and beat the floor with his fists in perfect agony of conviction.' The meeting went on till 2am. Goforth wrote: 'Day after day the people assembled now and always it was manifest that the Refiner was in His temple.' Writing about Elder Keel's confession he wrote: 'It hindered the Almighty God while it remained covered, and it glorified Him as soon as it was uncovered; and so with rare exceptions did all the confessions in Korea that year.'

On Tuesday afternoon, the whole community assembled to give thanks to God. The previous night, Elder Kang You-moon, of the Central Church confessed his hatred of Elder Kim, who was Blair's assistant in the Pyongyang Church. Kim sat silent. At the noon prayer meeting on Tuesday they prayed for Elder Kim. In the evening meeting, Elder Kim stood behind the pulpit and confessed his hatred not only of Elder Kang, but also of Blair himself and asked for Blair's forgiveness. Blair began to pray, "Father, Father" and got no further. Blair wrote: 'It seemed as if the roof was lifted from the building and the Spirit of God came down from heaven in a mighty avalanche of power upon us.' Blair fell at Kim's side and wept and prayed as never before. Some prostrated themselves before the Lord whilst hundreds stood with arms outstretched towards heaven. 'The cry went over the city until the heathen were in consternation.' The missionaries had prayed for an outpouring of the Spirit and it had come.

Blair wrote: 'Every sin a human being can commit was publicly confessed that night. Pale and trembling with emotion, in agony of mind and body, guilty souls, standing in the white light of that judgment, saw themselves as God saw them. Their sins rose up in all their vileness, till shame and grief and self-loathing took complete possession; pride was driven out, the face of men forgotten. Looking up to heaven, to Jesus whom they had betrayed, they smote themselves and cried out with bitter wailing, "Lord, Lord, cast us not away for ever!" '[6]

Christians even confessed their sins to non-Christians for their past actions and attitudes which greatly affected the city. Even Japanese soldiers came under conviction! Soon Pyongyang became known as the "Jerusalem of the East."

In Korea, every fifth day was a market day and the merchants would make more money on that day than on eight other days, but when the market fell on the Sabbath, 10,000 men and boys were found in the Sabbath school at Chung-Ju preferring to honour the Sabbath rather than make money.[7]

Mr Swallen, who was one of more than twenty missionaries in Pyongyang said, "It paid well to have spent the several months in prayer, for when God the Holy Spirit came He accomplished more in half a day than all of us missionaries could have accomplished in half a year. In less than two months more than two thousand heathen were converted.' By the middle of 1907 there were 30,000 converts connected with the Pyongyang Centre.

Mr Swallen, Graham Lee (who was a good singer) and William Blair were the main leaders prior to the revival, but it was Samuel Moffet and Kil Sun Mojo (this Korean rose before dawn to pray for revival) who brought them together from the missionary prayer meeting onward. During the revival, Elder Keel (who had confessed his sin of 'Achan') was raised up as a Korean leader. He held meetings everywhere and got the people praying.

In 1907, the Pyongyang Theological School saw seven Koreans graduate and they became the first Korean Presbytery of Korea. Bible study groups increased and there was acceleration in missionary building growth. Illiterate people, especially women learnt the Hangeul script (Korean alphabet), and the understanding that God created all men equal in His eyes led to a greater status for women. The revival also crossed the border into Yeonbyeon and Manju, China.[8]

George McCune who personally witnessed the outpouring of the Spirit on the Korean Church reported that the movement greatly surpassed the ones in Wales and India, describing it as the most empowering presence of the Holy Spirit ever and in 1909, the Movement of Saving One Million Souls began.[9]

The revival was still going strong in 1910 and the afterglow of revival continued for a least a few years after that date in various towns. Goforth wrote: 'It was clear that the revival had not died down by 1910, for in October of that year 4,000 were baptised in one week [Korean Presbyterians receive a person publicly for Catechumen (catechism) after three months and then after a period of one year examine them to see if they are ready for baptism] and thousand besides sent in their names, saying they had decided to become Christians...' In Seoul, 13,000 'signed cards saying they wanted to become Christians, and in September...the Methodist churches...received 3,000 by baptism.'[10]

Blair, writing in 1910 wrote: 'In all Korea today there are no less than 250,000 Christians worshipping God in more than 2,000 places.' In this year, the Old Testament was finally translated into Korean and The British and Foreign Bible Society through its Bible Colporteurs sold 666,000 books to the people of Korea, most of them single gospels! In August 1910, Korea was annexed by Japan which was the beginning of organised persecution, especially amongst the Christians.

Rev. Robert Jermain Thomas and North Korea

In September 1866, Rev. Robert Jermain Thomas[11] with his clothes on fire leapt overboard at Pyongyang with his remaining Bibles and wadded to the bank and frantically gave them out. The entire crew were executed. Thomas' executioner accepted the last red Bible from this martyr, and as Tertullan said, "The blood of the martyrs is the seed of the church." The executioner used the Bible as wallpaper for his house and one day was converted as he read the decorative classical Chinese Scriptures. During the Pyongyang Great Revival an old man, Chun-Kwon Park, (who attended a Presbyterian Church in Pyongyang), during a time of public confession went to the front and confessed that he had been Rev. Thomas' executioner, forty-one years ago.

In 1893, this house was turned into an inn which was later bought by three western missionaries and turned into the Chowlangli Church (also known as Nuldali Church), the Thomas Memorial Church, in memory of Rev. Robert Jermain Thomas. As the number of indigenous Christians grew they bought more land and built the Jangdaejae Church. Numbers increased again so they moved location and built another church, called Jangdaehyun Church which was where the 1907 revival first broke out. This church was eventually demolished sometime after 1957 under Communist rule in what became known as North Korea.

After the Korean War (1950-1953) though there had been fighting since 1946, Korea was partitioned at the 38th parallel. Communists ran the North whilst the South was democratic; North Korea declined in prosperity and freedom, whilst South Korea prospered economically and spiritually.

A Boy Schools Palace (slightly similar to the Scout Movement) was built on the foundations of the Jangdaehyun Church. Next door is the recently built Pyongyang University of Science and Technology (PUST) which is financed and run by Christians and is known as project Zerubbabel – "Not by might, nor by power, but by My Spirit says the Lord of hosts" (Zechariah 4:6). When workmen were digging the PUST foundations they found a bell tower, (which in Korean tradition sits next to a church building and not on top of it as in the West; some reports say they found the remains of the bell) which would have belonged to the original and subsequent churches which were built in memory of Rev. Thomas; thus completing a circle from the beginning of Korean Christianity to the re-birthing of Christianity in North Korea. On the 16 September 2009, the building dedication service for (PUST) was held.[12]

Dr. James Chin-Kyung Kim, founding president and co-chairman of PUST wrote: 'While the skills to be taught are technical in nature, the spirit underlying this historic venture is unabashedly Christian. A century ago, the northern half of the Korean peninsula was steeped in Christian and modern influences, so much so that Pyongyang, its centre, was known throughout Western Christendom as "the Jerusalem of the East." God in His Providence has granted us a second opportunity to teach modern subjects to new generations of young North Koreans to encourage them to become, once again, eager to learn and borrow from the outside world.'[13]

There are an estimated 40,000-60,000 Christians in North Korea today and they are the most persecuted in the entire world; most of whom who are in prison camps. Communist North Korea is the last ultra-extreme Communist bastille. God, may its walls come down peacefully, allowing the Gospel of salvation and hope to flood in, bringing the healing balm of Gilead and salvation of Jesus Christ for all who call upon His name. Amen.

Chapter Thirteen

Mighty to Save

'The fruit of the righteous is a tree of life and he who wins souls is wise' Proverbs 11:30.

South Australia 1914

In 1912, Rev. Lionel B. Fletcher saw revival in his church, the Port of South Adelaide Congregational Church in South Australia and in the surrounding churches in the district. Towards the end of 1914, (the first few months of World War I, which began in September), Rev. Fletcher was holding a mission in an unnamed country town in a northern district in South Australia. Word was sent to him that several people were under great conviction. Rev. Fletcher wrote: 'Long before I reached this town there had been signs of revival in some neighbouring towns and hundreds had professed conversion.' At the opening service, there was a deep seriousness, but few came forward for salvation. 'Fear had laid hold of many and some were staying away lest they become converted' whilst 'others came to listen with all their defences up, determined not to be led to confess Christ...we [Rev. Fletcher and his wife] had never before been in a place where it was evident that most of the population was being deeply moved by religion...'

Rev. Fletcher's wife was requested to call on a woman who was in deep distress. The woman's eyes were red with weeping, and her cheeks were red with tears. She confessed that for three days she had worked about the house under conviction, knowing herself to be a sinner, but she could not find salvation. Rev. Fletcher talked and prayed with her and found also that her husband and a number of other men were in a like condition. Rev. Fletcher wrote: 'We were young and rather inexperienced...we sought for help from an old saint in God in the matter, the wise man said, "Leave them to the Holy Spirit; He will lead them through in good time. You must not hurry His working with these people."...We had never been accustomed to hearing religion talked about in the streets, nor had we ever before been stopped by strangers and requested to step into a shop or a house to speak to someone who was in trouble of spiritual things. But this was now happening to us everyday..."

'On the following Sunday afternoon, Mrs Fletcher met the husband and led him to Christ...' then his wife found light and liberty. Others began to come to Christ; and the large church no longer lacked a congregation, but was crowded to excess night after night. There was joy in many houses but sadness in others as some still held out in rebellion. Some of these were ringleaders in sin, and the church leadership were afraid that they would drag the young converts back into sin. Special prayer was made for these people, especially for a well known gambler and drinker, who was the brother of one of the church workers.

At the close of one of the services, after Rev. Fletcher had preached his heart out, a hymn was sung; the well-known gambler and drinker, with a groan covered his face with his hands and then walked to the front with his brother's arm linked in his. The man confessed his sin before the Lord and sought Jesus as his Saviour (but did not find assurance until the next day), 'this produced a great impression. A small army of young men came forward and stood with him and afterwards there was a room full of those whom I instructed in the way of Christ.'

During this revival many hundreds of people were converted. In the neighbouring church, Rev. Sam Forsyth, a friend of Rev. Fletcher was preaching on a Sunday to the mining community (many of whom were Cornish), 'many of their relatives and hundreds of their friends had been converted...' At the end of the service and as the appeal was given, the soloist began to sing, "What will you do with Jesus?" two people came to the front. The singer's voice wavered and broke; he then flung the book from him and came to the front to surrender his life to Christ! Rev. Fletcher wrote: 'Something like a sob shook that congregation;' twenty-two men and women got converted that night.

The following night the whole community went to church without any announcement or arrangement. They went to pray, to rejoice and nightly people surrendered their lives to Christ. 'Towards the end of the campaign, two neighbouring publicans met to talk over their dismal future, each fearing bankruptcy. Their bars were empty, while the Mission meetings were crowded to excess.' On the final night, vehicles came in from the surrounding country, each bearing its load of people. All roads led to the Mission meeting and singing could be heard in various directions. At the end of the service, Rev. Fletcher felt compelled to ask a stranger to lead in prayer, at first he declined in great emotion, saying "...I could not. I think it would kill me," but then he did. This Cornishman, greatly loved for his piety, and unblemished character pleaded to his heavenly Father, confessing the sins of his people and then pleaded for souls to be saved. 'He asked that that night – that very moment – [that] the power of the Holy Spirit might be poured out upon the congregation.' Rev. Fletcher, after hearing the sound of many feet, opened his eyes and 'beheld what looked like the whole congregation moving. The aisles were filled with people coming towards the platform...when we left, one hundred and twenty-one young men stood about us singing – they had each decided to follow Christ – and there were many others, men and women and children.'

Rev. Fletcher wrote: 'This was no shallow movement destined to leave no trace behind, but it was a breath of real revival which gave the world some fine men for God.' Some of the converted went off to war and never returned. One middle-aged man rearranged his business affairs in such a way that he was able to give all of his time for the work of God, a Gospel Band was formed which set out to reach the un-churched for Christ.

In 1919, Rev. Fletcher returned 'to the district and found that several centres were visited regularly for preaching services; hundreds had been converted, homes of misery had been transformed into homes of glory, and a book could have been written concerning the miracles of grace...The preachers were the converts of five years before, and their ardour made me rejoice....'[1]

C. W Malcomson wrote the biography of Lionel B. Fletcher – *Twelve Hours in the Day* (1956). Fletcher wrote several books including *Conquering Evangelism* (1946), a series of talks in connection with the Sydney Missionary and Bible College, and *The Pathway to the Stars* (1933) which is a compendium of short address aimed at young Christians as part of discipleship, to build them up in the most holy faith.

Incidentally, Lionel B. Fletcher had six brothers, all of whom were preachers!

Rusitu Revival 1915-1917

In 1904, Rees Howells, a Welsh coal miner was converted whilst in America and returned home amidst the Welsh Revival (1904-1905). In 1906, he *fully* surrendered his life to the Lord and the Holy Spirit took possession of him and led him into a series of costly intercessions.

In December 1910, Rees married Elizabeth and in July 1915 they left for Southern East Africa, to become missionaries in the Rusitu Valley, Gazaland (also known as Rossitu outside a town called Chipinge in modern day Zimbabwe) under the South Africa General Mission (SAGM). Their fellow missionaries knew they had come from the land of revivals and asked them if they had brought the blessing with them. Rees told them, that the source of all revival is the Holy Ghost, and that He could do amongst them what He had done in Wales! Via a translator, Rees preached on revival, and within six weeks the Holy Spirit began to move upon the Christians as they met at the home of the Howells' at Rusitu Mission Station. Elizabeth taught them the chorus, 'Lord, send a revival, and let it begin in me.'

One evening the four missionaries of the Rusitu station met together and the Holy Spirit told them that their prayers were heard and that revival was coming to their district. On the 10 October 1915 (Rees' birthday), revival came. A young girl broke down in tears and within five minutes the entire congregation had followed suit, the meeting went on late into the night. Rees wrote: 'You can never describe those meetings when the Holy Spirit comes down. I shall never forget the sound in the district that night.'

There was prayer, confession of sin and testimonies etc. which continued for six days until the Rusitu Christians were right with God. For the next fifteen months there would be two revival meetings a day, without a single break, and meetings all day on Friday. Hundreds were converted and as the news of the revival spread, other mission stations were affected. The head office of the SAGM requested all mission stations to spend thirty minutes each morning in prayer for revival. Rees received the promise of Malachi 3:10 and *saw* revival descending on every mission station. In 1917, under commission of the SAGM, he travelled over 11,000 miles to Swaziland, Pondoland, Bomvanaland, Tembuland and Zululand and saw revival in every mission station![2]

The full accounts of the revival can be found in two very hard-to-obtain booklets: *Advance in Gazaland* and *Retrospect and Revival in Gazaland*, both by Mrs Bessie Porter Head; sister-in-law to Albert Head, chairman of the SAGM. Head was also the chairman of the Keswick Convention in England and the Llandrindod Conventions in Wales which were held annually.

Abyssinia 1920s

During the fourth century, Christianity began to make an impact in Abyssinia (modern day Ethiopia), Africa. Two nephews of Meropius, a Christian doctor of Tyre sailed the Red Sea when their ship was wrecked on the coast of Ethiopia. Only the nephews survived, Frumentius and Edesius were sold as slaves to the King of Abyssinia who learnt to love them and raised them to honoured positions. Shortly before the king's death, he gave them their liberty and made Frumentius, the administrator of his kingdom, and the guardian of the heir to the throne. Frumentius brought Christian merchants from Egypt to settle in Abyssinia and visited Bishop Anthansius at Alexandria and sought his help in evangelising his country. Anthansius ordained Frumentius Bishop, along with the title Aba Salama 'Father of Peace' and made him the head of the missionary party which he sent with him. 'Christianity made such rapid progress that by the year 500 it had covered the land...and carried the Gospel to the tribes in heathen darkness around. It also created the Ethiopian translation of the Bible.'

Theological discussions separated the Abyssinian Church from the rest of Christendom and as the North African Church was extinguished by Islam in the sixth and seventh centuries, the stronghold of ancient Christianity 'held its own against the false prophet...though Christianity gradually sank to the level of paganism' as was witnessed in the twentieth century.

Abyssinia had the distinction of being the last remaining indigenous kingdom of Africa to hold its own against European overlordship. This land had been closed against direct missionary effort since the first Protestant missionary, Peter Heyling of Lubeck arrived in 1635. Lubeck was robbed and executed by a Turkish Pasha in Cairo, Egypt in 1652.

The Abuna (Archbishop of Ethiopia), had under his care an estimated 216-230 or so tribes which spoke many languages. The Abuna is appointed and consecrated by the Coptic Patriarch of Alexander. During the time of the revival the country had two million Coptic Christians, three million Muslims and six million pagan inhabitants.

In 1914, Mr Hooper of the British and Foreign Bible Society opened a depot for the sale of Holy Bibles in the capital, Addis Ababa after the Abuna of the Coptic Church granted permission. This opening led to a steady sale in Bibles in the languages of Tigre, Galla, Amharic and Ethiopic. Most literate Abyssinians were probably able to read one or other of the last two languages and for those that could not, there already existed some portions of the Scripture in half a dozen languages.

From 1920 onwards, for the next five or six years, as Coptic Christians read the Bible they were enlightened to the old truths of the New Testament, including justification by faith, thousands of Abyssinians left their historical church with its ceremonies and traditions alongside large numbers of Muslims, both of whom received Christian baptism from the Evangelical Abyssinian Church. Many of the former followers of Islam, were from amongst the higher classes with limited education, but able to read and this revival brought many of them into the new Evangelical Church.

The Rev. J. J. Jwarson of the Swedish Mission in Eritrea retold the story. He stated that the centre of the movement was in Sokota in the Amhara country which was led by the ex-Sheik Zaccaria. Zaccaria, a person of great influence had his name changed to Noaye Kristos and became known as the Apostle of the movement. Two of Kristos' disciples, also ex-Sheikhs, Alaka-Paulos of Tigrae and Alaka-Petros of Sokota visited him in order to acquire copies of the Holy Bible and to consolidate their acquaintance with evangelical Christians. The Bibles were obtained from the Addis Ababa depot and the new converts 'were very anxious to study the Bible, and they organised amongst themselves a numerous body of teachers, said to number about 500, with the object of teaching their youth to read the Scriptures.'

This movement in turn opened doors for Christian missionaries and by 1926, two such Societies had entered the land and were involved in successful work. The American Presbyterian Mission in Sudan, on account of the beneficial work of its hospitals across the frontier of Sudan at Nasser, was invited by the Abyssinian authorities to open a hospital within its boundaries, this was done at Sawi. The authorities after seeing the results then invited them into the capital, whilst the Swedish Mission worked in the north. By 1926, there were only 150 Europeans within Abyssinia.[3]

Latvia 1924
Oswald J. Smith, pastor of the Alliance Tabernacle, Toronto, Canada, visited the Russian Mission Fields of Europe in 1924. Travelling around Europe, Smith in his book, *The Revival We Need* wrote: 'I saw God working in a most remarkable way. The

people would walk thirty miles, or drive with horse and wagon two hundred miles, to attend meetings. Services lasted three hours or longer, and in some cases, three services were held each day, and then the people complained that they were not getting enough. In one place they met in a meeting of their own in the early hours of the morning, before even the workers appeared on the scene, making four services in all each day.

'One told another, and everybody came, until they were standing in the aisles, sitting in every available space on the platform, crowding the largest auditoriums, so that scarcely another person could squeeze in. Well do I remember preaching to three thousand in a Lutheran Church [in Libau, Latvia in the summer of 1924], Oh, how they listened! Yes, and in the open air it was the same. For three hours I have seen them stand in rain – men, women and children – so hungry were they.'

Three thousand people turned up for an open-air meeting in Riga, Latvia, and Pastor William Fetler, director of the Russian Missionary Society of Riga translated. Oswald Smith first met Fetler in the Alliance Tabernacle, Toronto, Canada. Fetler had invited him to be associated with him in the work, but instead Smith agreed to visit the mission field. Oswald Smith wrote: 'And oh, how God worked! From the very commencement the spirit of revival was in the air. They prayed, sang and testified, the tears streaming down their cheeks. With stricken hearts they listened to the messages and when the invitation was given, flocked to the front, and falling on their knees, their eyes overflowing with tears, cried to God for mercy.'

From his diary, Oswald Smith wrote: 'To describe the scenes that have been enacted by the Holy Ghost would be simply impossible; for what God has wrought is nothing less than miraculous. Each night the great auditorium was thronged [packed full], and during the closing day, crowded beyond capacity, gallery, platform and all, with people standing everywhere. Night after night souls came forward for salvation, and the altar was filled over and over again. Great numbers accepted Christ for the first time. How many I do not know.' On the fourth day, at the morning meeting at ten o'clock, 'was the great time of the feast...The choir seats were filled. Extra chairs were then placed on the platform and wherever there was space. Still the people came, until, at last, many were compelled to stand in the aisles. Then the power of God fell on the audience. Men and women knelt everywhere, and oh, such prayers! Such tears! Such penitence and confession! Such joy and peace! Such testimonies! And how they sang! Truly, it was heaven on earth.' Three more services were held that day.

In the evening after Oswald Smith had retired to his room, a student came to see him and said, "I have determined to pray all night, for I will not cease until I know the power of the Holy Ghost in my life." We prayed together, and he sobbed aloud. Thus the break started. A few minutes later Oswald was asked to meet with some people in an adjoining room. 'When I entered I found a group from the office on their faces. To them also God had spoken. Prayer again, agonising, definite prayer, ascended to God. Sin was dealt with and put away and a full surrender made, once more the Holy Spirit had His way. Presently in trooped all the students in a body and kneeling down, in Russian, German, Lettish and English, they poured out their hearts to God. Oh, what a melting time! How they wept before the Lord! What a joy it was to be in such an atmosphere of revival and to see the Holy Spirit Himself at work.'

The next morning, Oswald Smith preached in the main auditorium where over 1,200 were present. In the afternoon there were over 1,500 present, Oswald recorded, 'at seven o'clock I faced my third congregation and the power of God was most real. There was a holy hush on the large audience, so that at the close, so many came forward that the after meeting lasted an hour. This was in the lower hall. At 8pm, Oswald went upstairs to his fourth meeting of the day where 1,300 were present. At the end of the service Oswald returned to his residence and wrote: 'When I returned to the Mission House I found a room full of Russians, all on their faces before God, praying quietly, earnestly, as only Russians can. For a while I joined them, then left, and at twelve o'clock and went to bed.'

Oswald Smith travelled onto other cities and saw similar results as the Holy Spirit met with spiritually hungry people as God worked mightily. He wrote: 'Many of their faces seemed literally glorified, so great was their joy.'[4]

J. Edwin Orr in *Always Abounding – An intimate Sketch of Oswald J. Smith of Toronto* (1940) wrote: 'One of the most obvious reasons for the abundant blessing outpoured upon the Peoples Church [Smith's second pastorate in Toronto] is its missionary programme. God always honours people who honour the Great Commission.'[5] Oswald J. Smith wrote *The Enduement of Power* (1933). Edwin Orr first met Smith in 1935 and wrote about their meeting in *Times of Refreshing* (1936).

Chapter Fourteen

Saved to Serve

'As cold water to a weary soul so is good news from a far country' Proverbs 25:25.

Estonia 1929
In 1929, Oswald J. Smith returned to the Russian Mission Fields of Europe (he had previously seen revival in 1924 in Latvia). On his 114 day mission trip, he travelled through fourteen countries as the Director for Canada of the Worldwide Christian Couriers (WCC) and preached 143 times. J. Edwin Orr (who later held an associate-pastorate with Oswald Smith), in his book *Always Abounding* an intimate sketch of the life of Oswald Smith's life, wrote: 'The Salvation Temple of the Russian Missionary Society was his field of labour in time of real revival. Many people accepted Christ.'

Orr stated that throughout his journeys, sometimes Oswald Smith had rapt attention whilst at other times there was organised interruptions. In Riga, Latvia, at the close of his message a man loudly demanded to know why he closed his eyes as he prayed and would not look at the people. Smith, through his translator (Pastor William Fetler, director of the Russian Missionary Society of Riga), explained that it was his custom to pray with his eyes closed. The *Greek Orthodox newspaper in Riga (*who are unable to conceive prayer without a crucifix) falsified his explanation by saying that he claimed to be too holy to look on such sinners!

In April 1929, Oswald Smith preached at Tallin (Revel) the capital of Estonia. His first service was half full, but there was the beginning of a breakthrough at once. In the next meeting the church was unable to hold the mass of people with many standing. The third meeting was moved to an auditorium which held over three thousand people, but that was too small. Oswald Smith wrote: 'So great was the crowd, and so deep the interest, that numbers were compelled to stand throughout, in spite of the huge throng, many came forward and knelt at the altar to accept Christ, and deep conviction settled on the congregation.' The next day saw an even greater response. Orr wrote: 'A real revival atmosphere was present, with open repentance and confession. On one night, 2,500 waited behind for the after meeting (for those who were interested in knowing more about becoming a Christian) and genuine seekers sat and filled the front rows. Oswald Smith, writing about this after-meeting wrote: 'Carefully I explained the Gospel. As I spoke tears flowed down their cheeks. Soon they were on their knees. Sins were confessed and forgiven, Christ received, and notes of praises offered to God. Oh how changed their countenance when they arose! How their eyes glistened with joy! Then they testified one by one, until some twenty had told of a born-again experience, then and there. Two were doubtful. With these I dealt again, and soon one was weeping with joy, and adoring God. Thus ended one of the most wonderful series of revival meetings I have ever held...as for myself, I feel deeply humbled.'

Under Oswald Smith's official capacity as the director for Canada of the WCC, he recommended to the Couriers the needs of two Baltic struggling missions, the Russian Refugee Mission and the Russian Border Mission. Six years later, when J. Edwin Orr travelled across Europe in 1934, returning from Soviet Russia, in Latvia (where he saw localised revival) he met pastors and missionaries who spoke very highly of Oswald J. Smith because of the great help in the evangelisation of people who lived on the borders around Russia.[1]

Tsinan 1930-1931 and Pingtu Revival 1931-1933 – China

The Tsinan Revival (1930-1931) was part of the Shantung Revival (1930-1932) in China. Shantung is a province in the north of China with Tsinan as its capital. In the summer of 1930, a group of five spiritually hungry missionaries from the Southern American Baptists went to the annual Summer Conference in Chefoo. They were 'hunting a new experience in the Lord. Miss L. never stopped stressing in prayer and laying upon the hearts of others the fact that there was seventy "dead churches" in the North China Association. During the summer a definite prayer list was made on which it was agreed to pray for revival in Tsinan, Tsining and Hwanghsien' and revival came![2]

During the Pingtu Revival (1931-1933) a missionary in a letter, dated the 15 July 1932 wrote: 'In the densely populated county of Pingtu, Shantung [Province], where the revival began and the churches have become greatly revived, there are now villages in which every family has one or more saved persons, and in some villages nearly everyone has accepted the Lord. Is this not glorious news to all who love the Saviour!?'[3]

Eggon Revival 1930 – Nigeria

In and around 1930, a young medical missionary, Mr Sanderson was at the Wana Mission Station, Northern Nigeria; a single outpost amongst 60,000 Eggon inhabitants in the Wana and Eggon foothills. He would later translate the Gospel of St. John with the help from Auta, a former spirit priest who was converted during the revival.

The demands for medical work and school work could have occupied Mr Sanderson's whole time, 'but *it was for their souls that he was burdened.*' He called the Christians together for a week of prayer. About six met, morning and evening to plead for blessing in Eggon. 'It was not until the last two days that they seemed to catch the vision and come through in victory.' Medical and school work were cut down to a minimum and 'aggressive evangelism took their place. They went everywhere preaching the word [and] it was then that things really began to happen. Souls were won for Jesus and fierce persecution purged the Church.'

At this time, an old chief had a sudden conversion to Christ after he came to the mission station and the missionaries unfolded the plan of salvation to him. He had been burdened over the murders and others sins he had committed in his youth. He had sacrificed to the spirits, but the burden on his heart still remained until he accepted the gift of Jesus' cleansing blood which washed him whiter than the snow.

'Persecution arose as the fire spread.' A girl with a bad ulcer was brought by her mother to the dispensary and for three months they heard the Gospel and then believed. Her brother, Atyuku got converted and won many others to the Lord, but he caught a fever and within less than five days died. But just before he died, he asked his mother to, "Call the young men of the Jesus way." They came to his hut and he asked them to sing. They sang songs about God and heaven and then prayed. To everybody's surprise, Atyuku got to his feet and looking out the door of his hut said, "Adilidzi ode onjen o wo odzi ekahé!" (Indeed are the houses in heaven beautiful like that!). Then he returned to his mat and passed into glory. The Holy Spirit used that experience to confirm the Gospel (alongside the dignity and composure of his mother), to prove that he went to heaven as the Eggon people traditionally wail loudly at bereavement.

Men and women followed Christ and abandoned their old faith of spirit worship, which included young and old men, grey-haired women, subordinate chiefs and spirit priests. The senior tribal chief was outraged from the loss of allegiance to him and the material loss of beer, goats and sheep which the priesthood need for its sacrifices. He opposed Sunday services and ordered the Christians to appear for compulsory government labour at the hour of morning worship. The Christians complied with the work and in the evenings they would 'flock to the mission station to learn more about Him who was capturing their whole affection.'

The chief set the hill alight as they were gathering thatch to build a large church. Two Christians were poisoned, but after time in hospital they recovered. He had those who preached about Jesus beaten in his presence 'in some cases leaving their backs scored with deep lines of clotted blood.' A betrothed Christian woman was arrested and asked to marry the chief's son. As she was promised to a Christian man she refused 'which resulted in severe floggings for two consecutive days and then her total dismissal from her own village.'

Auta, a former spirit priest was working fifteen miles away from his home and returned to find his entire possessions stolen, sheep, goats, chicken, grain, stools and even his pots and pans. However, the Christians, upon hearing of his plight, from far and near replaced all the stolen items. Eventually, Mr Sanderson's life was threatened by the chief, and thinking of the Eggon believers he informed the District Officer. After a public inquiry it was recommended that he leave the station for a while.

In 1935, Miss Eva Stuart Watt, Home Secretary of the Sudan United Mission arrived at Wana Mission Station. Her personal comment was that whilst Mr Sanderson had the best of intentions by informing the District Officer, it was an unwise move. At Wana, Eva was welcomed by Mr and Mrs Judd and wrote: 'What...[a] privilege...to see and hear at the stations of our own South African Branch, especially at Wana...' On Sunday morning she noticed 'groups of people strolling down to hear God's word.' Some had walked from eight to fifteen miles, 'young men and white haired veterans, mothers with babies on their backs and girls carrying bundles of grain (for the offering).' They were more than two hours early for the 10am service! Eva 'spoke on Jesus and their faces were aglow,' "We know Jesus" they said "and we love Him." 'The reflection of inner radiance bore witness to that fact...Their love flowed from a pure fountain of Calvary and I could feel its warmth.'

At 9:30am, at an elders prayer meeting, 'forty-six Eggon fathers, including three lesser chieftains, opened their hearts to God in short earnest prayers that went straight up to the throne of God...I could not understand a word (nor could Mr Judd who was in charge, for he came from Randa Mission Station), but I felt we were at the very gate of heaven.'

'God was present' at the Sunday morning service 'which was a seething mass of black faces,' as four hundred of them met under the partial shade of a giant locust bean tree. Eva wrote: 'What I had seen took me to my little hut and drove me to my knees. I could see beyond all missionary struggles, the Mighty Rushing Wind sweeping through Africa. I could see God's sledge hammer breaking up the barriers of stone and Pentecostal fires melting hearts of ice...'Praying always' is a secret they have learnt of the Holy Ghost.'

Before the Christians begin work they meet for prayer and after they finished hoeing their fields etc., they would kneel down 'in the hot and dusty soil and pour out their hearts to God.'[4]

Kuwo Revival 1933 – China

A missionary from the China Inland Mission, Webb of Swindon, wrote to J. Edwin Orr early in the year 1934, telling of God's blessing. Webb returned to Sinkiang, China, in 1933, and was praying for three more fellow labourers for an autumn tent campaign. The tent was set up in the social centre of the district, outside the south gate of the city. Unbeknown to them at the time the whole row of houses immediately opposite them were brothels. One of the sins aggressively denounced was the sin of prostitution, and many of the young men who got converted used to frequent those establishments. After a two month campaign, preaching twice a day there was 120 professions of faith, but much of it proved to be 'shallow soil' as many quickly withered under persecution. Though all the houses of ill repute, were mobbed by the locals and 'leaving one or two places in ruins.' It was not long after this that the City Magistrates arrested the occupants and closed the places. Webb wrote: 'We heard to our joy that it was all the doing of the Jesus religion.'

Some of the workers were able to meet together to wait on God for the fullness of the Holy Spirit. A fellow worker, from another district who had been used mightily in revival in a neighbouring province, who was 'full of the Holy Ghost,' came to help. Day after day, they sought the face of God, praying from eight to ten hours on their knees, far into the night, or till near break of day and one after another were filled with the Spirit of God.

Many of the workers had prejudices, preconceived ideas and reservations which all needed to be dealt with, but soon as God met with them, they became 'of one heart and one mind.' Some of them had to deal with sin and as Webb wrote: 'This cost us a good deal; the price had to paid for blessing. In my own case the Lord dealt with my darling idol, smashed it both and me and when sobbing at His feet like a little child, He gave me the assurance that my request was granted. That afternoon, whilst waiting on Him, meditating on the cross of Christ, the Holy Spirit fell on me. With a great shout of hallelujah the joy of the Lord flowed through my whole being and for over an hour all I could do was praise the Lord with laughter and song. We were like men drunk with new wine. Like a flash my life was transformed.' Webb began to pray more; he took a trip to Hungtung to put a matter right with a fellow missionary. 'This done the way was open for blessing.' On the Sunday evening twelve of the boys from the Middle School surrendered to Christ, and the next day saw another four or five, the blessing continued.

A week later, on the Sunday, certain workmen attended the worship service and returned on the Tuesday, being Christmas Day. Webb took the opportunity to talk to those who were already saved, and found the others under deep conviction. In his room, as they got on their knees, 'they burst out crying, sobbing out their confession of sins to God, five or six (one being a woman) got converted on this occasion and two were filled with the Spirit. The blessing next overflowed to the three sons of the house and the father went to the meetings at Kuwo (the centre of this revival movement) and came back filled with the Holy Ghost.' The father was so on fire for God that at his own expense he organised a week's meeting, which started two days later. 'The local talent was not able for it' Webb recorded, but God had His man ready as 'an evangelist recently filled with the Holy Ghost came along and carried on till the end.' Webb concluded in his letter, 'praise Him, all the glory is His...the number at worship on Sundays has trebled itself; victory is before us; pray us into it.'[5]

Chapter Fifteen

One Generation Shall Tell Another

'Be diligent to present yourself approved to God, a worker who does not need to be ashamed, rightly dividing the word of truth' 2 Timothy 2:15.

New York and Eastern Nazarene College 1936 – USA

On the 28 September 1935, J. Edwin Orr began a world tour to circumnavigate the globe. For the two preceding years he had travelled extensively around Britain, Eastern and Western Europe, into Soviet Russia and as far away as Palestine (Israel) and had seen localised revivals in many countries.

In late February 1936, Edwin Orr was on the last week of his one hundred day, forty-eight State tour of America. He had taken as many as twenty meetings a week for the past few months and travelled an average of one thousand miles a week across Canada and America. He arrived in Boston, Massachusetts, (land of the New England revivals from previous centuries) where he first spoke at the Christian and Missionary Alliance Tabernacle (C&MA), on Kenilworth Street, as the guest of Rev. Robert Kilgour. In the Sunday evening service there were several decisions to accept Jesus Christ as Saviour.

Edwin Orr stayed in New York City, from the first till the sixth of March, where he held a series of sixteen meetings which had been arranged by Miss Jennie Johnson of the Pocket Testament League, New York. Orr was in and around the area (and visiting other cities) for just a week and made his headquarters in the Brooklyn home of the Sudan Interior Mission.

On Monday the second of March, Edwin Orr spoke in the evening meeting on what he saw in Soviet Russia when he travelled there in 1934. The evening meeting was held under the auspices of the Business Women's Council and New England Fellowship. After preaching about his travels he did not feel at liberty to preach his sermon on 'Why I am a Revolutionist,' and so began to preach a direct message from the Lord. Orr was very strong in his words and told those present that Boston strongly reminded him of a refrigerator! Orr wrote: 'Boston is one of the most spiritually dead cities of America.'

At first, there was an uncomfortable silence; Edwin Orr discerned that the devil was stirring up resentment. So, to defuse the situation he asked a question to which came no reply, "How many Christians here are in bondage to secret sin?" Orr then went on to explain why Boston had no revival. As the custom was in Boston, if the preacher spoke past nine o'clock, people would get up and leave. Fifteen minutes later, a man began to leave, Orr sensing that the devil was using this to try to break up the meeting, told those present that they could either go home to sleep or stay for an awakening!

Edwin Orr preached the word and then the breakthrough came. People began to publicly confess their sins and get right with God and each another, Orr wrote: '...The meeting went on and on, revival began to reach hearts, prayers began to ascend, and the Lord was victorious over all the obstacles...the meeting closed at a late hour. Hundreds had sought publicly to get right with God, a couple of decisions were made, and the meeting created a sensation among the folks.'

The next morning, Edwin Orr had to do a radio address and from there, he and the Rev. Kilgour drove over to Eastern Nazarene College. As Orr spoke there was a strange outbreak of revival similar to that of Columbia Bible College which occurred just eight days previously. Orr wrote: 'Just as at Columbia, the break came when a student, uninvited, came forward to confess his great need. The meeting seemed to be taken out of my hands, scores were broken down into tears, and a wave of real revival swept over the school. So the early morning chapel service went on till midday.'[1]

Bible Training Institute 1936 – New Zealand

In 1936, J. Edwin Orr was in New Zealand as part of his world tour, promoting full surrender to the Lord Jesus Christ and encouraging prayer and participation for local and national revival. In the previous two years, he had travelled round Europe, Canada and America and had seen localised revivals in several countries, notably Latvia and at various Bible Colleges / Institutes in America.

In Auckland, North Island, New Zealand, on Tuesday 7 April 1936, Edwin Orr and Jack Sherriff (who was also assisting Orr in this leg of the tour) got together to pray that revival would sweep the Ngaruawahia Easter Convention on the Saturday.

The next day Edwin Orr spoke at the Bible Training Institute, in their morning service. Orr wrote: 'The students listened well to the message, and a break came in the meeting when one after another rose to confess hindrance and sin. Criticism, prayerlessness, secret sins were amongst the most honest confessions – and a little local revival broke out as soon as these hindrances were cleansed away...the meeting was really revival in first fruits.'

In the evening Edwin Orr, attended a service in a marquee tent in the Mount Eden district, under Mr Keith Rimmer. The speaker was to be Dr. Charles Rolls, who felt that it would be more appropriate if Orr would address the young people and therefore graciously stood down. As Orr spoke to the Christians, in an air of expectancy the Lord began to do a work in their hearts. One after another, they stood and asked for deliverance from sin, some were in tears; some broke down whilst speaking, two or three prayed at once. One person sang a hymn, "Calvary covers it all" and 'the hush of God fell on the place, backsliders were restored and after an appeal, around fifteen people were converted.' Keith Rimmer wrote: '...After the benediction was pronounced, no one seemed willing to go home...revival has started.'

From there Edwin Orr visited the Ngaruawahia Easter Convention (the Keswick of New Zealand) which ran from Thursday the ninth till Monday the thirteenth of April and on the Friday night revival began.[2] The account of the revival at the Ngaruawahia Easter Convention (1936) can be found in *Revival Fires and Awakenings* (2010) by the author.

Sudan 1938-1940s

In April 1938, Richard Jones, a teacher for the Church Missionary Society (CMS) and his wife arrived at Juba, southern Sudan (1,000 miles from Khartoum). Jones alongside a more seasoned missionary visited the CMS Nugent School, Loka and preached in the evening. Oliver C. Allison (future bishop of the Sudan) had met Jones in Salisbury, England in 1937 at their final interview with the CMS, he arrived in Juba in November 1938. Looking back over his life, Bishop Allison wrote: 'Richard Jones preached an impassioned sermon to the whole school that evening with a call to instant and radical repentance, addressed both to staff and school boys, condemning the missionaries for betraying the Gospel.'

Richard Jones was posted at Yambio amongst the Zande people who had only recently received the Good News. A few months before his arrival, the pioneering missionary Clive Gore had passed into glory; the two remaining missionaries, Arthur and Grace Ridley from Australia held a large convention at Yambio on the pattern of "Keswick" and many young Christians had been stirred. The Ridley's had returned home on sick leave before the Jones' arrival, so he was alone and the Mission was leaderless.

Richard Jones as at Loka, began preaching 'the same urgent and prophetic message of repentance.' The Zande people, former heathen 'were more than usually subject to fear of the unknown.' Certain people had an encounter with the Holy Spirit, which began to cause schism in the Anglican Mission, with those who had met Him being less than loving towards the weaker brethren. Some of the Christian teachers and evangelists who had come under Richard Jones' preaching (himself an Anglican) decided to quit the Mission. The teachers and evangelists sold their possessions including their bicycles in some cases which had been provided by the missionaries to aid travel in evangelism (maybe they were trying to live by faith or to be part of a Christian community which was more akin to the early apostles) – whatever the reasons why, it does appear to be a case of zeal without tempered maturity or accountability. The District Commissioner (DC) 'wisely allocated' these former Anglican's a plot of land which they could build their huts and cultivate the soil, which Jones publicly condemned (with the DC present) from the pulpit in Yambio Church. Without a wage, they soon ran into debt with the local merchants and 'owing to some regrettable incidents on the mission...the government felt bound to intervene and ordered Mr and Mrs Jones to leave the Sudan at short notice.' Bishop Allison wrote: 'A sad end to what might have been a promising missionary career...'

I was reminded of what Charles Finney, under the title, 'When can Revival be Expected,' wrote: 'Whenever Christians are found willing to make sacrifices necessary to carry it on – their feelings, business, time, work etc. The minister must be prepared if it be the will of God, to be driven away from the place and leave the entire event with God!'

Bishop Allison wrote: 'In the mysterious providence of God, Richard Jones in his brief few months set of the spark which resulted in a new spiritual forest fire, burning up the dross and purifying the young church. I saw plenty of "gold, silver and precious stones" in the process. Perhaps inevitably also some "wood, hay and stubble" which were only perishable! Those of us who followed saw the fruits of the labours of others, and more importantly the fruits of the Spirit.'

In early 1939, Bishop Morris Gelsthorpe and Dr. Joe Church a leader from the Ruanda Revival (1937-1950s), tempered with maturity and experience 'helped provide stability to the new situation.' The Riley's returned from Australia to find the Mission Station torn by bitterness and resentment. Slowly relationships were restored, and one by one, those who had left the Mission returned 'in penitence for their lack of love, but at the same time renewed in the Spirit for future effective service to the Mission and the Church that was already growing in numbers and depth.' As time progressed, the lack of love formerly shown to the weaker brethren was balance by the fruit of the Spirit. As decades passed, Christianity was no longer the religion of the white man (missionaries) or the school boys (trained at the Christians Schools) but quickly became rooted in the soil of the hearts of the Sudanese people. Old racial hatreds between tribes broke down and 'a new sense of brotherhood realised' and 'the Sudanese Christians became real missionaries, prepared to go at the call of God to serve in other tribes.'

Bishop Allison recalled: 'What started as a renewal developed into a revival as fresh and spontaneous pockets of revival sprang up from place to place...The Movement spread like wildfire in some areas, such as the Moru country; in others it led to an awakening, particularly in parts of the Dinka country, such as Akot...I can only thank God that I was privileged to be there at such a time of new opportunity and challenge to us all...As the years went by there was more and more evidence of the work of the Holy Spirit in individual and in unlikely places. These fresh pockets of revival as it then became, with a big growth of the indigenous church in the villages, were a source of real blessing, as well as sometimes a cause of division, and even embarrassment to civil authorities. The term "Balokole" widely used in Uganda for the revival "brethren" was replaced by the vernacular words meaning the "Praising Ones." '[3]

From the mid 1930s, the East African Revival broke out in Uganda and touched Kenya, Tanganyika and adjacent territories up to and until the 1950s. In Kenya the word "Balokole" so wrote Max Warren (whom Bishop Allison called a 'Missionary Statesman and Prophet.') meant "saved ones" –

members of the revival fellowship.[4] Bishop Oliver Allison asked one native pastor at a crowded congregation, "How is it that those elderly people seem to be able to read their Bible so well? How did they learn? The pastor replied, "Oh! Those are some of the Praising Ones. We used to think that old people could never be taught to read! but since they were 'revived' they have been so keen to read their Bible that they have learned to read in their special classes. It is the work of the Holy Spirit."[5]

A blind bard called Malek in an unnamed area of southern Sudan, in his sleep received a vision of Jesus Christ and heard the angels sing. On awakening, he sang the song to himself and later to his friends who wrote down the words. The blind bard used to sing the song and his friends in true African style would join in the chorus. Malek began to compose Christian lyrics and visited local villages. Bishop Oliver Allison wrote: 'Through his influence and others like him, little groups of "revived" Christians sprang up all over the countryside. They would meet by day and by night as the Spirit moved them, to sing their songs and to read the Bible together and to pray. Here was a spontaneous movement of the Spirit. Many were won for Christ; others repented of their sins and found release from their fears and sins. It was a joyful experience.' Many of the Praising Ones were accused of breaking the peace, and of being disloyal to their local customs and chiefs as they preached repentance towards God and faith in Jesus Christ. In some areas, they were forbidden to sing their hymns and on one occasion, a group of Christian were arrested for singing at the graveside of a believer – the exact opposite of the customary wailing over the death of a heathen! Many were thrown into prison where they enjoyed fellowship meetings together and became great witnesses among fellow prisoners.[6]

Bishop Oliver Allison concluded by saying that the praises to the Lord from the Praising Ones was their strength, especially during the civil wars of the 1950s and 1960s; 'Indigenous "songs from the forest" and from exile, caught on and encouraged others who had to face sore trials.'[7]

Chapter Sixteen

To The Uttermost

'The law of the Lord is perfect, converting the soul; the testimony of the Lord is sure, making wise the simple; the statutes of the Lord are right, rejoicing the heart; the commandment of the Lord is pure, enlightening the eyes; the fear of the Lord is clean, enduring forever; the judgments of the Lord are true and righteous altogether. More to be desired than gold, yea, than much fine gold...by them your servant is warned...in keeping them there is great reward' Psalm 19:7-11.

Buenos Aires 1954 – Argentina

American evangelist, Tommy Hicks from Lancaster, California, held a two month healing and evangelistic campaign in Buenos Aires, Argentina, from the 14 April until the 13 June 1954 which broke forth into revival. This sixty day campaign only took place because of God's Divine intervention in the life of Argentina's President, Mr Peron who was healed in Jesus' name as Hicks' prayed for him who then sanctioned the gatherings with free media coverage!

The campaign began in the 25,000-seat Atlantic football stadium, but this proved too small, so they moved to the 180,000-seat Huracan bullfighting ring and upwards of 100,000 flocked in around the clock, with 200,000 on the final night. Around six million people attended and thousands were healed. Hicks for two months hardly slept or ate and the members of the local churches who were ushers were rushed off their feet, working in twelve hour shifts.

Louie W. Stokes, in the foreword to his booklet, *The Great Revival in Buenos Aires* wrote: 'These notes were written during the rush of the campaign, oftentimes after the night meetings, and claim no literary skill or value. However, it is a faithful and conservative record of what was happening, written by one whose heart was one hundred percent in the work from the beginning.' Also, Stokes wrote: 'Over thirty local churches lent their cooperation and the Lord used Brother Tommy Hicks as the evangelist. The revival continues and will have lasting effects upon the life, not only of the Evangelical groups in Argentina, but in all spheres of religious life.'[1]

Ed Silvoso, Director of Harvest Evangelism was one of many evangelists used during the Argentinean Revival (1982-1997). In an interview with Noel Stanton, senior pastor of the Jesus Fellowship, he said, "I came to the Lord at thirteen. I was the first born-again Christian in the High School in a city of 100,000...Being a born-again Christian in Argentina in 1958 was like being a Christian in Mecca, that's how tough it was."[2]

The total attendance for the duration of the two month campaign in 1954 varies between authors, from two, four, or six million, though the latter is the correct figure, but conversion statistics range from eighteen thousand, half a million and up to three million! During future research it was recorded that more than eighteen thousand new church members were officially taken into fellowship at the time which was the largest figure in the history of Argentina.

A figure of around 20,000 conversions is more accurate rather than Tommy Hicks who "naively concluded," so said J. Edwin Orr, that three million people made a confession of Christ because half put their hands up. Orr said, "Latin American's will raise their hands for any invitation..." And regardless of the facts that 100,000 took decision cards, "If you're piling out of a stadium and someone is holding out cards, you'll take one."[3]

Rhinehard Bonnke, founder of Christ For All Nations (CFAN) said, "Evangelism must always lead into the Church of Christ otherwise it is not biblical evangelism." From 1987 till 2006, Rhinehard had preached to 98 million people in person, with 46 million making a profession of faith.

A Tribe in Indonesia – 1959

On the 9 September 1959, Paul Pontier of the Missionary Aviation Fellowship flew the first Indonesian national missionaries. They witnessed for three days and 1,000 tribes-people committed their lives to Jesus Christ.[4]

Nagaland Awakening 1960s

Nagaland is a mountainous region situated in the north-eastern State of India, bordering Myanmar (formerly Burma) and the Indian states of Assam and Arunachal Pradesh. Its people, the Naga's, (geographically inside of Nagaland) consist of thirteen tribes and are former head-hunters. Before Christianity came, the Naga's were tribal animists who worshipped spirits and were very superstitious. They have strong social bonds, a sense of community, a belief in the immortality of the soul and judgment after death.

The first missionaries arrived in 1840; they saw their first convert, Hube, seven years later, but he died within a month; the Naga Church was founded in 1872. The Ao Naga Church was founded in this year whereas the Khiamhgan (also spelt Khemongen) Naga Church, was only founded in 1950, yet no more than fifty miles separated these two tribes. As Christianity came, heathen practices came to lose their grip and were abandoned, though from one village to the next, the stories differ. When the British left India a few years after World War II, Nagaland raised its flag of independence. The Indian Government retaliated, all missionaries (and foreigners) were expelled for allegedly inciting independence and the Indian Army began a fifty year war of terror and ethnic cleansing in which around 200,000 Naga's were killed.

During the 1960s awakening, the principle date of the revival was 1966, though the timing and duration of the revival and its effect in each tribe and its hundreds of churches differs greatly. It was in this awakening that the final clash came between the conservative traditional Baptists and the Holy Spirit filled revivalists. As the Holy Spirit came, demoralised Christians were revitalised and the heathen were converted.

In the early 1960s, Christians who were revived at different villages returned home and began praying for revival but many of their Churches refused them the use of the building so they prayed in their homes. Some were imprisoned, others were killed. The following year the Nagaland Christian Revival Church was formed, because of the split between the traditional Baptist churches, who denounced what was happening and the revivalists themselves, who saw thousands come to Christ, while the Baptist's still denied the gifts of the Holy Spirit and the miracles which were happening all around them.

The awakenings of the 1950s and 1960s brought rapid church growth and a change in the morality of many of the villages. Some villages were entirely converted, whilst others were entirely untouched and Christians were still marginalized in society. As in all revivals, like the nation of Israel, there was ebb and flow. As one example, the Sendenyu Baptist Church had seen seven amazing years of revival during the 1950s awakening but 'by 1967 onwards,' as records their own Church souvenir booklet 'the believers began to turn backward to their former state of sinful life again...(2 Peter 2:22)...leaving their first love.'

In 1932, the first church amongst the Konyak tribe was established. The former practice of the Konyak's included not burying their dead. They would place the corpses on a bamboo platform and after nine days or so they would separate the head from the dead body. They would then prepare a feast, place the head on the table and the family would talk to it as if it were a living person. This is what the early missionaries faced.

By 1936, the Konyak Church had fourteen baptised members, in 1940, there were 145 baptised Christians and at the end of 1949 there were 1,600 members. A. Yanang Konyak wrote: 'Village after village came to Christ year after year. During the years 1949-1952, they saw more than a thousand conversions to Christ and the year 1951 is officially accepted as the year of the founding of Konyak Baptist Churches and the Baptist Banjem (association). In 1955, there were more than 4,600 church members in 23 churches and 1955 was also the year that Christianity first came to the Tobu area which is known locally as Upper Konyak.

In 1959, the Konyak's sent out 108 Gospel Teams. In May 1960, the campaign "Nagaland for Christ" began with five members and Christians freely began to proclaim their faith throughout Konyakland. A. Yanang Konyak wrote: 'Once again the churches got their strength back. In spite of many disturbances and opposition from within and without – especially from the Indian Government at the beginning – the churches could stand firmly. No one could extinguish the work of the Holy Spirit. The more the trouble, the faster the Christians increased in number.'

In many places, the Konyak Christians were beaten, their property was confiscated and their crops stolen, but when the ahng (leader) of the village submitted to Christ then so would his people. By 1964 the Konyak's had 52 churches with 10,733 members and by 1967 they had 12,148 members.

In the northern Sumi territory in 1960, a few members of a church where Hevukhu Achumi Sema was the pastor, (who would become the director of the Nagaland Missionary Movement) returned from a prayer meeting in Changtongya with assurance of their salvation. Some of the Church 'became suspicious' recalled Sema, recalling what happened when revival first broke out 'and persecuted them by throwing stones at them, taking away their Bibles, beating them and [performing] many forms of torture.' The Holy Spirit filled Christians prayed and practically helped the people, but despite this, persecution grew more intense against them. One day, 'the village joined together with three other surrounding villages. We took hold of fifteen female revivalists, took off their clothes and paraded them naked before all the people [remember these were so-called Christians perpetrating this act and not the heathen!]. We hoped to shame them and humiliate them...Some cheerfully received the humiliation and prayed for their persecutors' and stated that even Jesus was naked on the cross. 'God started to use the revivalists through healings and within a few years the whole village was touched by the fire of revival.'[5]

Paul Hattaway in his book, *From Head-Hunters To Church Planters* briefly wrote about the Zeliangrong Revival (1959) which occurred when local evangelistic teams shared the Gospel in animist villages and a number of people got converted. But, a woman, with mysterious powers started up her own movement which 'taught bizarre doctrine... and many were deceived.' She was worshipped as a goddess and this movement became a threat to the church. Consequently, the Zeliangrong Church did not grow as fast as those within other tribes and it was not until the late 1970s that this woman's influence began to decline.

A group of believers were at a village in Phek District when they saw a ball of fire fall from heaven onto the Indian-Myanmar border. They rushed to the village of Lephuri to discover that revival had broken out, even though no preacher had visited it. In other places revival spread as 'fire carriers' moved from village to village preaching about the Lord Jesus Christ.

In the beginning of January 1961, a four day conference was held amongst the Ao tribe at Keruma. Neihulie Angami wrote: '...the Spirit of God moved upon the people in a wonderful way.' Many of those present 'saw visions of angels coming down to the meeting place. On the Sunday, the communion service lasted seven hours, 'the presence of God was so real...Everyone was so moved by the Spirit that people began to cry aloud in prayer. Even those who were serving communion could not lift up their heads because of weeping. Prayer continued for hours.'[6]

Paul Hattaway, is founder of Asia Harvest, a ministry which is committed to evangelising and working in cooperation with churches across Asia. He wrote: 'By 1965 every Angami village in Nagaland had a church.'[7]

Nagaland Awakening 1970s

During the Nagaland Awakening of the 1970s, the principle dates of the revivals were 1972 and 1976, but each tribe and its hundreds of church had its own story to tell. In November 1972, Billy Graham held a crusade at Kohima, Nagaland to a crowd of 100,000 people, when the town's population was less than 33,000! Many educated people and Nagaland leaders 'dedicated their lives to Christ.' In 1978, Dozi Phuveyi wrote: 'The fire continued to burn till a dynamic movement of revival took place beginning from 1975 to this day.'[8]

Rev. Ayang Sor is from the Ao tribe whose parents were affected during the 1952 revival. This led to his dad becoming a pastor. He stated 'Prayer carried on for a long time and in 1976 another major revival broke out. The effects of this are still being felt today [2006].' It was during the 1970s awakening that really inspired the Naga's for world mission, their 'eyes were opened, really for the first time, to see the neighbouring states and countries where the Gospel had not taken root.'[9]

In the third week of September 1976, a 'spiritual awakening week' was held at the Sumi Baptist Church. Five revival preachers had been invited and on the sixth day, a Saturday 'a mighty visitation of the Holy Spirit took place.' Hevukhu Achumi Sema wrote: 'Many people fell down to the floor...and there were endless confessions of sin and ceaseless prayer and crying to the Lord.' The service finished at 6am on Sunday morning! Every night people came to the church for prayer, but 'strong opposition arose' from some Church members because what was happening was contrary to Baptist doctrine! The pastor and all born again Spirit filled believers were locked out of the church. However, one night, as they were praying the Lord told them to pray inside the church. A man laid his hands on the lock of the church as directed by the Lord and it fell to the ground. The opposition leaders sent nine half-drunk men to attack them. With broken bottles in their hands, they waited outside the church, but the Lord sent twenty-four police officers to deal with the offenders. 'After five months of prayer a new Sumi Baptist Church emerged which contained all the revived people.' The church building was completed within forty days! 'God used the Church to spread revival all over the region. Spreading the revival was the sole intense burden of the Church.'[10] See Appendix J.

Chapter Seventeen

The Least of These

'Defend the poor and the fatherless; do justice to the afflicted and needy. Deliver the poor and needy; free them from the hand of the wicked' Psalm 83:3-4.

Eastern Zimbabwe 1982

In and around the year 1982, revival broke out in a remote tribal area in Eastern Zimbabwe, transforming the whole area into a Holy Haven. Michael Howard, a Rhodesian, who has seen at least six revivals across Africa and who has a Bible School in Malawi wrote: 'No records were ever kept, but it was the Holy Spirit visiting in response to the heart-wrenching sobs of God's people.'

The Rhodesian Bush War (1971-1979) was the Rhodesians defending themselves against the black terrorist army. In 1978, the country became known as Zimbabwe Rhodesia, but after elections in April 1980, the country gained independence under Robert Magabe. He eventually went on to ruin the once prosperous country. By 2008, inflation had risen faster than it could be calculated! White farmer had been evicted from their farms, farm machinery was sold as scrap metal, seeds rotten in the ground, and innocent Zimbabweans began to starve.

Michael Howard and his small team of evangelists and Intercessors were in a rural secondary school in an unnamed place in Eastern Zimbabwe in around the year 1982. There was no electricity. The Friday evening meeting in the school hall was lit by dim lanterns and the students had turned up 'more out of curiosity than to show interest in things spiritual.' Michael wrote: 'As we arrived, I distinctively felt His brooding presence and I knew that He, the enabler, the Holy Paraclete [Holy Spirit] was there to glorify Jesus.'

Prior to this revival, a young black pastor called Jemu, when he first left Bible School had for a time lived with Michael at Chipinge. Back in 1982, in the crudely built school hall, Jemu led the singing and the Africans 'who love to sing' enthusiastically joined in, 'but this was altogether different' and after the first song the Holy Spirit 'seemed to latch on to the next and He became the Divine worship leader. The fourth or fifth song was of native worship to God' and was so simple, yet profound. The more they sung 'the higher and higher the Spirit took us, finally spiralling right up into the heart of the Father.'

After an hour or so of singing the same song, 'the atmosphere was so drenched with His holy presence that I was beside myself.' Michael wanted to cry out, "Enough Lord or I die" and yet another part wanted more of Him. 'Jesus had indeed come and was being glorified by the Holy Spirit.'

A junior teacher called Esther, who had been worshipping the Lord, arms outstretched and tears streaming down her face, 'suddenly collapsed under the full power of the anointing as great heavy sobs came from deep within.' This breaking happened to one and then another and 'before long there were bodies lying everywhere and such a cry was ascending to God that it sounded like a thousand native funerals all taking place at once.'

Michael wrote: 'This was something out of the book of Acts; this was Joel's prophecy [Joel 2:28] coming to pass before our very eyes…' After many hours, Michael went outside the hall to discover that more people were outside the hall than inside! News of God's visitation had already been carried to the neighbouring villagers. The locals were crying out, "Come and see! God has come to our land."

People were prostrate before the Lord, others were kneeling, standing or lying on their backs. Every now and then a wail would ascend, 'the noise was deafening, but the Spirit was touching the deepest recesses of the lives of the natives, many of whom had been badly affected by the war. They were being delivered and healed as they were brought into living reality with the cross.'

The revival continued in the following days as the Spirit was poured out on teachers, students and the surrounding villages. Vast numbers of people were saved and on one Saturday there was at least fifteen people baptising the new converts, 'the Holy Spirit was awesomely present and sifting every heart…groups of students and villagers were gathered everywhere.' Some were praying, singing, weeping or shouting, 'but all were ordered under the control of His mighty hand.' The baptism services went on for hours and hours and as the 'Spirit descended in heavenly waves and baptised hundreds in Himself so that many came up out of the water speaking in tongues glorifying God.'

During the baptism, some 'demoniacs' began to manifest and began to thrash around because the devil hates water. The demons were cast out in the mighty name of Jesus, 'with horrible shrieks they fled' and then the candidates were baptised again and finally handed over to others for counselling. Michael wrote: 'Revival demands, absolutely *demands*, our fullest attention to this urgent agenda of God. The best resources of Christendom; men, money and machinery, must be commissioned for this task and this is what we did...People longed to sacrifice themselves and their entire resources in order that the lost might be saved...We are called to reach our generation *and* to train up the next generation to reach theirs. Without the two operations dove-tailing to work together, there would be a major bottle-neck of God's purposes.'[1]

El-Minya Revival 1991 – Egypt

In 1991, a move of God broke out in El-Minya (also known as Minya), Egypt under a former architect who got converted and felt called to become a Coptic monk, his name was Father Daniel. Father Daniel dressed in the traditional Coptic clothes wearing a robe and sandals. Because he was Coptic, some of the missionaries at the time held him in suspicion, though not my two sources (from the UK), one of whom said, "We certainly had great fellowship with him."

In February 2008, I spent a few days in Minya. It is situated along the Nile River approximately 200 miles south of Cairo and has many tall blocks of flats. After getting off the train from Cairo, it was very noticeable that Minya was different than other Egyptian towns and cites I had visited, and it was not because of their love for neon signs! Just crossing the railway bridge, I saw a large church with twin 'bell' towers under construction and there were large numbers of women who did not cover their heads, which is common within Muslim communities. After asking around, it turned out that 25% of Minya's population are Coptic Christian (one man said it could be as high as 30%) and there are five evangelical churches in the city, with the sixth one being built (the twin 'bell' tower).

This revival (though Father Daniel does not call what he has started a revival. He says that the word 'revival' could not apply in Egypt unless Muslims were radically affected) was mainly amongst the students of the middle to upper classes (of the Coptic Christians). It soon spread to their families and into the business community in other cities.

Operation World, 21st Century Edition, 2001, reported: 'There has been a growing renewal movement since 1973 and many young people are now coming to the Lord and a new generation of bold leaders is emerging. Several Pentecostal and evangelical denominations are growing significantly.'

Father Daniel received much persecution, including physical beatings so that now one eye is out of sync with the other. Eventually, Father Daniel was thrown out of the Coptic Church because of his insistence of preaching the Gospel and was excommunicated from his position. He began to travel and preach, but he urged his disciples not to leave the Coptic Church wanting to see reform from within it.

A Christian worker who witnessed some of the events of the El-Minya Revival wrote to me in September 2006: '...It was kept quiet because of [the] police and Islamic influences, but as many as 20,000 found the Lord in a few months. It is the only 'old fashioned revival' I have ever been part of. Meetings were held nightly in different locations – no churches would allow it. They would start at 7pm and run until 3-4-5am. They grew from the prayer of Father Daniel, though in reality they had no leader. Daniel would turn up during the night or early morning. It is the only time when I had to join a hundred or more on the roof of a building looking down an airshaft at that was happening inside. I had to queue for my turn to come round!'

Another Christian worker who went to some of the meetings told me in October 2006 that in one of the meetings, all the furniture of the house was moved out. The people were so squeezed in that they all had to stand up and if you put your hands in the air, you could not put them down again! There was, "Singing over and over again, there were little kids, three or five years old, lost in worship" whilst others pleaded with their parents to take them to church.

In Minya in 2008, I had a Divine appointment with a man who, when he was just nineteen years old, as a student, attended a meeting under Father Daniel where 2,000 people were present. It was at this meeting that he got converted! This man whom I will call Torrey (not his real name) was the son of a pastor and was named after a famed American Evangelist. Minya was where Torrey grew up and he had returned with his family on holiday. Torrey informed me that home meetings called 'Daniel Meetings' still take place, which I understood to be house churches / cell groups that meet at peoples' homes.

In Cairo, Father Daniel hired a stadium, "How, I do not know?" said one of my sources, "But there were queues to get in – [and] healings, deliverances and conversions." Not all of the revival was quite so overt; much of it went underground when persecution arose.

I was informed that "love" was the mark of the revival, "Love, love, love" and that the brethren were so accepting of people. This Christian worker informed me that she went to Egypt to recruit labourers for another mission field. She returned to her mission base without having accomplished her objective but informed her colleagues, "I have now fallen in love with Jesus again." To which they were all ecstatic about, having prayed that she would be blessed whilst in Egypt. Since then Egyptian labourers have gone to the desired mission field.

Father Daniel, now Pastor Daniel used to live in an undisclosed location, but despite death threats continues to minister publicly. He is now married, works under the Assembles of God in a rented building and resides in Cairo. Dr. Rev. Menes Abdul Noor is the founder of Kasr El-Dobara Evangelical Church in Cairo, where up to 7,000 people attend a week. It is the largest evangelical church in the Middle East. His life story is told in *A Pastor From Egypt* by Naiim Atef (2003). In February 2008, I visited the church and alongside my brother, was allowed to film and interview Dr. Rev. Menes Abdul Noor and Dr. Rev. Sameh M. Tawfik, the senior pastor. The church can seat 1,500, with Monday evening being the main service. Rev. Menes informed me that Daniel and himself are good friends and that when members of Daniel's AOG congregation get married they use Kasr El-Dobara Church.

Naiim Atef wrote: 'Since Kasr El-Dobara was founded, the vision has always been to evangelise not only the local church, but all of Egypt and the whole region. This is very well expressed in the strong prayer movement that has been growing since the end of the 1970s and beginning of [the] 1980s. The passion of its leaders is not only to see a one strong church, but a revival that touches many churches and places in the community.' Genesis chapter twelve reveals this, Abraham had been blessed so that he could bless others. 'Kasr El-Dobara has received many blessings. It has grown both spiritually and numerically and God has given it many opportunities for ministry. It has not kept these blessings to itself, but has shared them to bless others with the blessing it has received.'[2]

Dr. Rev. Menes Abdul Noor also informed us of the work of the Lord amongst Coptic Christians, who are truly born again; one congregation consisting of 10,000 Christians who faithfully adhere to Coptic traditions, with all their incense and bells, but have a living relationship with Jesus Christ.

Pastor Daniel has travelled to the UK on a few occasions and will only turn up at the conference and speak when the Lord has given him something to say. One of my sources, several years ago, organised two meetings at which Father Daniel was the main speaker (his wife would be the translator), though he would generally arrive to speak as the people were leaving, which was unfortunate for those who left, because he always had a message to share. In London, he has held conferences, though they were more of an evangelistic event rather than the European concept of a Christian conference and wherever he travels Arab speaking people come to the Lord.

Many of the converts from this revival, having been discipled and trained are now Christian leaders whilst, "many young people from the revival are now in [Christian] ministry planting churches."

Pastor Daniel has appeared on the Al-Hayat channel (Arab Christian TV) and Rivers of Life (which he founded) has now some kind of recognition in Egypt, though I am not sure exactly what that means in a Muslim country, as they are still very restricted. All the Coptic Christian I spoke to in Egypt informed me that they are treated as second-class citizens.

Eritrea 1993
Eritrea sits above Ethiopia on the continent of Africa. It has a population of around four million people equally divided by Christians and Muslims. If you are a Christian in Eritrea it is because you were born into a Coptic family, most of whom never become "born again" as Jesus stated (in John chapter three) nor are filled with the Holy Spirit.

For thirty years there was a war between the Eritrean's who were trying to gain independence from Ethiopia. In 1991 independence came which was a "big turning point" for the nation so an Eritrean born Christian labourer informed me.

In April 1993, in an internationally monitored referendum, ninety-eight percent of the registered voters voted, and of these, ninety-nine percent voted for independence. A transitional constitution from May 1993 was replaced by a new constitution adopted five years later, but by April 2010, it had not been implemented.

There are several streams to this revival, but at the present I am only permitted to share one tributary. In 1993, some ten to twenty Eritrean high school and university students from the Full Gospel Church who had been studying in Ethiopia returned home to the capital of Eritrea, Asmara. The students, former Coptic Christians had been converted and baptised with the Holy Spirit whilst in Ethiopia and in Asmara began to see many young people coming to Christ as they taught about the Holy Spirit. The older generation refused because "it's like becoming a Muslim to them." My source, a native Eritrean who is used in intercession informed me, "It was so radical, the songs the worship" and so very different than the traditional Coptic Christian tradition.

The revival had been continuing for about five years when a border conflict brought Eritrea and Ethiopia back into war against each other from 1998-2000. However, this only helped fuel the revival as sixteen year old boys and older were conscripted in training camps. Many of these conscripts were born again, Spirit filled, Christian young men. My source informed me that these men "excelled in all that they did [like Daniel] and were more favoured than those who did not know Christ." Many of these Christians did not know church, with its traditions and set formulae and began to share the Good News and pray for their fellow comrades – many were healed in Jesus' name and set free from addictions.

Prior to the revival, prayer had been ascending to the throne room of God for many years, not only for Eritrea but for Britain as well, I was told, "We expected revival to come like in Britain – free [from persecution], but God moved in unexpected ways...Intercession is very important." At first the government ignored these conversions from Islam to Christianity as all these young soldiers lives were on the front line anyway, and as had already been stated, they were a cut above the rest and a credit to their country to which they were loyal to.

One news source stated: 'Large numbers of Eritrean soldiers embraced a more evangelical brand of Christianity during the war with Ethiopia after listening to broadcasts in the local vernacular from FEBA radio, a Seychelles-based Christian station...There are unconfirmed reports of several young Christian soldiers having been shot after being discovered reading the Bible.'[3] Over a period of time the government got concerned about the shift in balance between the Christian and Muslim population, this is when the persecution arose and was quite severe amongst the military. Evangelical church leaders, those not belonging to the Coptic, Catholic or Lutheran Church began to be arrested; the Evangelical Church went underground and by 2005 all Evangelical church buildings were closed down, though this stance was officially sanctioned in May 2002. My source told me, "It's like Saudi Arabia, you cannot walk around with a Bible in your hands or legally meet in houses."

In 2001, severe persecution broke out in Asmara amongst two Orthodox churches as 'church leaders sought to deal with 'heretics' in their midst. Many young people were beaten, their property was vandalised and Bibles and other religious material were burned during this officially sanctioned attack. Government spokespersons then began comparing Pentecostal / Charismatic and Evangelical church members to Islamists, and branded them a danger to national security.'[4]

A few years after the millennium a group of four or five leaders locked themselves in an underground house, and for at least two years they prayed for revival and refused to come out. They were known as the "group of prophets" though in reality during the revival there were "many, many leaders." Other people were permitted to join them in prayer, I was told, "When we pray there, we just fly overhead."

Three to five years ago, my source revisited her homeland and again the following year, when she found her country was "very different, all the [Evangelical] churches were closed." They secretly met for prayer and were told, "Do not pray loudly" all the windows would be shut and one person would come to the house at a time so as not to cause suspicion. They would meet from one in the afternoon till ten at night.

Some of the fifteen-year-old girls and boys were having visions and prophesying, they were "full of fire." Before the churches were closed, "many, many evangelists came [to Eritrea] and many prophesied about the Eritrean's reaching Arabs in neighbouring countries."

Many of the Christians are put into steel cargo containers (like the ones you see on articulated lorries) where they suffer greatly in extreme heat. Many of my sources friends and her fellow labourers have been imprisoned, she stated, "[There is] so much persecution going on, we do this happily, having to suffer, but they choose to serve Him. They bring Christ before anything [allow Him to shine through their endurance]."

One man, Joseph a man who was "full of the Spirit" in his mid twenties received a word from God: "The Lord spoke to me, you'll go to prison for eight months." He was sent to prison, but the authorities did not inform him about the length of his detainment. My source visited Joseph in a prison in Asmara and told me how she cried over the condition that her brother in Christ was enduring. The place was dirty, terrible hygiene, the food was bad and there was no private space to pray, so he used to put his blanket over his head. During the months of March to May, the climate is very hot which only added to the discomfort and the prisoners were not allowed to use the toilet more than twice a day. But in prison Joseph saw conversions and healings take place, he "impacted very, many, many young people" I was told. Eight months to the day and Joseph was told by the guards, "Come on, pack your bags." Unexpectedly, he turned up at a person's house, my source informed me that she was present and thought that he must have been released a few days previously because, "his face radiated like Moses – so full of joy and laughing" but in actual fact he had come directly from the prison.

Elizabeth Kendal in a Religious Liberty Prayer Bulletin wrote: 'In January 2006, the regime forcefully took over the administration of the Eritrean Orthodox Church (EOC) and arrested those who protested. There is a renewal movement inside the EOC known as 'Medhane Alem' and dozens of its leaders also have been arrested, accused of heresy... Today some 3,000 Eritrean Christians are imprisoned for their faith. Some are in underground and solitary cells whilst some are in 'secret' prisons for the 'disappeared.' However, most are herded into unventilated shipping containers in the desert where dysentery and infectious diseases go untreated. Torture is routine... Open Doors reported that Yemane Kahasay Andom (43) died at Mitire Military Confinement Centre on 23 July 2009. Andom was a member of the Ethiopian Baptist Kale Hiwot Church (literally 'breath of life') linked with SIM.' For eighteen months he refused to sign the recantation form and weakened by continual torture and weeks of solitary confinement Andom died of malaria in an underground cell.

'On 5 December Eritrean authorities arrested 30 mostly elderly Christian women who were praying together in a house in the capital, Asmara. According to International Christian Concern, most of the detainees are members of Faith Mission Church, an evangelical church with a Methodist background. It had been active in evangelism and development activities in Eritrea for over five decades until 2002 when it was forced to go underground.'[5]

In September 2006, eritreanchristians.com reported: 'In the past few days the government of Eritrea ordered Kale Hiwot, Lutheran, and Catholic churches to surrender all their offices operating in the country. The churches have strongly objected to the order. This new development highlights the government's determination to eliminate any form of Christian worship from Eritrea. Kale Hiwot is an evangelical church and some of its properties had been spared from seizure by the government. All other evangelical churches have been forcibly shut down and their leaders and church members were thrown in jail and continue to be detained under inhumane conditions in many areas of the country.'

In closing my source said, "I love my country and pray for my country." Pray for Eritrea and please remember her and the other persecuted countries of the world where our brothers and sisters suffer for their faith in Jesus Christ. i.e. North Korea, Saudi Arabia, Vietnam, Laos, Iran, Burma, Somalia, Bhutan, China, Afghanistan, Algeria and many other countries.[6]

Tibetans in China 1996

The following is an excerpt from a 1996 article: 'Yet, there is light in Tibet, strong signs that God is moving with His Holy Spirit. According to a report in *China and the Church Today* from Gansu province [in China], an area worked extensively by several mission groups before the communists came to power, a few Christian households had gathered together to worship during a Chinese New Year's celebration. Their neighbours, seeking to wipe out Christianity, disrupted their meeting and told them to disperse. The Christians, unwilling to stop their meeting, were severely beaten by the crowd. The next morning, their persecutors found their herds of sheep, cows, and horses dying. Their family members also began to die one by one. Realizing that the wrath of God had fallen upon them, they pleaded with those who believed in Jesus to pray. The Lord heard the believers' prayers, and the sick and dying were healed. As a result, more than a hundred Tibetans turned to the Lord![7]

Chapter Eighteen

When the Grain Ripens

Jesus said, "...Behold, I say to you, lift up your eyes and look at the fields, for they are already white for harvest! And he who reaps receives wages and gathers fruit for eternal life that both he who sows and he who reaps may rejoice together. For in this the saying is true: 'One sows and another reaps.' I sent you to reap that for which you have not laboured and you have entered into their labours" John 4:35-38.

Malay Revival 1998

In the early twentieth century a Bible colporteur travelled south from the Battak Land (island of Sumatra, Indonesia) and arrived at 'the Malay [speaking] country [on Sumatra]' and to his 'astonishment sold 1,000 Malay Scriptures and probably could have disposed of thousands more' but for the fact that his stock was exhausted...' He wrote: 'I was particularly surprised when many of the Moslems [Muslims] showed a decided preference for buying gospels rather than the books of the Old Testament. The districts of Fort de Kock and Padang offer fine opportunities as mission centres...Too long has satan held sway in these populous districts, and the time is now ripe for soldiers of the cross to go up and possess the land.' On his eight week tour in Sumatra he sold 3,000 Bibles, Testaments and portions in the Battak, Malay and Chinese language and received orders from the missionaries for 8,000 more![1]

Travelling north to Malaysia, nearly a century later...

I read a brief account of the Malay Revival in Malaysia on the internet and was able to correspond with this humble "Christian layman" (as he refers to himself) who has furnished me with additional information to which I am truly grateful. He desires to be known only as a 'teacher from the United States' whom I will call Chuck. He wrote: 'I am still amazed at God's power to use the smallest and most flawed human endeavours for His glory. I never thought that this would be mentioned or chronicled this side of Christ's return, although the events of 1998 in Malaysia are well known throughout the Church in Malaysia and Singapore.'

This missionary couple with their tenacious commitment were determined to work in Malaysia until they either got thrown out of the country (which was very probable) or until a Church was planted amongst the Malaysian Malays so that they could no longer be called an unreached people group. *Operation World* states that in Malaysia, around 58 percent of the population adhere to Islam and it is illegal to proselytise a Muslim. In the 1980s, limitations on religious freedoms were introduced, but in 1999, one year after the revival, the government began to relax some restrictions, such as on places of worship, public meetings and missionary visas.

For the first seven to eight years, almost nothing happened during the ministry of Chuck and his wife, but from 1985-1987 about twenty missionary couples with the same calling and purpose arrived. Chuck wrote: 'By 1991 they were all gone. I remember vividly pleading with the very last couple that remained, but they were discouraged and would not be persuaded. They did not even acknowledge that it was God's will for them to go back. Then we were alone...' They knew no other families working with the Malays, but there was a Chinese Christian community that encouraged them.

Chuck with his Kingdom worldview wrote: '...If we are imprisoned or killed, so be it. The militant who thrusts a sword through my heart in the final years of my life will never realize what a wonderful thing he is doing for my descendants who will not have to pay thousands of dollars of the Lord's money to nurse my decrepit fleshly carcass as it decays into oblivion [at a] nursing home...Better to look an enemy of God in the eye and go down with a single bullet!'

In 2006, his friend wrote about him: 'He led me to Christ when I was in college and discipled me in the Navigators. At that time he was a grad student in nuclear fusion research. Really, a bright fellow. Great evangelist, memorized big chunks of the Bible (I tested him), and prayed two hours every day.'

After all the missionary couples had left, their 'attack came; the Malaysian government shut down the programme' he was working with, and it looked like he could find no position under which he could stay. He wrote: 'One of the last weeks I worked with this programme, I looked out my office window. A large mosque was there, and the midday call of prayer was sounding. I saw hundreds of Muslims heading over there, '... the flock doomed to slaughter ...' as Zechariah the prophet said [chapter 11]. I fell on my knees and started weeping uncontrollably. I told

God I was the last one, and I just didn't want to go.' Chuck, his wife and young child began to pray fervently.

They put all their belongings into storage, left their house and moved into a local hotel awaiting doomsday – the day the work permit expired. He wrote: 'Our prayers seemed not to avail…about two to three days before doomsday I sat with my wife and child…and told them, "We are just outgunned!" The voice of the Holy Spirit came back very clearly, "You are NOT outgunned; your guns are not rolled up!" "What do you mean?" I responded. I thought of all of my prayers – unaided by the prayers of other saints.'

In a flash of Divine inspiration, Chuck was reminded about retired missionaries and pastors, true prayer warriors, godly men and women who were looked after by the Christian and Missionary Alliance in four of their retirement homes. He made an agreement with God; if He would allow them to stay, then he 'would return to the United States for a few weeks, at first opportunity' find these homes and 'generate as much prayer support as possible from these godly senior citizens.'

Within a day, a local job came through, a three month contract which was taken without hesitation. Chuck knew the Malay language and by God's grace, three months turned into fifteen, until he was hired permanently by a university in Malaysia. Money was very tight and it took until the end of the first three years contract until the family could return home to America (with free flights) in the winter of 1995 and generate the much needed prayer support.

Chuck wrote: 'It was a very hectic time, but with only two to three days with each family, all-night drives through snow and ice; we generated enough prayer support to overthrow the power of satan amongst the Malaysian Malays. I remember standing before a group of godly men and women in Carlisle, Pennsylvania, on 20 December 1995 and saying, "There is enough power in this room to overthrow the power of satan in Malaysia and reach the Malaysian Malays for Christ." I believed it, and meant it.'

In 1996, they returned to the tropical island resort of Penang, (also known as Pinang), in the north-western tip of Malaysia, about 140 miles, as the crow flies from the capital Kuala Lumpur and began working in a few locations. Chuck's relationship with the Malaysian government was a delicate balance. He worked for the same salary given to a national worker doing the same job, which got as low as $800 per month

(£570 – summer 1996 exchange rate). In return, he asked for one thing, complete freedom to "answer questions" about his faith and the questions did come, hundreds of them, everywhere he worked. He wrote: 'There is an intense curiosity amongst all Malaysian Malays about this strange "religion" of love and acceptance of the most hideous people! A "religion" where the great prize of an eternity with God is given in advance and remains despite all of our failures and acts of hostility toward God!'

The authorities were initially VERY reluctant until they discovered that 'he never made a negative comment about Islam, never discussed politics and most importantly, never, ever went to a Bible School, Christian training centre, or anything' and to the authorities he was clean. 'Since I was so "untrained" [Acts 4:13]' he wrote: 'they did not consider me a threat. This gave me a tremendous amount of freedom, because I was just a layman making comments rather than a Christian worker doing Christian work. At one point I shared Christ with about 20-30 Malays right at a national training centre. In another situation I made a taped presentation of Christianity at a university in Malaya.'

On one occasion Chuck and his family were passing by a small public Hindu shrine / temple (Malaysia is about ten percent Tamil Indian), when the family shouted (including their young son who yelled the loudest), "THE LORD REBUKE YOU, SATAN!" out the window at the top of their lungs. The next day they passed by on the same route and the temple was closed and stayed shut down for several weeks. Chuck wrote: 'It REALLY made an impression on him – he walks with God to this day.' Recalling the event he wrote: 'I don't know what in the world possessed us to do this on that particular day.'

Chuck wrote: 'The first indication I had that something was up – I had been praying that God would break down the walls of Islam. About the time of our trip the wall around the National Mosque in Penang physically fell down! I have pictures of the wreckage. No one could figure out what in the world happened.'

God moved the Southern Baptists to consider ministering among the Malays in Malaysia. They sent out an investigative team who met church leaders in Kuala Lumpur who informed them that no one was working with the Malays, except one American. The entire investigative team showed up on Chuck's doorstep who after hearing of their business and their offer for help told them, "YES you should definitely come!" And come they did.

Chuck stated that his mission agency 'loaned me to the Southern Baptists, and I had the great privilege of working under one Dr. – (his Dr. is in "unconventional" ministry!). In the ensuing free-for-all, involving Indonesians, police raids, nightmares for the mission agency leadership, and the planting of Malay-language churches, hundreds came to know the Lord. By the beginning of 1998, several other Christian groups, including OMF and SIB, had arrived.

'Finally, a major revival broke out in mid-1998 which led the Malaysian government to finally throw in the towel and officially acknowledge the presence of Christian churches and groups amongst the Malaysian Malays. By this time about 500 Malays had actually registered as Christians. Some local church leaders set the actual number much higher, 7,000-10,000. I think this was an exaggeration. But I am fairly confident the number is in four figures. No one will truly know this side of the Last Day.' The Malaysian government were not fully aware of how this revival came about. All they know is somehow, for no apparent reason, large groups of Malays started registering as Christians in 1998. Chuck's Muslim colleague was following the issue closely and said about 600 had stepped forward and registered as Christians. After the official acknowledgement, Chuck phoned the mission agency president and told him to pull the Malaysians Malays off their unreached people group list.

Chuck and his family were only able to experience the thrill of revival a few months before the Lord pulled them out at the end of 1998. Their work was done and the work of many others would continue. This ministry amongst the Malays was very costly, more than most of us can ever imagine. This teacher from America informed me: 'To this day I am thrilled that the Lord allowed me to throw away my career and financial success (both worthless) for the sake of an unreached people group of 13 million.' He continued, 'One of the main lessons of this revival, to me, is the awesome prayer power resident in these retirement homes for Christian workers (especially the Christian and Missionary Alliance). This power is LARGELY UNTAPPED by most missionaries. The beloved seniors will pray, and PRAY A LOT. And God moves!'

In January 1999, heavily in debt, whilst in a country in North Africa, no university (or high school) would hire him (or even consider him for the interview stage) and back in America the same thing happened. To avoid bankruptcy he took a job as a waiter. Eventually whilst in America, a miracle occurred and a university with an emergency situation hired him, which soon led to a permanent position in another university, though with Divine assurance he still awaits the call back to North Africa.

Malawi 2001 and 2004

Susan Pillans is an evangelist to Africa and India. Her ministry began when she was in Jerusalem with David Hathaway and his team (who have seen revival across Russia) when at the Garden Tomb, God spoke to her about abiding in Him for wherever He would send her. The next day she was invited to Kenya, to assist in the children's ministry. Whilst in England, raising some financial support for the conference, four days before the work was to begin the main speakers had to cancel.

She flew into Kenya and ended up in an unnamed rural place near Lake Victoria, knowing that she would have to be the main speaker and pray for the sick afterwards. Driving to the bishop's hut, Susan (and her friend Ruth), passed by two funerals and Susan wondered what she had got herself into. The next day they got behind a rock and began to pray, telling God that they had nothing to give to the people. They prayed incessantly with tears streaming down their faces, knowing that many of the people would walk four days for a miracle, but they could not do it. After about thirty minutes God spoke through their tears of intercession and declared that as He could cry through their eyes He could also heal through their hands.

That same night, in a blue and white tent, three hundred people heard the Gospel message. After the altar call, an appeal was made for those who were sick to come forward. In 2005, Susan was at the Fire from the North Conference in Lerwick, Shetland. In an interview with Gareth Littler, she said, "I was hoping that there would not be, but thirty people rushed forward and to my horror, the first three were blind, totally blind." She remembered what Rheinard Bonnke said on his first miracle with the Holy Spirit, "In the name of Jesus, blind eyes open" and she asked the Holy Spirit if she could use the same words. She felt it was OK, laid her hands on her and repeated the words. The woman exclaimed, "I can see! I can see!" She told the woman to testify. The second and third blind people were instantly healed. The fourth had malaria which they cast out (a spirit of malaria) and within one minute the person's temperature was down. A man who had fallen down a cliff, who had a lame arm was healed, as were all thirty people! The people just praised and worshipped the Lord. During that conference 250 people were healed, and the doors began to open. Susan said, "Prayer is the heart of everything that God does."

In 2001, Susan travelled to a small church in Malawi when she was sent to speak to one person, a man called Duncan and a small church was birthed. During a devastating drought in which three people had already died, God answered their prayers for rain within one hour; because of this, the entire community of 2,000 people became Christian and a church was built.

Malawi is known as the 'Warm Heart of Africa' and in May 2008, I spent more than three weeks in this beautiful country, Dr. David Livingstone, the missionary explorer first 'discovered' Lake Nyasa (now Lake Malawi) in 1859. In Blantyre, the lodge owner (a black African), proudly informed us that Dr. David Livingstone – was the 'Father of our Nation' which reiterated what the government tourist brochure stated. It was Livingstone who informed the world of the vile slave trade of the shores of Lake Nyasa where entire villages and town were decimated in the 1860s as boats transported the captives across the Lake, where they were forced marched to the East Coast and sold at Zanzibar slave market, the last open slave market in the world. Livingstone encouraged others to follow in his footsteps as Christianity and commerce would replace slavery and bring civilisation. Some of the places I visited were Karonga (in the north), Livingstonia (founded in 1894 by missionary, Dr. Robert Laws of the Livingstonia Mission), Mzuzu, Lilongwe (the capital), Blantyre (in the south, named after Dr. Livingstone's birthplace in Scotland), Liwonde, Mangoshi and Monkey Bay.

In December 2004, Susan returned to the church to hold meetings. She was very ill with diarrhoea and so just spoke whatever came to mind. After the altar call, being weak and dizzy she sat down upon a chair and told those who were sick to come forward, put their hands on their own body and receive their healing in Jesus' name and when they know they have been healed raise their hands. Within ninety seconds all hands had been raised. The next day, she returned to Blantyre and asked the Lord why she was not healed when all the others were? The Lord replied, "To cause you to depend on Me completely and utterly." Then she realised, "there was none of me in that meeting, less of me, more of God, none of me, all of

God," then the Lord said, "Do not limit Me, let Me be God..." The Lord then told her about Elijah and that if he did not soak the sacrifice with water and fill the trench then he would have limited the miracle, 1 Kings chapter 18.

Susan's next crusade was down on the Mozambique border, only twenty-five people turned up. Susan said, "It sometimes happens, if you're a girl." With the words, 'Don't limit God' she ordered the people to go and find the sickest person in the village they could, and call the entire village to see a miracle in Jesus' name. That night, the church was full, a lady was brought in who had been bedridden for two years, and she was skinny and was shivering under her grey blanket, unable to walk or stand. Susan pointed at her and prayed, "In the name of Jesus, disease leave that body. Body, be healed in Jesus' name. Strength come back into the body in Jesus' name." Then she told this woman, "in the name of Jesus stand up" which she did. A further command in Jesus' name to walk and she walked in front of the church. Susan then told her to run down the aisle, the woman looked horrified but Susan told her, "In the name of Jesus you can." The lady ran down the aisle and back. Everybody became a Christian after that, and the next day, two chiefs surrendered their lives to the Lord. Two girls aged twelve and fourteen were converted and gloriously healed, both were born deaf and dumb and the Lord opened their ears so that they could learn to speak.

Back in England, God spoke to Susan and told her that His people (the Church) are limiting Him by unbelief, by lack of prayer, through lack of commitment, and by putting other things before Him. The Lord showed her that when Judas received the thirty pieces of silver, in that moment he loved that silver more than Jesus. God told her, "My people are doing the same." They are loving their homes, their business', their money, their sport, their comfort, their lifestyles more than Me."

Since January 2005, Susan began preaching repentance and has seen whole congregations repent before the Lord, crying. After these times of open repentance and during the times of praise and worship, lifting up the Lord she has seen people healed and set free without the laying on of hands as the silent presence of God has come amongst them.

In November 2005, Susan went to India and spoke to 1,000 pastors and 10,000-15,000 youth during a three-day meeting.[2]

Chapter Nineteen

That All May Know

'Therefore God also has highly exalted Him [Jesus] and given Him the name which is above every name, that at the name of Jesus every knee should bow, of those in heaven, and of those on earth, and of those under the earth, and that every tongue should confess that Jesus Christ is Lord, to the glory of God the Father' Philippians 2:9-11.

Sapiranga Revival 2005 – Brazil

A fresh move of God, a blessing, a refreshing, a renewal began on the 20 January 1994 in the Airport Christian Vineyard, Toronto, Canada amongst a strong congregation of around 350 people. It became known as the 'Toronto Blessing.' The church is also referred to as the Toronto Airport Vineyard or Toronto Airport Christian Fellowship (TACF).

John Arnott, the senior pastor of TACF and his wife Carol had invited Randy Clark of the St Louis Vineyard, Missouri, USA to hold four-night series of meetings (that extended to ten) which began on the twentieth. At the ministry time at the end of the service, the entire congregation came forward for prayer and for the next one and a half months (on and off) he stayed as the fires of God burned brighter. However, it was imperative that he returned back to his family and home church. TACF began to have meetings six nights a week with the Monday evening off. The blessing quickly circumnavigated the globe and affected thousand of churches, mostly from those who had been to the Vineyard Church where it began and had brought the blessing (often unbeknown to them) back to their home church of differing denominations. Due to the influx of so many visitors from around the world, on a Sunday morning, the locals began to wear nametags so that they would know who would be there next week and the week after that!

By June 1994, an estimated 30,000 people had visited, among them at least 2,000 church leaders from all different denominations, all of whom came and drunk deeply of the fresh outpouring. Within eight months, it was estimated that it had touched 2,000 churches (Toronto Vineyard had received 90,000 visitors). At the time, there were optimistic Christian newspaper reports within several months that revival had broken out in different part of the world, whilst the debate as to the authenticity of this move of God had spread much further afield. Numerous churches were denouncing it as a delusion and a counterfeit of the enemy whilst others were jumping into the stream of God. To know more about God's workings in times of revival and renewal, as well as the devils infiltration and human imitation, see my book, *Understanding Revival and Addressing the Issues it Provokes* (2009). For more information about the Toronto Blessing see: *The 'Toronto' Blessing* by Dave Roberts (1994), *Catch The Fire* by Guy Chevreau (1994) and *Manifestations & Prophetic Symbolism* by John Arnott (2008).

In 2006, John Arnott, senior pastor of TACF in their in-house magazine, *Spread the Fire* wrote: 'Today there is a worldwide network of "River people" who have experienced the Father's blessing...' John went on to say that whilst the movement grows numerically the greatest blessing is to see lives transformed. 'Hundreds of people have written books and articles how God has renewed and transformed their lives through this outpouring. The stories come from everywhere, Japan and Australia, India and Russia, Europe, Africa, North and South America.'

John went on to write about a group of pastors from Sapiranga, Brazil, from Ministerio Internacional da Colheita who attended a conference in Toronto, which TACF hold annually. Having been touched by God they returned with fresh fire, revival broke out in their congregation, (the senior pastor is Vania Rorato) which soon spread across the city. Now the city has a Christian mayor and a Christian Secretary of Tourism and Business Development.

The pastors of the city began to form a network and are now working in greater unity. The church sponsors pastors to attend Leadership Schools sponsored by TACF in Sapiranga and minister to the poor in the countryside. The church also founded a large youth conference, *Historymakers* in which more than two thousand youth from across Brazil attend.

John Arnott wrote: 'Hundreds have been born again and filled with the Holy Spirit and added to the church as a direct result of the touch of God on their lives which they received in Toronto.'

The pastor, Vania Rorato hosts an evangelistic outreach television programme and the church also reaches out to neighbouring Uruguay 'with the Gospel of Jesus Christ preached in the context of the Father's love.'[1]

For a general overview of the blessing of God in Brazil, see *Fire in Brazil* (2007) a 47-minute DVD by HFC Productions and OLI International.

Burkina Faso 2006

Burkina Faso is a landlocked country of the Sahel in West Africa. It is prone to drought and famine and has an estimated population of 13 million, half of whom adhere to Islam. In 1960, Burkina Faso received its independence from secular France. During the 1960s evangelical Christianity began to rise steadily and especially within the last two decades where around eight percent of the country are now Protestant.

In 2006, *The 700 Club* (of the Christian Broadcasting Network) began a strategy of soaking the unevangelised Muslim and pagan villages with the Good News of Jesus Christ.

The Senufo tribe do not have any electrical power, and even if they did have they are still far away from any TV transmitter, so *The 700 Club* brought Christian programmes to them using their portable generators to screen Christian videos in their tribal language. *The 700 Club*, September 2006 Newsletter reported, 'After one recent evening event, an entire village of 1,300 men, women and children joyfully accepted Jesus.' The chief of the village, a 90 year old man asked the team if they could build a simple brick building which would be their church and double up as a school, 'which has now been completed.'

The 700 Club sent them a pastor to build up the flock and to teach them the ways of the Lord, who states that miracles are routine. One three year old boy received a miracle who had previously been crippled in both legs. The report of such a spiritual breakthrough has enabled *The 700 Club* to enter other villages who are welcoming them 'to bring the video projector unit and tell them about the Son of God who saves and heals!'[2]

Shillong Revival 2006-2007 – India

During 1905-1906 the Khasi Hills in India saw a revival. The state of Meghalaya is known as 'Scotland of the East' and is a hill town in the north eastern part of India. Its capital is Shillong. The revival began on Saturday the 22 April 2006 amongst a large body of people in Mairang, the exact place where revival first broke out in Shillong in 1906! Hundreds of delegates were attending the afternoon service of the Presbyterian Revival

Centenary commemoration, whilst 150,000+ sat outside on the huge lawns. The Holy Spirit came and the delegates continued to sing and pray for hours, oblivious to the elements. The revival took place in an area of about 14,000 square kilometres and affected thousands of local churches (almost entirely Presbyterian) but a few other denominations were touched and churches in the adjoining state of Mizoram were affected. Families and whole communities were transformed and there were thousands of conversions. Barkos Warjri, a Khasi who formerly lived in Bangalore wrote: 'Miraculous events took place in many churches with thousands of children throughout these hills seeing visions of God, Jesus Christ, heaven, hell, resulting in conviction of these children, their relatives or the churches concerned.' The Holy Spirit has even descended on schools, and 'several, regular classes were disrupted. Children from the age of about five expressed strong desires to be in church or simply to sing praises to God and pray.'

Barkos Warjri, received the following report from family and friends and on the 21 October 2006 wrote: 'Bible studies are no longer small group meetings in the Khasi and Jaintia Hills these days. They are more like crusades. The church building [on the 19 October] was full and so were the church lawns. A young girl with visions had given her testimony, and had said that God would do wonderful things that night. God had been doing so many wonderful things that people half expected what would happen. That night, however, it was something a bit beyond the ordinarily wonderful things they had been used to...[the] heavens would open.'

Towards the end of the meeting, 9pm, the congregation was singing the hymn 'Showers of Blessing,' when suddenly there was a noise and commotion outside and people saw a bright light like lightning. 'The heavens towards the north seem to part and some saw what looked like hills, and then a rainbow...Then there were screams and shouts like, "Here, here," "There, on the right"...There were angels all around! Some fell down in fear or in shock. Some walking on the road dropped to their knees....'[3]

By February 2007, the Presbyterian Church in the Khasi and Jaintia Hills officially accepted the revival as a work of God, but there was no clear system for discipleship except in a few local churches. A more detailed account of the Shillong Revival can be found in my book, *Revival Fire – 150 Years of Revivals* (2010).

Kabylie Region 2009 – Northern Algeria

Mission News Network (MNN) reported in late 2009, that 'despite laws preventing conversion, Muslims are turning to Christ in what's being called an amazing move of the Spirit in Northern Algeria.'

In 2008, Algeria put into full effect a new anti-conversion law that prohibited efforts to convert Muslims to another religion. This law is a direct attack against Christians as Muslims consists of 97 percent of the population. MNN wrote: 'The new law could make nearly all Christian churches in the country illegal. Despite this new law, 2009 has been an incredible year for evangelical church growth, says Pastor Youssef Jacob with Operation Mobilization. "We have churches that have grown 802%. Many converts have come from Islam with no Christian heritage, no Christian background, no resources whatsoever, no training. But they just believe in God and His Word."

'Jacob says the Kabylie people [also spelt Kabyle] are the most responsive in the Kabylie region, which is home to more than 2,000 towns and villages. "In every village and every town there are Christians, and there are churches," says Jacob. "In one town, actually there are more churches than mosques, which is a big miracle to happen in the Middle East."

'Jacob said, "I know of many, many churches today who baptize about 120 to 150 every year. I have never been to a church in the west or anywhere in the world where the church is already packed 2½ hours before the meeting." With the large number of new Christians comes a need for training. Jacob stated that funding for training and discipleship is desperately needed. "If we fail to train, disciple, and empower the Algerian church today, I believe it will be one of the biggest mistakes in the history of missions to the Muslim world."

'As training takes place, Jacob believes these Christians could be the key to reaching the Muslim world. "The Lord has given to us a vision that first [we need to reach] the Kabylie, then the whole end of Algeria, North Africa and the Arab world, mainly. But also God has given to us a vision to send missionaries from Algeria to Europe."

'While the church is growing, Christians are facing persecution. Jacob says, "I am one of the targets of the Muslim fundamentalists there. But I am not scared. I am not afraid at all. We still have many court cases which is hanging over many of our workers." '[4]

Section III

The Why and How of Revival

Chapter Twenty

Why we Need Revival

God said, "By those who come near Me, I must be regarded as holy; and before all the people I must be glorified" Leviticus 10:3.

The Lost Church

Without revival the Church is lost in itself, its programmes, its routines, its religious rituals and trappings which are not effective in reaching out to the lost and hurting amongst humanity, and worst of all, the Church is not reflecting a true biblical representation of New Testament Christianity. Jesus is not being lifted up (in testimony, through evangelism and honoured) and therefore He cannot draw all men to Himself.

The Church in general, is weak, frequently stagnant, and all too often dishonouring to the Lord by the lifestyles of its members, which causes the heathen to blaspheme the name of God. Jesus said, "Why do you call Me 'Lord, Lord' and do not do the things which I say?" (Luke 6:46).

If the Church does not see revival then the Church is sunk and will sink lower than the depths of the Titanic, thus making the chosen ones, the frozen ones. If we are frigid like an ice box then we cannot be on fire for the Lord. John Wesley, with his passionate preaching used to set himself on fire and let the people come out and watch him burn.

Isaiah chapter five, the parable of the vineyard, is a good description of why we need revival. Whilst God is speaking about the inhabitants of Jerusalem and Judah; its spiritual principles and the parallel of the Church is very relevant for today. The Church should bring forth good grapes, but generally speaking, it has brought forth wild grapes (verse 2). Without God's intervention, judgment is the only just cause and is inevitable (verses 5-7). The people of the world increase in sin, (as do many so called members of the Church), they heap up for themselves sin upon sin and draw iniquity with cords of vanity as if filling up a cart (verse 18). There is a lowering of morals to a mineshaft depth, calling evil good and good evil; they become proud, wise and being prudent in their own eyes, anything goes (verses 20-21). They despise God's laws, the word of the Holy One, and therefore by rejecting Him, the anger of the Lord is aroused against His people (verses 24-25).

As in the days of Judah's idolatry 'they did not obey or incline their ear, but walked in the counsels and in the imagination of their evil heart, and went backward and not forward...This is a nation that does not obey the voice of the Lord their God nor receive correction. Truth has perished and has been cut off from their mouth' (Jeremiah 7:24, 28). Without revival the Church regresses when it should be showing signs of progress. A. W. Tozer wrote: 'The Church began in power, moved in power, and moved just as long as she had power. When she no longer had power she dug in for safety and sought to conserve her gains.'

Reasons for When a Revival is Needed – Charles Finney

1. When there is an absence of love, confidence, and unity amongst Christians. It is vain to call upon them to love one another while they are sunk in stupidity and coldness.
2. When there are jealousies, dissensions, bitterness, and evil speaking amongst Christians.
3. When the Church becomes worldly in dress, parties, amusements, reading novels and worldly books.
4. When professing Christians fall into gross and scandalous sins. [Thus they bring reproach on the name of Christ].
5. When a spirit of controversy prevails among Christians.
6. When the wicked triumph over, and mock and scoff at the Church. [It appears that the Church is powerless].
7. When sinners are careless and stupid (going down to hell unconcerned). The duty of Christians is to awake them, like that of a fireman in the case of a fire. Their guilt is similar to that of firemen who will sleep on when the city is ablaze.
8. Without a revival sinners will grow harder and harder under preaching. [More cynical and stubborn].
9. There is no other way in which a Church can be sanctified, grow in grace and be ready for heaven. Hearing sermons week after week is not enough and every week it is more difficult to rouse the believer to do his duty.

We need revival because without Jesus Christ no man can be saved. We should all be doing our bit for the Great Commission, financially and practically, witnessing about Christ (sharing the Good News and giving our testimony), by our lifestyle and a personal favourite of mine, distributing tracts and evangelistic pamphlets. Evangelism and personal witness, whilst sowing essential seed, compared to revival, has limited effectiveness as mans heart has grown harder and more cynical then ever before. Most people would not even dream of going to a church or to an evangelistic event, they're scary places, but revival (in a unique way) does comprehensively what we cannot do effectively. Without revival people are damned and doomed for an eternity in hell, a place of eternal torment where there will be weeping and gnashing of teeth. Those who have not believed in Christ stand condemned already (John 3:18) and the wrath of God abides on them as they have stored up wrath for the Judgment Day (Romans 2:5).

'When the Lord Jesus is revealed from heaven with His mighty angels, in flaming fire taking vengeance on those who do not know God [the unbeliever], and on those who do not obey the Gospel of our Lord Jesus Christ [sounds like church goers with the nickname Christian, those who profess Him in name, but deny Him in lifestyle]. These shall be punished with everlasting destruction from the presence of the Lord and from the glory of His power' (2 Thessalonians 1:7-9).

- Charles Spurgeon said, "An unholy church! It's useless to the world, and of no esteem among men. It's an abomination, hell's laughter, heaven's abhorrence. The worst evils which have ever come upon the world have been brought upon her by an unholy church."
- Leonard Ravenhill said, "Get rid of this bunkum about the 'carnal Christian.' Forget it! If you're carnal, you're not saved."

For His Names Sake

There is a very present risk in seeking God's hand for revival, for what *He can give us*, rather than seeking His face for what *we can give Him*, for a more intimate relationship, Jesus has to be at the centre of our lives, otherwise we may spin counter to His ways which He has planned for us. In times of revival, God will be supremely glorified and Jesus is exalted! Many of us want to see revival, but not many of us want to pay the price. Isaiah declared: 'O Lord, we have waited for You; the desire of our soul is for Your name and for the remembrance of You' (Isaiah 26:8). We need revival so that God can be glorified and given His rightful place within people's hearts, instead of being blasphemed by foolish, unwise and perverted people.

The young shepherd boy David, went out to fight the mighty man of war, the giant Goliath. David, who had his trust in God, was indignant when Goliath shouted, "I defy the armies of Israel this day" and no soldier rose to the challenge. David, with contempt on his lips asked, "Who is this uncircumcised Philistine that He should defy the armies of the living God?" (1 Samuel 17:10-26). David went to King Saul and offered his services, stating his credentials as a shepherd boy with a history of killing both lion and bear, because the Lord was with him and would be with him in this battle against the enemy. King Saul accepted his offer, wished him God's-speed and tried to dress him up in his own armour. It did not fit as Saul was head and shoulders above everyone else and anyway, David was not used to wearing such protection and had trouble walking. An important lesson can be learned here, we cannot use somebody else's experience to get us through a situation, we each have to have our own staff and weapons, knowing that God is behind us. Whilst we can learn lessons from each other, we each have to walk the path to victory alone. David ran towards Goliath and killed him with a stone slung from his slingshot. He cut off his head with Goliath's sword and saved the day for Israel who then pursued the enemy, thus Israel had victory (1 Samuel 17:32-52).

Society Mocks God
Whilst there is nothing new under the sun, there is a greater need of revival now than ever before, because:

- The word of God, the Holy Bible and the precepts contained within have been disregarded and are often laughed at as archaic and made null and void by many of our government laws. 'It is time for You to act, O Lord, for they have regarded Your law as void' (Psalm 119:126).
- For most people, there is no moral absolute, no conclusive right from wrong, and as in the days of the Judges of Israel, everyone does what is right in their own eyes, and those who try to live by the rules of God are mocked and sometimes even attacked. This was also very present in John Wesley's day. 'Justice is turned back, and righteousness stand afar off; for truth is fallen in the street, and equity cannot enter. So truth

fails, and he who departs from evil makes himself a prey' (Isaiah 59:14-15).

- There is no fear of God; morals have been so turned on their head by political correctness that people are unaware of what is right or wrong, whilst some deliberately try and pervert justice and truth. 'Woe to those who call evil good, and good evil; who put darkness for light, and light for darkness; who put bitter for sweet, and sweet for bitter!' (Isaiah 5:20).
- There is no shame or remorse for breaking God's laws as people have hardened their hearts and seared their consciences as with a hot iron. 'This is the way of an adulterous woman; she eats and wipes her mouth, and says, "I have done no wickedness" ' (Proverbs 30:20).
- Many people who profess to know God try to make an all inclusive religion; they shy away from denouncing sin, claim that all roads lead to God and that all people are good. Yet the Bible declares that all have sinned and there is none that is righteous. The only way to God is through Jesus Christ who is the Way, the Truth and the Life. 'You have wearied the Lord with your words; yet you say, "In what way have we wearied Him?" In that you say, "Everyone who does evil is good in the sight of the Lord, and He delights in them..." ' (Malachi 2:17).

'O Lord, though our iniquities testify against us, do it for Your name's sake; for our backslidings are many and we have sinned against You' (Jeremiah 14:7)

Why we Need Revival:
1. God must be glorified, Jesus must be exalted and the Holy Spirit needs to be given His rightful place within the Church. He is not a thing or an influence, but the Spirit of God, a Person.
2. The Church needs to be revived. It must be swept free and cleansed from sin. If revival does not start in the Church then it cannot move outside the Church amongst the graceless.
3. The graceless need to receive the grace of God, sinners need to be surrendered to Him and in times of revival they are drawn as if by an unseen hand to call upon the name of the Lord and to turn from their wicked ways.
4. Revival quickens evangelism and aids discipleship, 'Warning every man and teaching every man in all wisdom, that we may

present every man perfect in Christ Jesus' (Colossians 1:28). New converts are often the most passionate evangelists.

5. In times of revival, under the searchlight of the Holy Spirit, people are highly sensitive to sin, responsive to repentance and forsaking sin and desire to live righteously before a holy God, acknowledging the difference between, 'The holy and the unholy, and causing them to discern between the unclean and the clean' (Ezekiel 44:23).

6. Revival can so change a person in a matter of hours, which would have taken a Christian counsellor years to produce much lesser results. Some are instantly delivered from demons.

Mr Swallen was missionary to Korea. In a discussion about the fruit of the Pyongyang Great Revival (1907-1910) of which he was a part of, he said, "It paid well to have spent the several months in prayer, for when God the Holy Spirit came He accomplished more in half a day than all of us missionaries could have accomplished in half a year. In less than two months more than two thousand heathen were converted.'[1]

Rev. W. J. Patton, a minister in Dromara, Ireland, writing about the 1859 Irish Revival, wrote: 'For the time being business was very much suspended. The whole parish was a place of weeping, and praying, and singing, and reading. There cannot be doubt that there were more Bible-readers, more believing prayers, more loving thoughts of Jesus, in our parish in the month of August than had been in the five years previous.'[2]

Revival and Missions

To use an analogy, revival is needed because it can be likened to nitrous fuel in a turbo-charged car that descends from the heavens and penetrates the engine of the Church giving it much needed impetus, which quickens and aids holiness, evangelism and discipleship.

The Korean Church was only founded in 1885, yet during the first year of the Pyongyang Great Revival (1907-1910), 50,000 people were added to the Church. In comparison, the Battak people, on the Island of Sumatra, Indonesia, first received the Gospel in 1862 and just over fifty years later by the year 1910 there was nearly 100,000 converts.

The facts reveals that the Korean Church grew very rapidly in one year alone, with 50,000 converts, yet without revival the Battak Church (which grew at a healthy rate) only achieved

100,000 converts within fifty years. In this example we can state that the Battak Church without revival grew fifty times slower than the Korean Church that experienced revival! This is why revival is needed! During the Welsh Revival (1904-1905), in a six week period alone, 100,000 converts were saved, and it has been recorded that in total, 150,000 made applications to join a churches but as many as 250,000 could have been converted during this revival!

This is why revival is needed, because God is the same yesterday, today and forever, and He has no pleasure in the death of the wicked but desires them to be saved, because whoever calls upon the name of the Lord will be saved. And this is most effective during times of revival.

Are you active in evangelism and praying for revival? 'To him who knows to do good and does not do it, to him it is sin' (James 4:17).

Our Responsibility for Revival and Missions

We need revival because there are too many modern day blind leaders of the blind, and they with their multitudes of followers will all fall into the eternal ditch of hell. We need revival because like Nineveh, there are people who are ignorant of biblical truth, ignorant of the fact that they are sinners on the threshold of hell and they do not know their right from their left. We need revival because there is a major regress in morals, those who say that there are no boundaries, no moral absolutes and they call good evil and evil good and woe unto them! – But also, woe unto the Church for our lack of concern, compassion and commitment towards each other, the Great Commission and that God is not being glorified as He should be.

Charles Finney wrote about many hindrances to revival, but one of them was, 'neglecting the claims of world mission...' Finney went on to conclude that this neglect was because Christians generally 'focussed only on their own field of labour, their own church [or] their own circle of ministry.'

It is the responsibility of every concerned Christian to pray daily for revival (2 Chronicles 7:14 and Isaiah 44:3-4) and also to pray that God would thrust forth more labourers into His harvest field (Matthew 9:38). Those prayers need to be coupled with our practical and financial giving towards evangelism and world missions. All Christians are commanded to spread the Good News according to ones capacity. For those who are considering the claim of the Great Commission and how they (or members of their church) can responsibly and intelligently participate, see *How to Plan, Prepare and Successfully Complete Your Short-Term Mission* (2010) by the author.

- Go ye (Mark 16:15)
- Give ye (Luke 9:13)
- Pray ye (Matthew 9:38)

Charles H. Spurgeon said, "The question is not, 'Will the heathen be lost if they do not hear the Gospel?' but, 'Will we be saved if we do not take it to them?' "

Due to a revival that spread through Ruanda and the surrounding countries beginning in 1932, Joe E. Church wrote a series of Bible readings that were compiled into the book, *Every Man a Bible Student* (1938). Joe Church wrote: 'The call to be a missionary is the logical outcome of the changed life. We are changed into His image who said, "*As My Father sent Me, even so I send you.*" It is the outcome of true spiritual vision that sees a lost world as Christ saw it, and is willing to following in His footsteps. ...The opportunity of going to foreign lands is only possible for the few, although the call to active missionary service is binding on all Christians, those who remain equally as on those who go.'[3]

K. P. Yohannan, founder of Gospel for Asia (GFA), which supports more than 16,500 indigenous missionaries (with 30,000 churches planted in the 10/40 window), always poses two questions to Christian audiences. In essence, they are: "Why do you think that God has allowed you to be born in the wealthy Western world as part of the privileged elite rather than amongst the poor masses of Africa or Asia?" And, "In light of the superabundance that you have, what do you think is your minimal responsibility to the untold millions of lost and suffering in the Two-Thirds World?"[4]

'Deliver those who are drawn towards death, and hold back those stumbling to slaughter. If you say, "Surely we did not know this," does not He who weighs the heart consider it? He who keeps your soul, does He not know it? And will He not render to each man according to his deeds?' (Prov. 24:11-12).

Let us not forget the sober reality that on Judgment Day, we will not only be judged by what we said and what we did, but by what we did not say and did not do. It is the responsibility of this generation to reach our generation with the Good News, and this is most effective during times of revival.

Chapter Twenty-One

The Motive for Revival

'O Lord, though our iniquities testify against us, do it for Your name's sake; for our backslidings are many, we have sinned against You' Jeremiah 14:7.

What is my Motive?

What is the motive for revival? For many a person within the Christian ministry (and congregational members of a church) their motive for revival can appear a little bit self-centred, ignorant or perhaps mildly confused.

Human motives can be most fickle to say the least and many of us can be unaware of our true motives because as Jeremiah declared, "The heart is deceitful above all things, and desperately wicked; who can know it?" (Jeremiah 17:9) – Well the Lord knows and it is the Holy Spirit who can reveal our true motives of the heart in all that we think, say or do. Jesus condemned the scribes and Pharisees who were active in missions saying, "Woe to you, scribes and Pharisees, hypocrites! For you travel land and sea to win one proselyte [single convert - NIV], and when he is one, you make him twice as much a son of hell as yourselves" (Matthew 23:15). Here were the religious rulers of the day, evangelising, going on missions yet they themselves were not right with God!

Sometimes, those of us within the Church can have a pharisaic attitude believing that the reason we pray for revival, (whilst pointing our finger and looking down our nose) is for those outside the Church. However, what we fail to remember is that if we have the light, then why do so many of us still live in darkness? Jesus came to preach the Good News, to heal the broken-hearted, and to set men free from their chains of sin, but to those who thought they had the answers, the self-righteous Pharisees and Sadducees, Jesus had to sternly rebuke because of the hardness of their hearts, unbelief and for their ungodly attitude towards those who were less fortunate than themselves. They knew the law of God, but not His heart of compassion. They wanted to stone the woman caught in adultery, but Jesus told her to go and sin no more. They hated Jesus for working on the Sabbath and would have preferred the man with the withered hand and the woman who was bent double to have stayed afflicted rather than see them healed. The Church needs revival, but to pray for it only for those outside of the Church (as important as it is), is not our primary objective.

Charles Finney posed the question, 'What is your motive for revival? For the denomination, for the church or for the glory of God; an increase in attendees and more money for the church? Sometimes ministers want revival because their church is going through difficulties which the minister needs to deal with and address, but is afraid to face the issue. At other times another denomination is being blessed more than them and the minister or congregation member wants to even the score.'

'All a man's ways seem innocent to him, but motives are weighed by the Lord' (Proverbs 16:2) NIV.

Why People Followed Jesus

Nearly two thousand years ago, prior to the resurrection, when Jesus' followers, were at their peak, He revealed the different motives as to why they followed Him. There is also a parallel between the motives of those who followed Him then (and now) and those who are present during times of revival. Some followed Jesus for the excitement; 'a great multitude followed Him, because they saw His signs which He performed on those who were diseased' (John 6:2). Others followed Him for what they could get from Him; 'you seek Me, not because you saw the signs, but because you ate the loaves and were filled' (John 6:26). But Jesus challenged His followers to identify with Him; 'whoever eats My flesh and drinks My blood has eternal life, and I will raise him up at the last day' (John 6:54). It was 'from that time many of His disciples went back and walked with Him no more' (John 6:66).

We are not called to follow Jesus, (or to pray for revival) for our benefit but for His. Steve Hill from the Brownsville Revival (1995-2000) in Pensacola, America said, "Ask not what Jesus can do for you, but rather ask what you can do for Jesus."

Evangelist and revivalist, Reuben Archer Torrey wrote: 'Many prayers for revival are purely selfish. The churches desire revivals in order that membership may be increased, in order that the church may have a position of more power or influence in the community, in order that the church treasury may be filled, in order that a good report may be made at the presbytery, or conference or association. For such low purposes as these, churches and ministers oftentimes are praying for a revival, and oftentimes too, God does not answer the prayer....'

Within prayer meetings you will often hear prayers which are semi-Scriptural in which people pray for something when God has entrusted to us the responsibility and made the provision for the fulfillment of it. As an example, "Lord, please send someone to witness to my work colleague." Yet, we are *all* called to evangelise and make disciples, not just ministers. "Lord, help me not to be so rude towards my boss." Yet, we are to be responsible for our actions and words, seasoned with salt, gentle, kind and courteous and self controlled. Whist we can ask God to help us, we have to play our part, as 'God helps those who help themselves' so stated Benjamin Franklin. Let us not forget that we negate our responsibility when we expect God to do for us, that which is our duty.

Many pray for revival without fully comprehending what they are asking for, and it has not been unknown for people (even Christian workers) to reject a heaven-sent revival (what they have been praying for) because it came differently than what they had expected or wanted! Whilst others have stood aloof, unsure whether it was of Divine or demonic origin – God's dynamic or the devils delusion. See *Understanding Revival and Addressing the Issues it Provokes* (2009) by the author.

Some people have a limited view of what revival is and / or in their preconceived ideas, what God will do, can do, is able to do or will not do. Whilst some struggle in their discernment of the flesh, the Spirit and the demonic. Others incorrectly believe that revival is *only* for saving souls, and for such a reason desire it, (but the Church needs to be dealt with first, renewed, refreshed, revived and transformed into the image of Christ). However, as commendable as saving souls is (because in revivals, sinners get saved and God has no pleasure in the death of the wicked, but desires all men to be saved) – the primary reason for revival is for the glory of God. For the vindication of His name, to exalt and honour Jesus Christ and to give the Holy Spirit His rightful place within the Church, which ultimately glorifies the Father and exalts and honours the Son. Also in our daily living, we are called to do all for His glory (1 Corinthians 10:31) and in times of revival this is highly enlarged, magnified and multiplied.

Andrew Murray McCheyne wrote: 'The Christian is just a person who makes it easy for others to believe in God.'

God's Glory and Vindication

- God said, "By those who come near Me, I must be regarded as holy; and before all the people I must be glorified" (Leviticus 10:3).
- The twelve memorial stones were set up, 'That all the people of the earth may know the hand of the Lord, that it is mighty, that you [the Israelites] may fear the Lord your God forever' (Joshua 4:24).
- God said, "For My own sake, for My own sake, I will do it; for how should My name be profaned? And I will not give My glory to another" (Isaiah 48:11).
- 'O Lord, though our iniquities testify against us, do it for Your name's sake; for our backslidings are many, we have sinned against You' (Jeremiah 14:7).
- '[The] Gentiles...glorify God in the day of visitation' (1 Peter 2:12).

Based on the five Scriptures we can see that revival is primarily for the glory of God and for the honour of His name. The reviving of Christians and the conversion of souls are secondary issues, as important as they are.

Duncan Campbell, from the Lewis Revival (1949-1952) said, "I sometimes say at the risk of being misunderstood, that we do not pray for revival in order that souls may be saved, but souls are saved in their thousands when we have revival, when the thirsty are satisfied, then the floods on the dry ground. If you want revival, get right with God. If you are not prepared to bring the "last piece," [of your entire consecration to God's altar] for God's sake stop talking about revival; your talking and praying is but the laughing-stock of devils. It is about time that we got into the grips of reality."[1]

Reuben Archer Torrey wrote: '...Why should we pray for revival? For the glory of God, because we cannot endure it that God should continue to be dishonoured by the worldliness of the Church, by the sins of unbelievers, by the proud unbelief of the day, because God's word is being made void; in order that

God may be glorified by the outpouring of His Spirit on the Church of Christ.'

God sends revival to the body of Christ, 'that all the people of the earth may know the hand of the Lord, that it is mighty, that you might fear the Lord your God forever' (Joshua 4:24). Revival is a vindication of Himself and asserting His own power and glory so that the people of the earth 'shall know that the living God is among you...' (Joshua 3:10). Revival reminds us that God dwells in the Church (Ephesians 2:21-22) and that 'the Gospel of Christ is the power of God to salvation' (Romans 1:16). "I must be glorified" (Leviticus 10:3) are God's words and only in times of revival will nations turn and truly glorify the Lord.

There is a story about a manager of a luxury hotel who had inscribed on a plaque the poignant phrase: 'My Reputation is in your Hands.' It was hung on the wall behind him so that as the members of staff were called to see him, they would be reminded of their responsibility. What they did reflected on their superior. How much more then for Christians reflecting (sadly, often in a negative sense) their Master? It was Steve Hill who frequently said during the Brownsville Revival (1995-2000) in America, "If you call yourself a Christian, act like one, or change your name to heathen!"

Andrew Bonar wrote: 'The rousing up and reviving of believers is not a small matter; it concerns the glory of God. If the lamps do not shine, it does not speak well for the oil, nor for the care of the keeper. And if the children of God do not testify for Him, it does not speak well for their High Priest in heaven, nor for the Holy Spirit within them.'

Our motives for revival – James, in his epistle wrote: '...Yet you do not have because you do not ask. You ask and do not receive, because *you ask amiss...*' (James 4:2b-3a). James is talking in the context of asking for wisdom which comes by prayer and we know that anything that is not of faith is sin. But using the above Scripture (and we can apply the spiritual principle) we do not receive (we have not seen or witnessed revival) because we ask with wrong motives. What is our motive for revival?

Colin C. Kerr said, "Why do we want blessing? That our churches may be filled, our addresses and sermons empowered? Let us be honest. Why do we want this great outpouring? That a godless people may be converted, and an immoral or careless people changed? Why are we seeking this experience? That we may be spiritually happy and others restored or converted? Whatever place there may be for such consideration, they cannot be the basis for seeking revival with any real hopefulness. One of the truths that the Church most needs to learn afresh is found in Isaiah 48:11, 'I will not give My glory unto another.' When the Church or the individual becomes consumed with a passion for the Lord's glory, and His glory alone, things will soon begin to happen. Great honesty is needed in this matter. Why do we want revival?'[2]

Claudio Freidzon, who was used in the Argentine Revival (1982-1997), wrote: 'True awakening occurs when society realises that Christ lives and begins to make decisions in recognition of the fact that He is Lord of lords. The fruit of such a move should lead believers to think outwardly, expressing concern for the souls that are perishing. Such a move should not be limited to manifestations, healings, miracles, and wonders; on the contrary, it ought to produce in the Christian a desire to pray for lost souls to be converted to the Lord Jesus Christ.'[3]

Ask and Abide
- Jesus said, "Ask and it shall be given" (Luke 11:9).
- Jesus said, "Abide in Me, and I in you. As the branch cannot bear fruit of itself, unless it abides in the vine, neither can you, unless you abide in Me. I am the Vine, you are the branches. He who abides in Me, and I in him, bears much fruit; for without Me you can do nothing. If you abide in Me, and My words abide in you, you will ask what you desire, and it shall be done for you. By this My Father is glorified, that you bear much fruit; so you will be My disciples" (John 15:4-5, 7-8).
- 'He who says he abides in Him ought himself also to walk just as He walked' (1 John 2:6).
- 'Now he who keeps His commandments abides in Him, and He in him. And by this we know that He abides in us, by the Spirit whom He has given us' (1 John 3:24).

Chapter Twenty-Two

How to see Revival – Our Lifestyles

John the Baptist said, "I indeed baptise you with water unto repentance, but He who is coming after me is mightier than I, whose sandals I am not worthy to carry. He will baptise you with the Holy Spirit *and fire*" Matthew 3:11.

Instructions for Revival

How to see revival? I suppose if it was as easy as the ABCs we would all being seeing revival now. Or perhaps it is easier than we think, yet we have not paid the price? Whatever our view, we have already seen that revival is conditional, and there is a big price to be paid. Personal revival, which we can all achieve, is always a precursor to heaven-sent revival. There is no shortcuts, no easy route and if we desire to see the heavens rent and God coming down then we must follow the Makers instructions as revealed in the Holy Bible and it all revolves around, holiness, crucified lives, full surrender and being endued with power from on high, for works of service.

Eva Stuart Watt who chronicled the Imbai Revivals of (1935) and (1935-1936) in the N. E. Belgian Congo wrote: 'We may read volumes on revival and attend conventions by the score, until we know it seems, everything there is to know about the working of the Holy Ghost; but one ounce of obedience will do more to loosen the bolts of the windows of heaven than tons of fundamental theorising.'[1]

The Individual Heart

We cannot expect God to pour out His Spirit corporately if we are individually not fulfilling the conditions. It is just a mockery to expect God to revive us, or our local Church whilst we participate in habitual sin without remorse and repentance (which includes forsaking sin). This is not to say that before revival comes there must be a perfect Church. On the contrary, revival is the Holy Spirit coming to revive the Church, but there must be a core, if only a handful who are correctly related to God and each other within each congregation or group, so that they can stand in the gap and ask God to pour out His Spirit from on high. But this all begins with the preparation of the individual heart which is then outworked into a person's lifestyle, character and demeanour.

After the restoration of the temple worship under King Hezekiah, (just before revival broke out), multitudes ate the Passover and participated in this important religious festival of the Feast of Unleavened Bread though 'they had not cleansed themselves' which 'was contrary to what was written' in the Law of Moses. But Hezekiah did not rebuke the fledgling Jewish multitude, but prayed for them saying, "May the good Lord provide atonement for *everyone who prepares his heart to seek God...*" (2 Chronicles 30:18-19). Verses 20-22 records that 'the Lord listened to Hezekiah and healed the people.' They then participated in worship 'accompanied by loud instruments,' the Levites taught them the word of God, whilst the people made offerings and 'confessions to the Lord.'

Young Christians are generally not as mature in the faith as those who have named the name of Christ for a longer period and will not have victory over sin and struggle in different areas of their lives, as do many mature Christians. Some Christians have more charisma than character, whilst others anointing is greater than the character of Christ formed in them. But like Hezekiah, we can pray for them and as long as their hearts are right before God, (even though their lifestyles or character may not always glorify God) the Lord will minister to their needs. We should be less hasty to judge and more quickly to love and to pray for the weaker brethren, or those who have slipped up.

Worldliness Verses Holiness

We are not to be conformed to this world, but conformed to the image of Christ. Friendship with this world in enmity towards God and the Spirit within us yearns jealously (James 4:4-5). God wants us to become disciples, not church-goers with the nickname Christian; not Sunday saints and weekday aints! It's all or nothing – no more compromising your testimony or two-timing Jesus; if you do you're a God-mocker, because you mock God with your testimony and His name is blasphemed amongst your work colleagues and neighbours because of you (Romans 2:24).

The Bible plainly declares that 'without holiness no man can see the Lord' (Hebrews 12:14). Holiness is not about keeping rules and regulations because we have to, but a heart attitude because we want to – we want to offer our 'bodies as living sacrifices, holy, acceptable to God' (Roman 12:1-2) which is only reasonable, just and fair. Jesus gave His life for us, so we should give Him our life in return. At conversion, we are 'sealed with the Spirit,' but we are called to be 'filled with the Spirit' and that is the 'baptism of the Holy Spirit and fire' as the Refiner comes to indwell and expunge sin from our lives as we die daily to self, crucifying the flesh with its passion and desires. We work in cooperation with God as we desire to do His will.

Experiential sanctification is a much deeper work of God in the believer's life than positional sanctification (made holy because of Christ's death and resurrection on the cross – imputed righteousness). It is the 'baptism in the Holy Spirit AND FIRE' – the "greater works" of what Jesus spoke about and "rivers of living waters" that will bubble and flow out of a sanctified saint so that people will know that they are very different than the average born again believer because their entire nature has been changed by the FILLING of the Holy Spirit. It is not so much as 'I' have the Holy Spirit (speaking in tongues, or other gifts of the Holy Spirit) but that the Holy Spirit HAS ME! Therefore, I live to please the Master. And because He has me (yielded to Christ, crucified life, full surrender), He come into to indwell in all His FULLNESS and I can be an overcomer and have victory over sin to the praise and glory of God.

Charles Spurgeon said, "Holiness is not mere morality, not the outward keeping of Divine precepts out of a strong sense of duty, while those commandments in themselves are not our delight. Holiness is our complete being fully consecrated to the Lord and moulded to His will. This is the thing which God's Church must have, but it can never have it apart from the Sanctifier, for there is not a grain of holiness beneath the sky, but what is of the work of the Holy Spirit. And, brethren, if a church is destitute of holiness what effect can it have on the world? An unholy church makes Christ to say that He cannot do many mighty works there because of its iniquity."[2]

Holiness Scriptures
*   'Who may ascend into the hill of the Lord? Or who may stand in His holy place? He who has clean hands and a pure heart, who has not lifted up his soul to an idol, nor sworn deceitfully. He shall receive blessing from the Lord and righteousness from the God of his salvation.

This is Jacob, the generation of those who seek Him, who seek Your face' (Psalm 24:3-6).

- 'Sow for yourselves righteousness; reap in mercy; break up your fallow ground, for it is time to seek the Lord, till He comes and rains righteousness on you' (Hosea 10:12).
- 'I acknowledged my sin to You, and my iniquity I have not hidden. I said, "I will confess my transgression to the Lord," and You forgave the iniquity of my sin. Selah. For this cause everyone who is godly will pray to You' (Psalm 32:5-6a).

Ian R. K. Paisley, in his book, *The 59 Revival* wrote: 'God's way to revival is the pathway of separation. 'Have no fellowship,' declares the Scriptures, 'with the unfruitful works of darkness'...Unity without purity can never command the blessing of God to descend...Let us learn the lesson of the Ulster Awakening [1859-1860], that a church sound in doctrine and separated from those who have separated themselves from God, is the only channel that God designs to use for the outpouring of His reviving grace.'[3]

George Mitchell, who chronicled the life of Jock Troup from the East Anglia Revival (1921-1922) wrote: 'God was more glorified...in sinners getting saved, than the church having correct liturgy...It is helpful and healthy to learn from revival times that God's emphasis has been on holy people He has mastered, rather than clever methods we can master.' And '...The Lord is more interested in personal holiness than theological correctness.'[4] And as the famous phrase states, it is not your ability that God is after, but your availability.

Ministers and Revival

Ministers are strategic players in helping to promote and stimulate prayer for revival, as they teach and preach on this vital subject and encourage their flock to pray. If the minister is on fire for God, like John Wesley was, people will come out and watch him burn! On the other hand, if the minister does not believe what he preaches then neither will the congregation. Like produces like. The minister is there to assist in building up the body of Christ, along with prophets, teachers, evangelists and apostles, to bring the Church into maturity, to the full stature of Christ (Ephesians 4:11-13).

When a minister speaks, then generally speaking, those under their authority act, even more so when they have an anointing from God upon their life and live what they preach in the fear of God, as a true shepherd. While Ezra was praying, confessing and weeping in the house of God 'a very large congregation of men, women and children assembled to him...for the people wept bitterly.' After a covenant was made, a proclamation was given and after three days Ezra addressed the assembled people at Jerusalem and told them to get right with God. The people responded, "Yes! As you have said, so we must do" (Ezra 10:1-12).

If the minister teaches and preaches on revival then not before long, many members of the congregation will begin to see the bigger picture of what God can do and what He has promised. As God is glorified, Jesus is exalted so that He can draw men to Himself as the Holy Spirit brings conviction of sin.

Within ones church or community, as the minister denounces sin and preaches holiness, focussing on Christ and the cross, individual members will apply the truths (as they confess and forsake their sin) become revived and better related to God and each other and this leads along the pathway to revival.

In the song of Deborah and Barak, after the defeat of Sisera and his army, it goes, "When *leaders lead* in Israel, when the people willingly offer themselves, bless the Lord!" (Judges 5:2). On the other hand, corporately the Church (and the leaders of any country) have much to repent of for causing and sometimes encouraging moral decline in their church (or nation), because when those in position of authority transgress (or do not denounce ungodly laws), it appears acceptable for the people under them to do likewise, see 2 Chronicles 28:19.

Complacency and at Ease

A minister is pulled in many directions, but perhaps one of the most disheartening things for a minister to see is ones congregation complacent and at ease; having no concern for the lost, disinterested in evangelism, outreach and world mission; with no concern over their own welfare, no victory over sin, no desire for holiness, no desire to be separate from the world and a blasé attitude about glorifying Jesus Christ, the Son of God; Saviour of the world.

Jonathan Edwards, in his most famous sermon, *Sinners in the Hands of an Angry God* said, "He is angrier with many who are now in the congregations of our churches, many who seem to be at ease, than He is with many of those who are now in the flames of hell."[5]

Isaiah prophesied, "Rise up, you women who are at ease, hear My voice; you complacent daughters, give ear to My speech...you will be troubled, you complacent women; for the vintage will fail, the gathering will not come. Tremble, you women who are at ease; be troubled you complacent ones; strip yourselves, make yourselves bare, and gird sackcloth on your waists. People shall mourn...on the land of My people will come up thorns and briers...the palaces will be forsaken, the bustling city will be deserted – until the Spirit is poured out from on high, and the wilderness becomes a fruitful field, and the fruitful field is counted as a forest" (Isaiah 32:9-15).

Isaiah is directing a message to those who live in Jerusalem, a prophecy of judgment and blessing, but as Christians we can see comparisons with the state of the Church and the majority of those who are within it. The complacent people, those who are at ease, without a care in the world perfectly portrays much of the body of Christ. We are called to humble ourselves and repent; we can see that our land is godless, the thorns and briers of sin entangle a plethora of people – we have turned our backs on God, so He has turned His face from us. Too many of the 'palaces' of our churches which were once filled are now closed down, turned into art galleries, shops, flats or even mosques! If we will but just humble ourselves, turn from our wicked ways and repent, things will change and God, in the fullness of His time, will pour out His Spirit from on high.

Treason against God

God is a covenant-keeping God and if we make a covenant with Him (a vow or a promise), then He expects us to keep it. We cannot make promises to God and then change our minds when it no longer suits us. In the days of Jeremiah, King Zedekiah had made a covenant with all the people living in Jerusalem to proclaim liberty to all the Israelite slaves, their brothers and sisters. This they did joyfully, until they changed their minds and again enslaved their brethren thus profaning God's name. Because of this, God declared judgment upon them stating that they would be given into the hands of their enemies (Jeremiah 34:8-20). In Ezekiel chapter seventeen, the parable of the two eagles, God declares to Jerusalem for breaking its oath and despising its covenant, that it is tantamount to treason against God and will be judged accordingly! (Ezekiel 17:15-20). How many of us have made promises or vows and not fulfilled them? See Eccl. 5:1-5.

Theft against God
To be called a thief is a title that none of us would like to have. I once had to confront someone under my authority over the action of their friend who whilst staying with us took an item which belonged to me. This person acknowledged that their friend had taken my property, but would not hear of him being called a thief. I asked the person, "What would you call a person who has taken something which does not belong to them?" 'Thief' was not one of the words.

Most of us would never even dream of pick-pocketing or mugging someone, making bogus claims on our insurance or tax forms, driving out of the petrol station without paying for our fuel or stealing, yet many Christians are unknowingly thieves! One preacher said to his congregation, "Some of you have come here today in stolen cars, with stolen money, wearing stolen jewellery" – he went on to explain that these people have stolen from God because they have robbed Him in tithes and offerings (Malachi 3:8-10).

We must also be just as careful as to whom we give our money to. If we have surrendered our lives to Jesus Christ, what is *ours* is now *His*. We are all called to be good stewards of that which is entrusted to us; our wage, a bonus, an inheritance and our legacy, (via our written will) is an entrustment and must be used wisely. Sadly there are many Christian broadcasts which would be funny; if they weren't exploiting the gullible, the naïve and the poor – those that make promises and claims which aren't Scriptural. Many of whom come up with new gimmicks to fleece our hard earned money, so that they can build their kingdom and not God's.

Generally speaking, we give our tithe to the church (to those who are spiritually feeding us), offerings as directed by the Holy Spirit or out of a heart of compassion (when you see someone is hungry, 'the least of these' or you have the ability to help a brother etc.). In essence sow joyfully and generously into God's Kingdom and make sure that it is fertile soil so that fruit can be birthed for the glory of God.

Many of us have robbed God by our sins of omission. By not doing things which we should be doing; loving our neighbours as ourselves, praying for those in authority, being salt and light, running a good race, blessing and not cursing etc. Have we robbed God in our time and commitment to Him, in our Bible reading, devotion and have we given God that which is our duty? – We should become disciples and not church-goers with the nickname Christian. Are we making disciples as we take up our cross daily and follow Him? Have we been loyal to God in our time, in our witness of Him and in our lifestyles? These are serious questions which we must honestly and humbly answer before God if we seriously want to see revival. As we ask the Holy Spirit to search our hearts, we may realise that we are not as close to God and to our brothers and sisters in Christ as we thought we were. But, if we acknowledge a problem we can rectify it. Confess and forsake all known sin (Proverbs 28:13).

Eva Stuart Watt wrote: 'We so often refuse our God even elbow-room in our everyday living and our continual planning. Our work for Him often crowds Him out. We look to Him to come to us along the narrow paths of our limited vision. We look to see Him work in some wonderful way, yet our circumscribed way it must be; where all the time it only matters that we meet Him, by whatever way He comes, and that He works His own sovereign will, no matter how it crosses ours...He may come when we least expect Him, to Paul He did. He may meet us as He met Moses, on the backside of the desert and make the thorn bush to blaze with His glory. He may come to us as He came to those Babylonians captives in the fiery furnace and bring us through the flames un-singed. He may call us from our threshing floor, as He called Gideon, and commission us to save a nation. We may find Him suddenly close beside us, as we travel the Emmaus road, when doubts and disappointments are challenged fiercely the citadel of our affections. And our heart will burn within us and then burn out for Him. But as sure as God reigns in heaven, He will come to His seeking saints, when they need Him and when they search for Him with all their hearts.'[6]

The Lord said, "If My people who are called by My name will humble themselves, and pray and seek My face, and turn from their wicked ways, then I will hear from heaven, and will forgive their sin and heal their land" (2 Chronicles 7:14).

Conclusion
In conclusion, if we desire to see personal, local or national revival, then Jesus must be at the centre of our lives and we

must be rightly related to God and with each other, and this begins with getting our hearts right before God, crucifying the flesh, full surrender and being baptised in the Holy Spirit and fire (Matthew 3:11). We cannot say we love God whilst we hate our brother. We cannot pray for God to have mercy on the graceless whilst we pass them by and do not help the least of these. We have to be outwardly and inwardly right with each other. Disunity and hating each other in our hearts are both wrong, as is jealousies, contentions and backbiting – it is all sin.

We need to pray and plead the Scriptures so that they will be fulfilled in the fullness of time. Our motives must be pure, God must be glorified, Jesus must be exalted and the Holy Spirit must be given His rightful place within our lives (individually) and the Church (corporately).

We have to be submitted to God and a channel through whom the Holy Spirit can use. To fully surrender our lives as a living sacrifice means that our will, emotions, time, job, family and money etc. are all under the Lordship of Jesus Christ. Then and only then, will we understand the concept that we are just unprofitable servants doing the will of our Master, so that He can get all the glory when revival comes.

- 'And it shall come to pass afterward that I will pour out My Spirit on all flesh. Your sons and your daughters shall prophesy, your old men shall dream dreams, your young men shall see visions; and also on My menservants and on My maidservants, I will pour out My Spirit in those days' (Joel 2:28-29).
- 'For the earth shall be filled with the knowledge of the glory of the Lord, as the waters cover the sea' (Habakkuk 2:14).
- 'O Lord, though our iniquities testify against us, do it for Your name's sake; for our backslidings are many, we have sinned against You' (Jeremiah 14:7).

Our Responsibility for the Great Commission

Just because we are praying for revival does not exempt us from our responsibly of the Great Commission. The fields are white unto harvest and need to be reaped. Whilst we may not be an evangelist, we are called to evangelise and for those who are ashamed of Jesus, He will be ashamed of them at His coming. We must go into the highways and the byways and compel people to enter into the Kingdom of God through the narrow way, because broad is the way that leads to destruction.

We should be preaching the Gospel, in season and out of season; always prepared to share our testimony of the wonderful saving power of God's grace and mercy, through the atoning death of the Lord Jesus Christ, who took the punishment that we deserved, so that in His death, we can live, through faith in Him.

We must sow the seed of the Gospel and pray for the former and the latter rain; pray for the seed to sprout and grow as fellow labourers till the ground so that a harvest can be reaped. Pray that the Lord will send forth more labourers into His harvest field so that fruit can be picked and remain for His glory.

Great Commission Scriptures

- Jesus said, "Go therefore and make disciples of all the nations...teaching them to observe all things that I have commanded you; and lo, I am with you always, even to the end of the age" (Matthew 28:19-20).

- Jesus said, "Go into all the world and preach the Gospel to every creature. He who believes and is baptised will be saved; but he who does not believe will be condemned. And these signs will follow those who believe: In My name they will cast out demons; they will speak with new tongues; they will take up deadly serpents; and if they drink anything deadly, it will by no means hurt them; they will lay hands on the sick and they will recover" (Mark 16:15-18).

- 'If you confess with your mouth the Lord Jesus and believe in your heart that God has raised Him from the dead, you will be saved. For with the heart one believes unto righteousness, and with the mouth confession is made unto salvation. For the Scripture says, "Whoever believes on Him will not be put to shame." For there is no distinction between Jew and Greek, for the same Lord over all is rich to all who call upon Him. For "whoever calls upon the name of the Lord shall be saved." How then shall they call on Him in whom they have not believed? And how shall they believe in Him of whom they have not heard? And how shall they hear without a preacher? And how shall they preach unless they are sent? As it is written: "How beautiful are the feet of those who preach the Gospel of peace, who bring glad tidings of good things!" ' Romans (10:9-15).

Chapter Twenty-Three

The Revivalists Observations

'Sow for yourselves righteousness; reap in mercy; break up your fallow ground, for it is time to seek the Lord, till He comes and rains righteousness on you' Hosea 10:12.

Those who have been used in revival are always those with the greater authority to speak on the subject of revival. Regardless of what we think, say or write, the following revivalists, to use modern language, 'have been there, seen that, and bought the T-shirt.' Therefore, they know what they are talking about, having participated and tasted of the fruits of revival. Whilst the majority have passed into glory, these men of faith, through their writings still speak. We need to listen and heed the advice and warnings of those who walked much closer to the Lord than we do, because if we walked as close to the Lord as these spiritual giants did, we would see revival.

Conditions for Revival

Charles Finney stated that before revival can come, there needs to be a necessity of union (Matthew 18:19 – 'If two of you agree on earth concerning anything...'). Obstacles of disunity and other factors that hinder revival are:

1. Rotten members of the church (so called 'mature members') need to be removed if they refuse to repent and change whilst in gross sin. Sometimes when an attempt is made to cast them from the church, a division will arise, causing a bad spirit, an uneasy atmosphere to prevail – away with all the dross! Deliberate wilful sinning needs to be punished as a little yeast will work through the whole batch of dough. Correct young converts and help train them, teach them and don't beat them, be tender and faithfully watch over them.
2. Whenever wrong has been done to any, there should be a full confession.
3. Unforgiveness is a great obstruction to revival which can lead to a revengeful and unforgiving spirit towards those who have injured them.

- 167 -

4. What is your motive for revival? For the denomination, for the church or for the glory of God? An increase in attendees and more money for the church? Sometimes ministers want revival because their church is going through difficulties which the minister needs to deal with and address, but is afraid to face the issue. At other times another denomination is being blessed more than them and the minister or congregation member wants to even the score.

5. Parents who pray for their child's conversion need to realise that their children are rebels against God, obstinate in their rebellion against Him; a sinner through and through, having a depraved heart who is deserving of the fires of hell; but is in desperate need of the Holy Spirit's quickening. The same is true of believers who pray for non-believers who feel that the sinner is not to blame for his or her actions! The sinner is to blame for his or her actions and will stand before God on Judgment Day to give an account!

Evan Roberts of the Welsh Revival (1904-1905) stated that there were four conditions for revival, which he frequently emphasised in his public appearances:

1. Is there any sin in your past with which you have not honestly dealt with, or not confessed to God? On your knees at once. Your past must be put away and cleansed.

2. Is there anything in your life that is doubtful – anything which you cannot decide is good or evil? Away with it. There must not be a trace of a cloud between you and God. Have you forgiven everybody, EVERYBODY? If not, don't expect forgiveness for your sins. Better to offend ten thousand friends than grieve the Spirit of God, or quench Him.

3. Do what the Holy Spirit prompts without hesitation or fear. Obedience, prompt, implicit, unquestioning obedience at whatever cost.

4. Make a public confession of Christ as personal Saviour. Profession and confession are vastly different. Multitudes are guilty of long and loud profession. Confession of Christ as Lord has to do with His workings in your life TODAY!

Practical repentance does not merely consist in putting away all known sin; it may and generally does involve certain acts of restitution, reparation and confession – and here we need much grace, wisdom and discretion.

God said, "When I say to the wicked, 'You shall surely die,' if he turns from his sins and does what is lawful and right, if the wicked restores the pledge, gives back what he has stolen, and walks in the statues of life without committing iniquity, he shall surely live; he shall not die" Ezekiel 33:14-15.

Rev. Duncan Campbell writing about the Lewis Revival (1949-1952) stated that the praying men and women of Barvas, Scotland, UK had a spirit of expectancy before he arrived on the Isle of Lewis, Outer Hebrides. Four things were made clear, and to them they became governing principles:

1. You must be rightly related to God and this is based on Psalm 24. You cannot see revival if you are living in sin; you must have 'clean hands and a pure heart.'
2. God is a covenant-keeping God and therefore must keep His covenant promises. God has promised 'to pour water upon him that is thirsty and floods upon the dry ground' (Isaiah 44:3). This is something that exists in the field of possibility and in the fullness of God's time (with man's cooperation – his pleading and prayers) it will happen.
3. You must be prepared for God to work in His own way, how He wants to. God is sovereign and will act according to His sovereign purposes – but while God is sovereign in the affairs of men, His sovereignty does not relieve men of responsibility.
4. There must be a manifestation of God, demonstrating the reality of the Divine in operation. This will force men to declare, "This is the Lord's doing, and it is marvellous in our eyes" (Psalm 118:23 and Mark 12:11).[1]

Colin C. Kerr, (not a revivalist), stated five principles for revival:

1. Revivals have nearly always started with a few people getting together to plead with God. Little groups have been organised and have studied the revivals both of Bible times and since.
2. There has to be very honest dealing with personal sin. Unconfessed sin has been confessed definitely to God,

and to any who have been hurt by it. [This includes restitution, see Luke 19:5-10].

3. There has been a humble desire to confess Christ as distinct from professing Him – the confession of a Person rather than the profession of a faith.
4. Prayer has been offered up for those churches and their leaders which seem dead or powerless. Remember that though revival has nearly always come in spite of the Church rather than through it, it has always started within it.
5. However much you get together with others in prayer and so on, revival must start individually. You must get alone with God and with your Bible, to seek Him; and to learn His will. There must be the daily response on your part to the voice of the Holy Spirit.[2]

When Revival can be Expected

Charles Finney stated that revival can be expected when:

1. Christians have a spirit of prayer for revival – they feel anxious for souls, he or she thinks of it day and night and dreams of it by night. (Pressing into God and pleading His promises until the blessing comes).
2. When this feeling of, 'My Little children, of whom I travail in birth' (Galatians 4:19, as said the apostle Paul), prevails in a church, then there will infallibly be a revival of Christians generally and will involve conversion of sinners to God.
3. Christians confess their sin one to another (Proverbs 28:13 and James 5:16).
4. Whenever Christians are found willing to make sacrifices necessary to carry it on – their feelings, business, time, work etc. The minister must be prepared if it be the will of God, to be driven away from the place and leave the entire event with God!

Dr. Horace Philip who saw revival on his mission station in 1920 said, "Whence comes revival? From God the Holy Ghost alone, the Lord and Giver of Life (John 3:8, Ezekiel 37:39). And He cannot be commanded, but must be obeyed (Acts 5:32). Obedience, faith and prayer are still the only human factors that can bring revival."[3]

Chapter Twenty-Four

Prayer for Revival

'And when they [the apostles] had prayed, the place where they were assembled together was shaken; and they were all filled with the Holy Spirit, and they spoke the word of God with boldness' Acts 4:31.

Prayer from the Heart

If we are going to pray for revival, for a spiritual awakening, we need to know what we are praying for; a distinction needs to be made by the trumpet of our heart in response to God. It is not praying a formula, a special prayer or praying by rote that will induce God's ear to hear our plea, but it is a deep felt heart-cry. Crying out for God's glory to come and that His name be known (especially amongst the unevangelised) and that He will be vindicated amongst the heathen (especially among blasphemers and God-mockers). Jesus must be exalted and the Holy Spirit given His rightful places in our lives and within the Church and this can only happen when we are fully surrendered to the Master as we live to please Him, crucifying the flesh and daily take up our cross and following Him.

It is difficult to pray corporately when we are praying different things. Not every Christian knows what revival is, the condition for revival, our responsibility (to get right with God and each other) and more importantly, *why we should be praying for revival? *This was addressed in chapter twenty-one; our motive should be for God's glory.

God's Spirit and God's Glory

- Thus says the Lord: "And it shall come to pass afterward that I will pour out My Spirit on all flesh; your sons and your daughters shall prophesy, your old men shall dream dreams, your young men shall see visions; and also on My menservants and My maidservants I will pour out My Spirit in those days" (Joel 2:28-29).
- 'For the earth will be filled with the knowledge of the glory of the Lord, as the waters cover the sea' (Habakkuk 2:14).

- The Lord said, "But truly, as I live, all the earth shall be filled with the glory of the Lord" (Numbers 14:21).

Our Responsibility and God's Nature
- 'If My people who are called by My name will humble themselves, and pray and seek My face, and turn from their wicked ways, then I will hear from heaven, and will forgive their sin and heal their land' (2 Chronicles 7:14).
- '...But You are a God, ready to pardon, gracious and merciful, slow to anger, abundant in kindness...' (Nehemiah 9:17).
- 'The eyes of the Lord are on the righteous and His ears are open to their cry' (Psalm 34:15).
- 'Search me, O God, and know my heart; try me, and know my anxieties; and see if there is any wicked way in me, and lead me in the way everlasting' (Psalm 139:23-24).
- 'O Lord though our iniquities testify against us, do it for Your name's sake; for our backslidings are many, we have sinned against You' (Jeremiah 14:7).

Our Responsibility
- Jesus must be at the centre of our lives, we need to be living a God-glorifying lifestyle, walking in holiness (1 Peter 1:16) and abiding in God (being in obedience to His will, see John 15:1-11, 1 John 2:6 and 1 John 3:24).
- We must be fully submitted to the Father's will, having offered our bodies as a living sacrifice, which is our reasonable service, discerning God's acceptable and perfect will, living for Him and crucifying the flesh (Romans 12:1-2 and 2 Cor 5:15 and Galatians 2:20).
- Jesus said, "Blessed are those who hunger and thirst for righteousness for they shall be filled" (Matthew 5:6). Are you hungry and thirsty for more of God? Will He not fill those who desire more of Him? See Isaiah 44:3.
- Confessions of our sins, the sins of our forefathers and our nation's sins are paramount, (Exodus 20:5-6, Judges 2:6-19 and 1 John 1:9). We need to make sure that we are right before God. Unless we deal with the sins of the past it is impossible to move forward into *all* that God wants for us. This may include restitution and reparation where and if possible.

- Does our heart condemn us? Is our conscience pricked with unconfessed sin because we have not kept God's commandments and therefore we are not pleasing in His sight? (1 John 3:21-22). See also Proverbs 28:13 and Leviticus 5:5.

As Brian H. Edwards wrote: 'If the Church today assailed heaven for the right thing, to the right end and with the right reason then we could expect to see God respond.'[1] Joyce Meyer wrote: 'We can pray but we cannot avoid our responsibilities.' We must understand the Scriptural conditions and promises, we must understand our responsibilities (to live holy) and be ready to respond in whatever way His word directs and in daily fellowship and obedience to the Holy Spirit, with Jesus at the centre of our lives. In the most basic sense, if we are not living right with God and each other, then our prayers will reach no higher than the ceiling, because the heavens will be as Iron and our cloud of sin will cover us from the presence of God, see Leviticus 26:14, 18-19 and Psalm 66:18.

'One who turns away his ear from hearing the law, even his prayers shall be an abomination' (Proverbs 28:9).

Many years ago an evangelical church held Friday night revival prayer meetings. The people would be praying and pleading for revival, for a spiritual awakening in their land. Being a Friday night, the end of a tiresome week, only the truly committed (except those who had to work or had children to look after) would turn up. Whilst there would be chairs to sit on, some used to stand, kneel, walk around and plead the promises of God. There would be periods of silence, waiting upon God, tears, rejoicings, prostrations, and words from the Holy Spirit, a Scripture read aloud and praise and worship. These prayer meetings in the side room of the church were active and joyful, anyone was welcome, and they began at a set time and generally finished around two hours later. There was freedom in the Holy Spirit, who was welcome to do what He wanted, when He wanted, how He wanted, through whom He wanted. The Spirit moved the people to pray and worship, to glorify Jesus, to pray for revival within their own lives and the nation. Soon numbers began to increase as more brothers and sisters became alive. There was on many occasions, unison in prayer as they prayed out loud simultaneously. However, things began to turn. Certain leaders came to the fore and decided that it was getting too noisy, the people were told to keep their bottoms on the seats, the Spirit was quenched and this lively revival prayer meeting began to stagnate under the restrictive bonds of fleshly rules and regulations – the Spirit was grieved and finally quenched. The numbers rapidly dwindled until the prayer meetings eventually stopped.

'Let the words of my mouth and the meditation of my heart be acceptable in Your sight, O Lord, my strength and my redeemer' (Psalm 19:14).

What to Pray For
We must be careful that whilst praying for revival we do not forget other important prayers that we are commanded or encouraged to pray. The Holy Bible reveals that we should be praying for many things on a consistent basis; this also includes the fulfillment of certain Scriptures:
- Asking for His Spirit to be poured out on all flesh (Joel 2:28-29).
- For the latter rain (Zechariah 10:1).
- For people to be saved (2 Peter 3:9, 1 Timothy 2:4 and Ezekiel 22:30).
- For the nations (Psalm 2:8).
- For the harvest (Matthew 9:38 and John 4:34-38).
- For fruitfulness as we abide in Him (John 15:1-17).
- For the Holy Spirit (Luke 11:11-13 and Acts 1:8).
- For the greater gifts of the Holy Spirit (1 Cor. 12:31).
- For our leaders and those in authority (1 Tim. 2:1-2).
- For the persecuted Church (Hebrews 13:3).
- For the peace of Jerusalem (Psalm 122:6).
- And lest we enter into temptation, we should all watch and pray (Matthew 26:41).

God Coming Down – The Spirit of God Descending
- Thus says the Lord: "For I will pour water on him who is thirsty, and floods on the dry ground; I will pour out My Spirit on your descendants, and My blessing on your offspring" (Isaiah 44:3).
- Thus says the Lord, "Rain down, you heavens, from above, and let the skies pour down righteousness; let the earth be open, let them bring forth salvation, and let

righteousness spring up together. I the Lord have created it" (Isaiah 45:8).

- 'He shall come down like rain upon the mown grass, like showers that water the earth' (Psalm 72:6). This Scripture is in the context of the Messiah's reign but can still be prayed for God to come down and meet with His people.
- 'For behold the Lord is coming out of His place; He will come down...The mountains will melt under Him, and the valleys will split like wax before the fire, like waters poured down a steep place' (Micah 1:3-4). The Scripture is in the context of Judgment, but before God can heal and bind up, He often has to chastise / discipline His children and judgment has begun at the house of the Lord! See 1 Peter 4:17.

Covenant-Keeping God
The Creator of the universe, the Giver and Sustainer of life, our covenant-keeping God (see page 39) has declared:

- "*If My people* who are called by My name will humble themselves and pray *and* seek My face and turn from their wicked ways, *then I will hear* from heaven, and will forgive their sin and heal their land" (2 Chronicles 7:14).
- "*If* you will keep My commandments and execute My judgments, *then will I do it!*" (1 Kings 6:12) AV.
- "Ask of Me, and I will give You the nations for Your inheritance" (Psalm 2:8). This is God speaking to Jesus, but we can also pray it because the Great Commission is the Church's responsibility and God has no pleasure in the death of the wicked.
- 'Thus saith the Lord, the Holy One of Israel, and his Maker, "Ask Me of things to come concerning My sons, and concerning the work of My hands *command ye Me*"' (Isaiah 45:11) AV.

'The Lord is not slack concerning His promise...but is longsuffering towards us, not willing that any should perish but that all should come to repentance' (2 Peter 3:9).

Why Pray for Revival
- We plead with God for an outpouring of His Spirit, primarily for His name's sake and for His glory (Leviticus

10:3, Joshua 4:24, Lamentations 3:22-25 and Jeremiah 14:7). The Church needs reviving! God's name is blasphemed by the heathen we live amongst everyday, these people are the graceless who like Nineveh do not know their right from their left and are unable to discern between the holy and the unholy. Many have seared their conscience as if with a hot iron and now call evil good and good evil.

- God wants us to ask for the nations as He desires all men to be saved and has no pleasure in the death of the wicked (Psalm 2:8, Ezekiel 18:23 and 1 Timothy 2:4). There is only one way to God and that is through His Son Jesus Christ. He is the Way, the Truth and the Life and no man can come to the Father except through Him. When the Holy Spirit descends in times of revival, He will bring conviction of sin even on those who are outside of the sound of a preacher, or those who have never entered through the door of a church building.

G. J. Morgan, minister of Albion Baptist Church, Brisbane, Australia, wrote: 'True prayer and true intercession means taking God's promises into His presence and requiring the fulfillment of them at His hand; presenting His own words to Him and seeking a fulfillment of those promises.'[2] Morgan continued: '…Matthew 18:19 is our sheet anchor ['if two of you agree on earth concerning anything that they ask, it will be done for them']; 1 John 5:14-15 is our confidence when we know we are praying according to the will of God; 1 John 5:16 is our assurance when we are pleading for an unsaved soul; couple that promises with 2 Peter 3:9 and 1 Timothy 2:3-4 ['God our Saviour who desires all men to be saved']. Come with me to Isaiah 45:11, where we have one of the most wonderful commands of Scripture, "Command ye Me," as well as "Ask Me." He promises to do the "impossible" if we will only call upon Him (Jeremiah 33:3).'

Daniel was a godly man and knew that Israel's seventy year exile (as prophesied by Jeremiah), was about to come to an end (Daniel 9:2) and so he prayed to see the fulfillment of Scripture. Daniel prayed and made requests through prayer and supplication, with fasting, acts of humility and repentance for the past; his personal sins and for the sins of his forefathers (Daniel 9:1-19). He did not sit back passively stating that as it was God's word it would come to pass regardless, but he actively prayed it through on behalf of his people. Daniel pleaded with God based on His great mercies (not because of his righteous living) and pleaded for His great name's sake (Daniel 9:18). The Lord stirred up King Cyrus of Persia, to make a declaration that any Israelite who wished to return to Israel and rebuild Jerusalem was free to leave, and under Ezra (and under Nehemiah) many did (Ezra 1:1-4). Thus Scripture was prayed through and Scriptural results were seen.

Prayer, Mercy and Revival – Faith is Substance
Most Christians accept the statement that prayer is vital for the life of the believer, and still acknowledge their inadequacy in prayer. Perhaps it's because we think that we have more important things to do. On the other hand, there are numerous distractions lurking around every corner – the lusts of the flesh which would consume our precious time and distract us from the more important issues in life.

The Holy Bible clearly reveals through the pages of Scripture that God wants us to ask in prayer, and He wants us to receive, though there are conditions for prayer:

- Forsake and confess all known sin (Psalm 66:18, Proverbs 28:13, Isaiah 59:1-3 and 1 John 1:9).
- Ask in Jesus' name (John 16:23).
- What is our motive in praying for -----? (James 4:3). Is the Father glorified through your prayers? (John 16:23).
- Is it a need or a want? (Matthew 6:9-13 and Phil. 4:19).
- Is it God's will? (1 John 5:14).
- Believe and have faith (Mark 11:24). Faith is substance, see Hebrews 11. "Ask and it will be given you" (Luke 11:9), "If you ask anything in My name, I will do it" (John 14:14) and "Ask and you shall receive" (John 16:24).
- "If two of you agree on earth concerning anything they ask it will be done for them" (Matthew 18:19), but *only* if they are in unity (Psalm 133, Ephesians 4:3).
- 'Let us therefore come boldly to the throne of grace, that we may obtain mercy and find grace to help in time of need' (Hebrews 4:16).
- Be persistent in your prayers (Luke 18:1).

Matthew Henry, the famous Bible commentator of the early eighteenth century wrote: 'It is the will of God that we should in everything make our request known to Him by prayer and supplication; not to inform or move Him, but to qualify ourselves for His mercy. The waterman in the boat that, with his hooks, takes hold of the shore, doth not thereby pull the shore to the boat, but the boat to the shore; so in prayer we do not draw the mercy to ourselves, but ourselves to the mercy.'[3]

'Through the Lord's mercies we are not consumed, because His compassion fail not. They are new every morning; great is Your faithfulness. "The Lord is my portion," says my soul, "Therefore I hope in Him!" ' (Lamentations 3:22-24).

All revivalists were praying people – being burdened for souls and the state of the society that they lived amongst. They put their faith into action, prayed, interceded, soul travailed, evangelised and preached (whilst continuing with their daily duties and responsibilities with family and work) and understood the more important issues of life – life and death, heaven and hell, and proclaimed the wonderful riches of Jesus Christ.

Jesus frequently got up before dawn, or went away into a solitary place to have communion with the Father. Jesus set the benchmark for prayer and we have to strive towards that goal. The Spirit is willing, but the flesh is weak (Mark 14:38). We all need to crucify the flesh and take up our cross daily and follow the Master. How much time do we spend doing 'things' which are of non-eternal value? The object therefore is to get our priorities in orders and to glorify the Master. What you are doing may be good, but is it the best use of your time, or what God wants you to participate in? Joseph Caryl from the seventeenth century said, "According to the weight of the burden that grieves us is the cry to God that comes from us."

Leonard Ravenhill wrote: 'Revival tarries because we lack urgency in prayer…The biggest single factor contributing to delayed Holy Ghost revival is the omission of soul travail. We are substituting propaganda for propagation. How insane! The only power that God yields to is that of prayer…Who will storm hells stronghold? Who will say the devil nay? Who will deny himself good food or good company or good rest that hell may gaze upon him wrestling embarrassing demons, liberating captives, depopulating hell, and leaving, in answer to his travail, a stream of blood-washed souls?' Ravenhill continued, 'The secret of praying is praying in secret. Books on prayer are good, but not enough...We must learn to pray, and we must pray to learn...One may read about prayer, marvel at the endurance of Moses or stagger at the weeping, groaning Jeremiah, and yet not be able to stammer the ABCs of intercessory prayer. As the bullet unspent bags no game, so the prayer-heart unburdened gathers no spoil...At the judgment seat the most embarrassing thing the believer will face will be the smallness of his praying.'[4]

Billy Sunday, evangelist and revivalist from Mid-West, America, was converted in 1887. He later saw 40,000 'hit the sawdust trail' who were truly converted during one month in Philadelphia. He often said, "The carpet in front of the mirrors of some of you people is worn threadbare, while at the side of your bed where you should kneel in prayer is as good as the day you put it down."

Our we Concerned for Our Cities?

Those who profess to name the name of Jesus Christ and who choose not to pray for revival are in effect saying, "Who cares? I'm saved, I'm OK, that's their problem not mine, what's it got to do with me?" We should be concerned about our great cities (Jonah 4:11), our towns and our neighbours. There is no Scriptural basis to hide the light and to keep the truth to ourselves. This anti-Scriptural attitude is also prevalent in those who choose not to witness for Christ, whilst some deny Him by their lifestyles, attitudes and by their sins of omission (passive sins) and commission (active sins).

J. Edwin Orr wrote: 'No one will suggest that the spiritual poverty and smug self-satisfaction...is the ideal of the Lord for the body of Christ. The antidote is revival, and revival must always be the will of God. To refuse to pray for revival (as hopeless) is like impudently telling the Lord that His power is limited.'[5]

'Away with pessimism. It is the sin of unbelief. The pessimist says that revival is impossible. Such are seldom men of faith. They say that revival is impossible before Christ comes. While the Spirit of the Lord is among us, who dare tell Him what is possible and what is impossible. God forgive our unbelief. They will try to justify their statements from Scripture. Tell them all that I challenge them to produce one single verse which proves the impossibility of revival among God's people [Orr had just seen localised revival break out in three Bible Colleges / Institutes in America and three localised revivals in New Zealand – all in a space of three months!]. They will quote, "When the Son of man cometh, shall He find faith in the earth?" Faith is already missing in the earth, but what has that to do with the Church of Christ? Revival is a Church affair. They will quote that we are in the Laodicean Church. The Laodicean Church is the apostate, professing Church – and you and I have nothing more to do with it. The call in the days of Laodicea is, "If any man hears My voice, and open the door" – Have not we responded to that? Then we are free from the curse of Laodicea. It is a snare of the evil one to make us despair. Revival is always possible to the obedient child of God…'[6]

'One finds that the pessimist fulfils their own ideas in themselves ['as a man thinks in his heart, so he is' Proverbs 23:7]. As soon as a man starts talking about the impossibility of revival, his own work is beginning to shrivel up ['according to your faith be it done unto you' Matthew 9:29]. The man who believes in revival is the man who sees results.'[7]

Paul Y. Cho, former pastor of the largest church in the world, Yoido Full Gospel Church, Seoul, South Korea, saw 230,000 conversions within his church during 1982-1983! He wrote: 'If you desire revival, there has never been, nor are there now, any short cuts to revival. The only key to revival is prayer. However, it must begin in you and me. Allow the Holy Spirit to spark your life with the match of faith! Let the spark spread throughout your entire church, causing a fire that will eventually engulf your city, state and nation. Let it begin now! If not now, when? If not you, who? If not here, where?'[8]

'Seek the Lord while He may be found, call upon Him while He is near, let the wicked forsake his way, and the unrighteous man his thoughts; let him return to the Lord, and He will have mercy on him; and to our God who will abundantly pardon. "For My thoughts are not your thoughts, nor are your ways My ways, says the Lord…For as the rain comes down, and the snow from heaven, and do not return there, but water the earth, and make it bring forth bud, that it may give seed to the sower and bread to the eater, so shall My word be that goes forth from My mouth; it shall not return to Me void, but it shall accomplish what I please, and it shall prosper in the thing for which I sent it" ' (Isaiah 55:6-11).

Chapter Twenty-Five

Nurturing a Revival

'Who is this who comes from Edom, with dyed garments from Bozrah, this One who is glorious in His apparel, travelling in the greatness of His strength? – "I who speak in righteousness, mighty to save" ' Isaiah 63:1.

Resolution Card

An unnamed pastor from America in and around the 1830s was asked by his congregation to hold protracted meetings or some special effort for the salvation of sinners within their community. It was the autumn of the pastors first year at the church, yet he felt opposed to holding protracted meetings, but in the week was led to write the following *Resolution Card* which was handed to each member of the church the following Sunday. It went as follows:

Resolutions
Adopted by the bearer of this card

1. Resolved, that as I am sinner, redeemed by the blood of Christ, I will do all that I can to save souls from whom He [Jesus Christ] died.
2. Resolved, that to prepare myself to do good to others, I will strive to have the same mind in me which was also in Jesus Christ.
3. Resolved, that I will from time to time select from among my neighbours some one or more individuals with whom I will, in tenderness and affection, labour steadily, daily, if possible, or even many times a day, until God shall either bring them to Christ, or I shall be convinced that I shall give them up.
4. Resolved, that I will carry those with whom I thus labour on my heart and pray for them continually and with them frequently, if they will permit me to do so.
5. Resolved, that while I labour and pray for the salvation of sinners, I will depend alone on the Holy Ghost to make me successful in my work.

Every member of the church was given a *Resolutions Card* and was informed that as long as any individual retained their card that they should consider themselves bound by the resolutions. But if they desired to be released from them, then they must return the card to the pastor.

The unnamed pastor wrote: 'The next night after the distribution I was called from my bed to go and visit a distressed sinner, which was a commencement of a work of grace that continued with us all fall [autumn] and winter, and resulted, as I trust, in bringing many souls to a knowledge of the Saviour.'[1]

Community Resolution

During the Great Awakening in eighteenth century America, Jonathan Edwards and the small town at Northampton, Massachusetts were so fearful of losing the blessing of the Holy Spirit through division that they made a community resolution, a covenant which is dated the 16 March 1742.

1. In all our conversations, concerns and dealings with our neighbours we will be honest, just and upright.
2. If we wrong others in any way, we will not rest until we have made restitution.
3. We promise that we will not permit ourselves to indulge in any kind of backbiting.
4. We will be careful not to do anything to others out of a spirit of revenge.
5. When there is a difference of opinion concerning another's rights, we will not allow private interests to influence us.
6. We will not tolerate the exercise of enmity or ill will or revenge in our hearts.
7. If we find that we have a secret grudge against another we will not gratify it, but root it out.
8. We will not allow over-familiarity in our talk with others, or anything that might stir up licentious behaviour.
9. We resolve to examine ourselves on a regular basis, knowing that the heart is very deceitful.
10. We will run with perseverance the race that is set before us, working out our salvation with fear and trembling.[2]

Pastor John Kilpatrick, of Brownsville AOG church, Pensacola, Florida, America, during the Brownsville Revival (1995-2000) continually prayed, "Lord please give me wisdom to pastor this thing. Lord, I don't want to be so lenient that I let anything in, but Lord I don't want to be so hard either that I don't let what You're trying to do in – God please give me wisdom. Holy Spirit, help me to walk humbly before You. Holy Spirit, help me to keep my mind on the Lord and to keep my eyes on the Lord, and Holy Spirit, help me not to get distracted with things, where I begin to let the embers grow dim and cold in my life, and Lord, help me not to let the fire go out in this church; Lord, help me..."[3]

Pastor Kilpatrick talking to *Charisma* about the move of God in his church, said, "If we stopped the prayer meetings, I know this move of God would grind to a halt."

Evangelist Steve Hill said, "One thing that could stop this revival dead in its tracks is exhaustion. Charles Finney recognised this as well. You can work yourself to death, and it doesn't glorify God."

Steve Hill saw his submission to Kilpatrick as one of the keys to the continuance of the Brownsville Revival. Kilpatrick stated that he would not do anything that would disturb his [Steve Hill's] authority. "We discuss everything, and we make a lot of decisions together."

Steve Hill said, "We try to stay out of the picture as much as possible, the revival is about Jesus. It's not about man…It's the defects of revival that often result in the revival being quenched – not by problems they create but by control-oriented leaders who try to act as God's deputies."[4]

Pandita Ramabai was the founder of the one hundred acre Mukti Mission Station in Kedgaon, India, which was dedicated to helping the child widows of India. She had seen revival in her mission stations at Poona and Kedgaon in 1897, and again at Mukti during 1901-1902 where in three weeks 600 women and girls were converted.

Writing in the *Mukti Prayer Bell* for October 1905, Ramabai wrote: 'I beseech you, dear brethren and sisters, do not lay down rules for God in regards to the way in which He shall send the much-desired revival among us [which broke out in November 1905!]. The revival will certainly come all over India. It will pass us by if we do not allow it to get in us. I have tried to lay down some rules for God's work at the beginning of the revival at Mukti. I soon found out that I stopped the work of the Holy Spirit by interfering with it. I humbled myself unto His mighty hand after receiving serious rebuke and took my hand off the work. The Holy Spirit has full liberty at work in us and He takes charge of the revival meetings at Mukti.'[5]

About a month after the Mukti Revival (1905-1906) broke out at the Mukti Mission Station, India, a request came from Bombay for the mission (who had their own printing presses) to publish an account of the revival and their spiritual victories. Pandita Ramabai felt it was not God's will to publish the story throughout India fearing it would hinder the work of the Spirit, but shortly after the Spirit of power decreased, there were evident signs that the revival was waning and a time of depression ensued. The workers met for special prayer "and then" said Ramabai, "the Spirit revealed to me that the depression had come because we had refused to give glory to God by not allowing the account to be published. I made up my mind to praise God and give Him glory in public the first time He made it possible for me to testify before people outside of our home." The depression left her immediately after this and an article was written and sent to the Bombay Guardian (a Christian weekly paper, edited by Mr Dyer) and elsewhere and the revival fires rekindled.[6]

Father Dennis J. Bennett is an Episcopalian Priest (American Anglican). He can be accredited as the father of the beginning of the Charismatic Renewal which rapidly spread worldwide. It began in his church at St. Mark's, Van Nuys, Los Angeles, California, America in 1960 and continued in his new pastorate at St. Luke's, Ballard, Seattle. Writing about what happened at St. Luke's from 1960-1970, where five services were held each Sunday, with a total congregation of two thousand, he wrote: 'Many unsolved problems at St. Luke's? You bet! But they are ones of action, and not of passivity. The pastoral and other problems at this church are concerned with how to control and guide a fast moving vehicle, not how to get a lumbering and unwieldy one into motion! The people are eager to serve, but need guidance as to how to do it effectively.'[7]

Appendices

Appendix A – Revivals from the Holy Bible
1. From the godly line of Seth men began to call on the name of the Lord (Genesis 4:26).
The Lord delivered the children of Israel under:
2. Judge Othniel, the son of Kenaz (Judges 3:5-11).
3. Judge Ehud, the son of Gera (Judges 3:12-15).
4. Prophetess Deborah, and leader Barak (Judges 5:1-15).
5. Judge Gideon (Judges chapters 6-7).
6. Judge Jepthah (Judges 10:6-18 and chapter 11).
7. The Prophet Samuel (1 Samuel 7:3-17).
8. King Asa of Judah commanded his people to seek the Lord God (1 Kings 15:9-15 and 2 Chronicles 14:1-15).
9. The prophet Elijah on Mount Carmel, before King Ahab and the false prophets (1 Kings 18:20-40).
10. Priest Jehoiada made a covenant between the Lord, the king and the people that they should be the Lord's (2 Kings 11:17-18, 2 Chronicles 23:16-21 and 2 Chronicles 24:2).
11. King Hezekiah (2 Kings 18:1-8 and 2 Chron. chs. 29-31).
12. King Manasseh of Judah humbled himself as a captive in Babylon. God permitted him to return to Jerusalem. He removed foreign gods and commanded the people of Judah to serve the Lord (2 Chronicles 33:12-16).
13. King Josiah (2 Kings chs. 22-23 and 2 Chron. chs. 34-35).
14. Jonah in Nineveh (Jonah chapter 3).
In the New Testament
15. John the Baptist called the people to a baptism of repentance (Mark 1:4-5 and Luke 3:1-18).
16. Jesus was the promised Messiah, the Saviour of the world and was the Anointed One (Luke 4:18-19). He preached the Kingdom of God with signs and wonders following confirming the message and thus proving He was the Promised One (Matthew 11:2-5 and Luke 8:25). The people flocked to hear His teaching (and to be healed) and many followed Him from city to city so that Jesus had periods of revival (the Gospels).
17. The Day of Pentecost – 3,000 converts (Acts 2:1-41).
18. Peter and John preached and around two thousand people were added to the Church (Acts 4:1-4).
19. Many signs and wonders were performed and multitudes became believers in Christ (Acts 5:12-14).
20. The number of disciples of Jesus multiplied greatly in Jerusalem including many of the priests (Acts 6:1-8).

21. Philip in Samaria (Acts 8:5-8).
22. Peter visited Joppa and raised Dorcas from the dead; many believed on the Lord Jesus (Acts 9:36-43).
23. Peter preached at Cornelius' house and the Holy Spirit fell upon them all (Acts 10:23-48).
24. Some of the disciples of Jesus (not the twelve) preached at Antioch and a great number believed and turned to the Lord (Acts 11:19-24).
25. Paul and his friends preached at the synagogue in Antioch at Pisidia (and then to the Gentiles) and the word of the Lord spread (Acts 13:14-50).
26. The disciples preached at Iconium in the synagogues. Signs and wonders were performed and the city was divided against the Jews and the apostles (Acts 14:1-4).
27. Paul and the apostles preached itinerantly and the Church increased in numbers daily (Acts 16:1-5).
28. Paul and Silas went into the synagogue in Thessalonica and preached. A great multitude followed them, which led to a riot (Acts 17:1-9).
29. Paul and Silas preached in Berea and many believed; Jews from Thessalonica caused a riot! (Acts 17:10-15).
30. Paul preached on Mars Hill, some mocked, but other joined them and believed (Acts 17:22-34).
31. Paul, Silas and Timothy spoke at a house meeting in Corinth and many Corinthians believed (Acts 18:7-11).
32. All who dwelt in Asia (Minor) heard the word of the Lord, both Jews and Greeks (Acts 19:8-9).
33. Fear fell on the Jews and Greeks in Ephesus. Many who had believed on Jesus Christ publicly confessed their sins and burned their magic books (Acts 19:11-20).
34. Many people were healed on the Island of Malta as Paul laid his hands on them, including the father of the leading citizen of the island (Acts 28:1-9). There is no recorded mention of converts but undoubtedly, there were many who believed his message as a snakebite did not kill him and they thought he was a god (v6).

Appendix B – Revival Amongst the Angas Tribe, Nigeria 1930s
On very rare occasions, revival can come to a heathen people group (like the city of Nineveh), those who are completely dead in their trespasses and sin with no concept of Christianity.

In 1930, the Church Missionary Society (CMS) mission station at Kabwir, Nigeria, amongst the Angas tribe was handed over to the Sudan United Mission (SUM). The local chief, Sariki Yohanna, a Christian, retold the story to Eva Watts in 1935. The first missionary at Kabwir astounded everyone by his bold assertions, "I've been sent from God with a message of warning for you." At the time, Sariki's father was the chief of the tribe who listened to the white mans words with more than a passing interest and repeated them to his counsellors. They were unsure of whether the white man was telling the truth or whether their ancestor's had told them a lie, so they set a test to see if God was stronger than the Tsafi; the tribal religion with its fetishes and sacred spirit-groves where sacrifices were made.

A certain tall tree, standing above the sky line (which was still standing when Eva Watt's visited) was in those days visited by screech owls. The test was to see wherever God could for three days and three nights keep the screech owls away from the tree. The chief said, "If He can do that we'll know He's stronger and will follow Him – if not, we'll keep to our Tsafi!" And the people simultaneously cried, "Well spoken." That night they sacrificed to the spirits, so that they would be stronger and guardsmen were appointed to keep watch, day and night. The God who had ordered the ravens to feed Elijah ordered the screech owls to roost elsewhere and after three days, from every hut in the village, the fetishes were brought out and publicly destroyed, and so they followed God and listened to what the missionary had to say.[1]

Appendix C – Is it a Revival or Not

Without the full facts, there can sometimes be a blurred line as to whether or not a revival took place when a people group come to Christ. As an example, in 1952, ten million people lived in Nepal without a single known Christian. Christianity had been banned for two hundred years. Roman Catholics had arrived in the eighteenth century and saw 600 converts in 54 years. Missionaries were expelled from 1767-1951.[2]

By 1951, Nepal was the poorest nation on earth, with no electricity or running water with an average life span of just twenty-nine years. For ten years, Dr. Lily O' Hanlon had been working at Nautanwa, India, south of the Nepal border alongside Hilda Steele and with a few others they had formed the Nepal Evangelistic Band (NEB).

In 1952, the Ranas family of hereditary prime ministers was ousted in a revolution and the legitimate heir to the throne, the king was reinstated. He invited the world to help his nation and Dr. Lily and Steele alongside others of the NEB applied and was accepted. In November they walked six days until they reached Pokhara at the foot of the Annapurna Mountain in Nepal where they established a hospital.

In the late 1960s, a Tamangs tribesman (one of Nepal's largest tribal groups) whose religion was Tibetan Buddhism went to the hospital where he received medicine, prayer and a Nepali New Testament. He soon recovered from his illness and told his nephew, Lok Bahadur, about it and what little he knew about the Christian faith. Lok returned home with the New Testament which he could just about read and found out that his daughter was ill who had been seen by the shaman of the village for the last few days. He told his relatives about what he had learned from his uncle, but they scoffed at his idea of praying to a foreign God. At night he prayed to the Christian God and asked in Jesus' name for her to be healed. By morning his daughter was well, but the villagers were not convinced.

Over the next few months, Lok was asked to pray for other villagers all of whom were healed. One of those healed was the wife of a village leader, Bir Bahadur and both believed in the Christian God. Soon a dozen members formed what we call a Church and gradually broke with the religious observances of the community. They endured much persecution and eventually some of the Christian families decided to leave their village for a neighbouring district (the others followed later) and after a three days walk they arrived at Duradara and a Christian community was formed on land recently set aside by the Nepali government for the resettlement of landless people.

Within a few years, members of the Duradara community went on missions to their old tribe, where former neighbours asked them to pray for their sick. Many were healed and soon the numbers increased as more of the Tamangs became Christian, first a few, then by tens and twenties and eventually by the hundreds. Within a few years, other Christian communities sprang up, some shamans were converted who burned their former religious items and brought with them hundreds of new followers. Thomas Hale wrote: 'Entire villages were transformed.' Becoming a Christian was illegal until 1990.

In 2000, the Duradara Christian community had grown to over 600 while in the original Tamang homeland there were 40,000 Christians in scores of villages. Hale wrote: 'The old Buddhist flags still flutter in the wind, but the words written on them are no longer Buddhist prayers but verses from the Bible. The tridents on their houses have been replaced with crosses.'[3]

In 2006, Nepal became a secular republic. The following year Dr. Robert Sander visited the Himalayan Land of Nepal as part of a small team led by Norman Beale, a missionary who spent thirteen years in Nepal. He noted that there was probably around 800,000 Christians, the growth of which occurred as narrated in the Book of

Acts or the Gospels. When Buddhist and Hindus in Nepal see other suffering, 'they feel it is their duty to leave them to their suffering. To interfere would rob them of their opportunity to atone for karma. Regardless of what is taught in the West about these religions, this is how it works on the ground' observed Dr. Sander. 'For these reasons, when they hear that Jesus forgives all sins in one stroke, that something called karma has no power over them, that they can have a relationship with Christ and an all-loving Father...they are thunderstruck. They want God, a loving eternal, gracious, God. For these reasons, and many more, there is an explosion of the Gospel in Nepal.'

Dr. Robert Sander concluded that, 'the Gospel did not primarily come to Nepal as a "superior" culture,' but came 'as in the beginning, by the risen Jesus doing what He always does; healing the sick, casting out demons, forgiving sinners, reconciling families and giving the hope of eternal life.'[4]

The 25 December 2008 was the first time that Nepal, a former Hindu State celebrated its first official Christmas Day, when schools, government offices and other places of work stayed closed! Glory to God!

Appendix D – A Revival of Religion

A revival of religion is where people become interested in Christianity and possibly even convert, but this does not necessarily constitute a heaven-sent revival.

In April 2006, Canon Andrew White, known as the 'Vicar of Baghdad,' of the Foundation for Reconciliation in the Middle-East (FRME) declared that the Iraqi attendance at St. George's Church in Baghdad, Iraq, was increasing as people sought God to cope with the extreme difficulties in their lives after the fall of Saddam Hussein and the ensuing rogue fighters, armed gangs, suicide bombers and other criminal elements in the capital.

Among his congregation where he preaches every month (as he travels back and forth to the UK among other places in the world) are Western Protestants as well as Iraqi Assyrian Christians, and since the fall of Saddam Hussein, from 2003-2006 the number of Iraqis attending his services in Baghdad has increased to about nine hundred. For their own protection, members of St. George's Church currently have to be taken by bus to the Green Zone for their church services.[5]

Retired Iraqi General Georges Sada, a former air force fighter pilot who once served as a senior military advisor to Saddam Hussein until his dismissal from the military in February 1991, when he refused to execute American and British prisoners of war, became the chief spokesman for Iraq's Prime Minister, Iyad Allawi during the interim government, just after the war. In 2006, he served as a senior national security advisor to Iraq's President, Jalal Talabani and has helped in redesigning the new Iraqi military, along with his efforts to strengthen the Christian Church in Iraq. Sada, in an interview with New York Times best-selling author, Joel C. Rosenberg says that the name of Jesus is praised in Saddam's old throne room (once used to order thousands of people to be executed), in his main palace in Baghdad, which has now been turned into an Evangelical church.

Rosenberg wrote: 'Sada told me that some 5,000 Iraqis have publicly identified themselves as new followers of Christ since Iraq was liberated, and that an estimated eight out of ten Iraqi believers say they converted because Jesus appeared to them in dreams or visions.' Rosenberg also reported that Sada had stated that, 'tens of thousands of Bibles were being printed in Iraq,' while 'thousands more are being shipped into Iraq,' and 'Christian programming is now available to Iraqis on satellite television.'

Rosenberg asked Sada why he is taking such risks to share the Good News? Sada responded, "There is an Arab proverb which says, 'Don't be a mute satan,' if you know the truth, you have an obligation to tell everyone."[6]

Appendix E– The Criteria for an Awakening

Looking back on national revivals and based on my research from revival church history, there is a four point criteria as to whether a national revival can be historically classified as an awakening or not. This four point criteria is:

1. Simultaneous revivals breaking out in a complete geographical area such as an island, county, state, nation or within a people group, (whom may live both sides of manmade boundary, even straddling international borders).
2. The duration of the revival has to exceed a minimum period of four years.
3. A minimum of fifteen percent of its population must repent of their sins and give their lives to Jesus Christ, being "born again" as Jesus said.
4. It must affect the moral makeup of the island, county, state, nation or people group. There must be a notable change within society in general.

An Awakening or Not

Out of the four distinguishing factors which define the criteria of an awakening; two factors, its duration and percentage conversion per population appears to be unfair. However, I have based my conclusions (the four criterion points) from my research of a little more than one thousand revivals and awakenings, spanning the last eight centuries on six continents from the accepted titles as recorded in revival church history, from more than two hundred authors.

The majority of the older revivals or awakenings, especially those from previous centuries can be referred to by as many as four different names. As one example, the British Great Awakening (1739-1791) is also known as the Evangelical Revival, the Methodist Revival or the Wesleyan Revival and twenty-five percent of the population's five million inhabitants were converted during that awakening!

The majority of national revivals do not fulfil the four point criteria as designated by revival church history and have therefore not be classified as an awakening. Some of these national revivals are:

The Welsh Revival (1904-1905), swept across Wales, UK, ignited fires across the globe and radically affected Wales, but because of its short duration it was not classified as an awakening, though I personally think that it should have been.

The Lewis Revival (1949-1952) has also been called the Lewis Awakening most notably because of Duncan Campbell's booklet of the same name, but popular Christian terminology; (especially authors), still refer to this move of God as a revival. The percentage of conversion per population is unknown, but in many of the small communities the drinking houses were closed forever, and when that happens, you know that a community is God-fearing!

At the end of a series of national revivals in Nagaland (north-eastern State of India) in the principle years of 1949, 1952, 1956, (Zeliangrong Revival 1959) 1966, 1972 and 1976, they were classified as the Nagaland Awakening of 1950s, 1960s and 1970s. In 2006, the afterglow of the awakenings was still being felt and ninety-nine percent of its nearly two million former head-hunter inhabitants claimed to be Christian. The majority are Protestants, with more than sixty percent Baptists, the highest percentage of any Baptist's or Christians in any state or country of the world. The account of the 1960s Nagaland Awakening begins on page 114.

The Argentine Revival (1982-1997) was naturally named after the country of origin, but the entire country was not was affected, though out of this great move of God, ten percent of the population became evangelical Christians.

The Fulton Street Revival (1857-1859) was not classified as an awakening even though it affected more people (and spread a chain of fires to many countries and continents during the years 1857-1860) than the First and Second American Awakenings combined. I have to conclude that the duration of only two years did not permit it to be classified as an awakening. Yet its effect was also over a larger geographical area than the American Great Awakening (1735-1760) upon New England's Congregationalists and the *Second American Great Awakening (1800-1830).*The duration of this awakening varies, though the average general consensus between authors and revival enthusiasts is between twenty to thirty years. One revival researcher wrote: 'It was roughly 1799-1807, though some say it lasted into the late 1820s and that it linked up with Finney's revivals from 1820s onwards.' Lewis Drummond in *The Awakening That Must Come* states that the Second American Awakening began in the late 1780s ending in around 1812 which was the year the *Great War began when America declared war on Britain (*Not to be confused with the Great War of 1914-1918, World War I), resulting in spiritual stagnation. But, Dr. Edward D. Griffin, in 1828 preached at a dedication service of a chapel at William's College (of which he was then president), and from his own observations said, "The year 1792 it has often been said, ushered a new era into the world. In that year commenced that series of revivals in America, which has never been interrupted, night or day..."[7]

Appendix F– Mass Movements
Georgina A. Gollock in *Candidates in Waiting* (1892) wrote: '...Spiritual results are beyond all human comprehension in their origin and can be commanded by no methods... You will find that men who died after long years of apparently fruitless [missionary] labour have yet done service for which all succeeding workers have given glory to God; and you will learn that many apparent revivals and ingathering have proved but fleeting in real results.'[1]

Mass movements can happen for a variety of reasons, but more often than not, it is a dissatisfaction of a caste people group who collectively decide (or under direction from their leadership) to change their religion. Sometimes a mass movement is a step in the right direction towards individuals becoming 'born again,' passing 'from death to life' and living for Christ, but is more often than not, not revival. Within some countries there may be a large population of Christians (by birth, or by a census of religion), but they may be largely nominal – Christian in name only, not in lifestyle or culture.

In the 1861 government census of Sierra Leone, recorded a population of 41,000, with 27,000 Christians and only 1,734 Muslims. In 1854, 12,000 people belonged to the Church of England who took the entire cost of educating their children via the Church Missionary Society upon themselves. But, Henry M. Stanley (the man who 'found' Dr. David Livingstone) noted that whilst he 'heard the voice of praise and prayer from the numerous aspirants to clerkship and civil service employ' he thought that little good had been done; noting 'the only efficient force of Sierra Leone natives are the few constables who perambulate the town baton in hand to crack the heads of the unruly. As to being useful, the natives seem very much opposed to anything of the kind, and declined the ignoble task of carrying tinned meats at a shilling a day.'[2]

Mass Movements in India

In India in the nineteenth century, 'multitudes came to Christianity' so wrote missionary, Sherwood Eddy in *India Awakenings* (1912) 'and since caste conditioned all Indian life and for centuries has crushed out individuality, and punished all efforts at independence and progress, men have been compelled to act together. Minds move in mass in India. We have to take the people as they come.'[3]

Sherwood Eddy noted five areas of mass movements. They were the Travancore on the southwest; Tinnevelli adjoining it; the Telugu field north of Madras; the aboriginal area of Chota Nagpur (where some 80,000 Christians reside) and the Rohilkand district in the United Provinces of North India. Eddy wrote: 'In the latter area, the Methodist Episcopal Church grew from 20,000 to 90,000 in a decade; whiles the total strength of this mass movement is now over 100,000.[4]

In previous centuries, but especially in times of famine, villages, groups (and individuals) have professed to become Christian to receive the benefits of the mission station. This gave rise to the term 'Rice Christian' as those who 'converted' and move into the mission station compound, or who lived within a mission 'parish' received greater help in these times of difficulty.

As seen in the Telugu People (1878) in India (in chapter eleven), Dr. Clough (and his fellow missionaries) in the great famine of 1877 refused to baptise those in his employment for fear of their motives. Cholera, followed the famine and still the natives begged to convert to Christianity, which eventually saw nearly 10,000 baptism within a year!

Sherwood Eddy in relation to the five aforementioned mass movements, wrote: 'I hear some one say that these people are "rice Christians." Perhaps they are, and you might be if you were in their place. Suppose you had been crushed by Hinduism, and had scarcely ever been able to get a meal of rice, but had to live on grain and millet. What if you had never been permitted to go to school, nor your ancestors for a thousand years before you? Suppose you had never been able to own land, not anything else save broken dishes, scavenger dogs and asses, according to the code of Manu [see appendix H] ... What if you were considered too low to be even touched with a stick while your very shadow was polluting...? The fact that they endure persecution is proof they are genuine.'[5]

Bishop J. E. Lessie Newbigin in Madhurai and Ramnad of the Church of South India told the story of an unnamed village 'far up in the hills' of the Puliyan caste when 'nearly all the villagers became Christian, and a school was started.' This was in around 1937. The area was very malarial and was ten miles from which a wheeled vehicle could be brought. After some years, the school had to be closed, the Christian teacher (from the plain) left and the village was isolated from Christianity for some years. When the Bishop heard of the village, contact was resumed and 'the villagers were reported to be still loyal to their confession, though terribly ignorant (naturally) of what it involved. The Bishop visited the only Puliyan Christian group in around 1950. He heard the story of the other Puliyan families who refused to give their daughters in marriage to the Christians unless they renounced their faith, but 'in spite of the fact the Church had treated them with such shocking indifference [by abandoning them - they] absolutely refused to do so.'

The Christian Puliyan's solved the problem by the ancient method of marriage by capture! Thus was echoed the story in Judges chapter 21 (which they were not aware of), when the women of Shiloh were kidnapped by men from the tribe of Benjamin ('every man catch a wife for himself') because the tribes of Israel had sworn an oath at Mizpah, saying "None of us shall give his daughter to Benjamin as wife" (Judges 21:1, 21). After investigating the facts, the Bishop told them that in future this practice was not acceptable and as long as the captured wives (four off) were happy to be baptised (they were receiving Christian teaching from a catechist) they he would do so.[6]

Bishop J. E. Lessie Newbigin in *A South India Diary* (1951) wrote about an Indian village, only referred to as P------- in around 1950: 'There is a mass movement among the leather workers' community in this area, and hundred have either been baptised or placed under instruction for baptism. They belong to the lowest social stratum of the villages, and their conversion has been bitterly resented by the Hindu landowners. It's very hard for the beneficiaries of an ancient social system to endure such revolutionary changes.'

The Bishop was taken aback when he visited the leather workers' quarters, 'it is the most shocking congested slum I have ever seen' which consisted of 25 small one roomed mud huts, generally with three families to each hut. 'As I watch them [the Christians] I feel ashamed that we have done practically nothing to help them. Economically they are worse since they became Christians.' The Bishop noted that there was not even space for one more hut for a Christian teacher to live amongst them and was in the process of trying to get them some land, which had been blocked by the other castes. 'When that happens doubtless the cry, "rice Christians" will be raised. At the moment they are dull and listless from want of food... Meanwhile what have we given them? We have given them the Gospel. At the moment they don't look much like the apostles on the Day of Pentecost. But these men and women have judged that it is better to suffer starvation and persecution than to give up the Christ of whom they yet know so very little.'[7]

In a more contemporary sense, among the Dalits (the untouchables) and other low-caste groups in India, leaders representing approximately 700 million of these people have risen up, demanding justice and freedom, from persecution and caste slavery. On the 4 November 2001, tens of thousands of Dalits publicly declared their desire to 'quit Hinduism' and follow a faith of their choosing.[8]

Karoland Revival 1960-1966 – Sumatra, Indonesia
In 1945, there were 6,000 Christian Karo, two percent of the population in Karoland north Sumatra, Indonesia. From 1960-65 there was a five hundred percent increase in church membership. Two OMF missionaries, Martin and Elizabeth Goldsmith were invited to teach the Karo people (and engage in lay training ministry) as part of this 'mass movement' to Christ. The Goldsmith were missionaries in Karoland from 1960-1962. L. T. Lyall in the preface to Batak Miracle (1967) wrote: 'They found themselves in the midst of a spiritual movement within the Church, the result of which was a new vision for evangelism and an outreach to eighty-fiver percent of the Karo people still pagans.' This movement began before the *Indonesian Revival (1964-1974) of which the *epicentre was the island of Sumatra.

In Keleng, the only hospital in Karoland, an entire ward wanted to become Christian. The year 1962 saw the first every inter-Church Christmas, whilst the village of Lingga (with 600 families) celebrated its first Christmas, which was a great evangelistic witness to the community.

When people who held animist beliefs began to receive a school education, their fear of spirits and that natural object have souls quickly dispelled and the Truth filled the vacuum. Backlash against the failed Communist coup of October 1965 (and with a constitution that said you had to have a religion), helped the people to choose! In 1965 at the Tigabinarga High School – nearly everyone converted to Christianity and this high school had been a former centre of Communist activity! The Karo Church trebled in size from 1965-1968.[9]

In 1966, 1,930 Karo Christians were baptised in one day with the assistance of fifty ministers! With more than 10,000 others preparing for baptism (after a one year church course). By 1966, the Karo Church was just one of forty recognised Protestant Churches in Indonesia. The following year the Karo Church grew to over 45,000.[10]

Appendix G – Caste and Indian Christians

It can be quite hard for those of us in the West who are born in a culture of freedom of individual action to comprehend the difficulties and complexities of the social caste system and Hinduism within India. Caste is still largely in force even today, though it does vary in each district and from village to village. Caste may be defined as a collection of families holding a common title or name, claiming descent from a common ancestor, originally professing to follow the same calling, and unified into a single community by a tradition of fixed rules and customs. They are separated from other castes by the prohibition of intermarriage, eating together, contact and similar barriers. There used to be four main castes, but now there are three principle ones: Brahams, Middle Caste and the Panchamas or outcasts, also known as the "untouchables" all of which can be subdivided into a few thousand castes!

For a Hindu to convert to Christianity, to break away from his old gods (of which there are as many as 330,000,000!), it is publicly confirmed by baptism, the outward sign of an inward faith. This is the dividing line between the two religions which will result in breaking caste. Many Hindus do not object to persons being secret believers, or even open followers of Christ, if only they will not sever themselves from the caste system by water baptism. The convert can suffer the wrath and retribution of family, friends and those within the same village. When I was in India, nearly a decade ago, a native missionary told us of a Christian being hung up in a tree and being beaten and that a converted Muslim had a fatawa (a Muslim ruling) pronounced upon him – a death sentence! Breaking caste within Hinduism means the loss of everything he or she holds dear – home, relatives, means of support, the hope of proper marriage and all social relations. The fact that they endure persecution is a proof that they are genuine.

I emailed an Indian Pastor (who I briefly worked with whilst on a short-term mission in India), he has a small mission organisation outside of Calcutta and I posed the question of how prevalent is the caste system in the twenty-first century? He replied: 'Caste system in Church is prevailing in many parts of India especially in South India (among nominal churches) and [is] not a big problem in churches in Calcutta. Outside of Church, it is [a] big thing.'

One convert and his family in and around the time of the Mukti Revival (1905-1906) had to endure; not being able to draw water from the village well and not being able to grind grain on the village grinding-stones. The family was boycotted and the villagers said, "We will never eat with you again and never darken your door in times of trouble. Your sons and daughter can never marry. We are dead to you and you to us." The next morning all his crops of onions and other vegetables had been uprooted and transplanted into a Hindus field a mile away, while the whole village was ready to swear that he had never had any crops in his field.[1]

Appendix H – Child Widows

The Indian census of 1910 revealed that ninety-nine percent of women were illiterate. The sacred code of the Manu has text written into it which completely degrades women and for those of the lowest caste they are worth less than an animal and can be treated as such, or even worse. Hinduism encourages girls to be married usually not later than when they are eleven or twelve years old, though infant marriage was not uncommon when a baby or toddler is pledged to be married to another boy or man who can be thirty or fifty years older, though the girl does not live with her husband until she is at least ten. This was raised in the last decade of the nineteenth century by the Indian government to age twelve by active indignant missionaries. The child wife is often placed under the control of the mother-in-law and as the Tamil Proverb declares: 'If the mother-in-law breaks a vessel, it does not matter; it is only earthenware. But if the daughter does so, it is gold.' Once a girl is widowed, according to Hindu custom she is never allowed to marry again, some are shut up at home until they die. A high-caste widow is supposed to be responsible for the death of her husband. Her head is shaved, her jewels torn from her, for a year she must eat but one meal a day, with frequent fasts and she is clothed in plain white cloth. Also girls and widows are taken to the temple to become temple prostitutes and slaves to the priests. The Hindu custom sanctions the nautch, or dancing girls, the Devadasis or "servants of the gods" – a life of religious prostitution and the practice in western India of dedicating girls for a life of immorality to the god Khandoba. In 1910 there was 144,000,000 women in India and one is six was a widow! These are the people that Pandita Ramabai tried to help.[2]

Appendix I – Famous Missionaries

Famous missionaries from the thirteenth to the twentieth century in chronological order of their arrival on the mission field. Names marked by an asterisk (*) are more readily available though many brief biographies can be found online on the Links Page @ www.MissionsNow.co.uk: Raymond Lull (North Africa), Francis Xavier (India and Japan), John Eliot (American Indian), Hans Egede (Greenland), *David Brainerd (American Indians) *William Carey (India), John Williams (South Sea Islands), Theodosius Vanderkemp (Southern Africa), *Adoniram Judson (Burma), *Robert Morrison (China), *Henry Martyn (India and Persia), *Robert Moffat (Southern Africa), *John Gibson Paton (New Hebrides – Pacific), Captain Allen Gardiner (Indians of Chile), Elias Riggs (Turkey), Miss Eleanor Macomber (Burma), Mrs Elizabeth Bowen Thomas (Syria), Titus Coan (Hawaiian islands), Miss Fidelia Fiske (Persia), *Hudson Taylor (China), *David Livingstone (Southern Africa), Guido Fridolin Verbeck (Japan), *Robert Jermain Thomas (Korea), *James Gilmour (Mongolia), Bishop Hannington (Uganda), Mrs A. R. M'Farland (Alaska), *The Cambridge Seven (China), *C. T. Studd (China, India and Central Africa), *Mary Slessor (West Africa), Christina Forsyth (Fingoland, Africa), Martha Croll (Jamacia), *Amy Carmichael (India), Marie Monsen (China), *Miss Gladys Aylward (China), *Helen Roseveare (Congo), *Jackie Pullinger (Hong Kong) and *Don Richardson (Irian Jaya).

Appendix J – Nagaland Statistics

By 2007, ninety-nine percent of Nagaland's former head-hunters inhabitants (a little under two million) claim to be Christian, though only the Lord truly knows those who have been 'born again' and have passed from 'death to life.' The majority of Christians are Protestants, with more than sixty percent Baptists, the highest percentage of any Baptists or Christians in any state or country of the world.

End Quote

J. Taylor Smith became Cannon-Missioner for the diocese of Sierra Leone in 1891 and then Bishop in 1897. The Rev. J, W. W. Moeran, looking back on his life (d.1938) noted: 'We can ill spare such a man in these days of increasing materialism and the craze for pleasure, when the greatest need of our country (and indeed the world) is a revival of true religion.'[1]

- JESUS CHRIST is LORD -

Sources and Notes

Chapter One
1. *The Bible in the World, Volume VII 1911*, British and Foreign Bible Society, 1911, page 90.
2. *The Great Dynamic* by Gideon L. Powell, The Christian Witness Company, 1923, page 87.
3. *Healing Rays* by George Jeffreys, Elim Publishing, 1932, page 118.
4. *How Revival Comes, The Two National Broadcasts* by Colin C. Kerr, Henry E. Walter, London, 1942, page 14.
5. *The Lewis Awakening 1949-1953* by Duncan Campbell, The Faith Mission, 1954, page 14.

Chapter Five
1. *How to Plan, Prepare and Successfully Complete Your Short-Term Mission – For Volunteers, Churches, Independent STM Teams and Mission Organisations* by Mathew Backholer, ByFaith Media, 2010, pages 10-11.
2. *Revival Sermons In Outline* by eminent pastors and evangelists edited by Rev. C. Perren, Fleming H. Revell Company, 1894, pages 18 and 20.
3. *Memoirs of John Smith* 1822, quoted in *Missionary Joys in Japan* by Paget Wilkes, Morgan & Scott, 1913, page 225.

Chapter Six
1. *The Lewis Awakening 1949-1953* by Duncan Campbell, The Faith Mission, 1954, page 10.
2. *Thirsting For God* by Eva Stuart Watt, Marshall, Morgan & Scott, 1936, page 152.
3. *The Scarlet Sin And Other Revival Sermons* by John R. Rice, Sword Of The Lord Publishers, 1946, page 152.
4. *When the Wind Blows, The Kilsyth and Cambuslang Revivals* by Rev. James Robe, Ambassador Productions LTD, 1985, pages 137-139.
5. *Lady Huntington And Her Friends* compiled by Mrs Helen C. Knight, American Tract Society, 1853, page 129.
6. *Historical Collections of Accounts of Revival* by John Gillies, 1754, Horatius Bonar, 1845, Banner of Truth Trust, 1981, pages 490-491.
7. *Missionary Band A Record* Morgan and Scott, 1887, page 37. *Paget Wilkes of Japan* by I. R. Govan Stewart, Marshall, Morgan & Scott, 1957, pages 35 and 59 and *Missionary Joys in Japan* by Paget Wilkes, Morgan & Scott, 1913, chapter 3 and page 314. *The Reward of Faith, in the life of Barclay F. Buxton* by B. Godfrey Buxton, Japan Evangelistic Band, 1949, 1971, pages 133 and 152-153 and *Missionary Joys in Japan* by Paget Wilkes, Morgan & Scott, 1913, page 52. *Pandita Ramabai, India's Christian Pilgrim* by Basil Miller, World-Wide Missions, undated, page 89. *Missionary Joys in Japan* by Paget Wilkes, Morgan & Scott, 1913, pages 111 and 52.
8. *Born for Battle* by R. Arthur Matthews, OMF Books, 1978, page 14 as cited in *Possessing the Gates of the Enemy* by Cindy Jacobs, Marshal Pickering, 1991, 1993, page 54.
9. *Prove Me Now! 10,000 Miles of Miracle to Moscow* by J. Edwin Orr, Marshall, Morgan & Scott, LTD, 1935, page 52.

Chapter Seven
1. *This is No Accident – Testimonies of a Trial of Faith in Congo* edited by Leonard C. J. Moules, Worldwide Evangelization Crusade, 1965, 1967, pages 108-109.
2. www.vision2025.org – September 2009.

3. *Mission Preparation Training* by Mathew Backholer, 2006, covers 29 subjects in 35 biblical lessons. *How to Plan, Prepare and Successfully Complete your Short-term Mission* by Mathew Backholer (2010) has forty-eight easy-to-read chapters – available from **www.byfaithbooks.co.uk**.
4. *Floods On Dry Grounds* by Eva Stuart Watt, Marshall, Morgan & Scott Ltd., 1939, 1943, page 10.
5. Other social pioneers are: John Howard, friend of prisoners, Granville Sharp, the slave's champion, Robert Raikes, father of Sunday Schools, Joseph Lively, pioneer teetotaller & Mathilda Wrede, the prisoner's friend.
6. *How Christianity Made the Modern World* by Paul Backholer, ByFaith Media, 2009 – available from **www.byfaithbooks.co.uk**.

Chapter Eight
1. Between various authors there is a difference between the day of the week and the date of the month during the second and third week of August and therefore to avoid confusion I have left the day of the week out in some paragraphs.
2. *Vanguards Of The Christian Army,* The Religious Tract Society, 1896, pages 383-384 and 390.
3. *The Pilgrim Boy,* Religious Tract Society, c.1900, pp.39 & 46-47 and *Vanguards Of The Christian Army,* The Religious Tract Society, 1896, pp.403 & 406.
4. *The Awakening That Must Come* by Lewis A. Drummond, Broadman Press, 1978, page 83. *Missionary Points and Pictures* by James Johnston, The Religious Tract Society, 1892, pages 113-114. *The History of Revivals of Religion* by William E. Allen (revival series No. 7), Revival Publishing Co., 1951, pages 15-16. *By My Spirit* by Jonathan Goforth, Evangel Publishing House, undated, pages 9 and 132-133. *In the Day of Thy Power* by Arthur Wallis, Christian Literature Crusade, 1956, pages 88 and 94. And *A History of the Moravian Church* by J.E. Hutton, 1909.
5. *The revival We Need* by Oswald J. Smith, Marshall, Morgan & Scott, 1933, 1940, page 29.
6. *Incidents of Missionary Enterprise – Illustrative of The Progress of the Gospel Among the Heathen* by Andrew Bonar, 1841, page 215.
7. *In the Day of Thy Power* by Arthur Wallis, CLC, 1956, page 174.
8. *The History of the Revivals of Religion* by William E. Allen, Revival Publishing Co., 1951, page 20.
9. *Vanguards Of The Christian Army,* Religious Tract Society, 1896, pages 372-380.

Chapter Nine
1. Ibid. pages 10-23. *India Awakening* by Sherwood Eddy, Missionary Education Movement, 1911, pages 12, 85 and 91-92. *Missionary Band, A Record and Appeal,* London: Morgan and Scott, 1887, page 71.
2. *Old Time Revivals* by John Shearer, Pickering & Inglis, undated, pages 55-60 and *The Ten Greatest Revivals Ever* by Elmer Towns and Douglas Porter, Servant Publications, 2000, pages 75 and 92.
3. *Times of Refreshing 10,000 Miles of Miracle Through Canada* by J. Edwin Orr, Marshall, Morgan & Scott, LTD, 1936, pages 43-44.
4. *Narrative of Remarkable Conversion and Revival Incidents – Great Awakening of 1857-'8* by William C. Conant, Derby & Jackson, 1859, page 224.
5. *The Revival We Need* by Oswald J. Smith, Marshall, Morgan & Scott, 1940, pages 2-3. *Titus Coan and the Revival in Hawaii 1837,* by Henry M. Field, 1880 and *Life in Hawaii by Titus Coan,* 1881, both on CD ROM.
6. *Incidents of Missionary Enterprise – Illustrative of The Progress of the Gospel Among the Heathen* by Andrew Bonar, 1841, pages 86-89.

Chapter Ten
1. *Missionary Triumph over Slavery* by Peter Masters, The Wakeman Trust, London, 2006 and *William Knibb - A Memoir* by Mrs John James Smith (1896).

2. William Knibb Freedom Fighter by G. A. Catheral, Janay Publishing Company, 1972, page 99.
3. www.news.bbc.co.uk/1/hi/england/hampshire/8398126.stm
4. Missionary Points And Pictures by James Johnston, The Religious Tract Society, 1892, pages 11-17 and John G. Patton, Missionary to the New Hebrides, Hodder & Stoughton, 1891, pages 75-78.
5. The Second Evangelical Awakening by J. Edwin Orr, Marshall, Morgan & Scott, 1949, 1955 abridged edition, pages 107-108 and 110.
6. Ibid. pages 12-13, 58 and 64. And Revival, Principles To Change The World, by Winkie Pratney, Whitaker House, 1983, pages 142-144.
7. The Net Cast In Many Waters, 1869, Bemrose and Sons, pages 23-24.
8. South African Methodism, Her Missionary Witness, edited by Rev. A. E. F. Garrett, Methodist Publishing House, circa 1966, page 37.

Chapter Eleven
1. India Awakening by Sherwood Eddy, Missionary Education Movement (MEM), 1911, pages 75 and 93-95.
2. Opened Windows – The Church and Revival by James A. Stewart, Marshall, Morgan & Scott, 1958, page 115.
3. India Awakening by Sherwood Eddy, (MEM), 1911, pages 94-95.
4. Spirit of Revival by I. R Govan, The Faith Mission, 1938, 1978 edition, (extracts) pages 20, 43, 71-74, 92 and 94.
5. Paget Wilkes of Japan by I. R. Govan Stewart, Marshall, Morgan & Scott, 1957, pages 15-17, 32 and 35-39.
6. Pandita Ramabai, India's Christian Pilgrim by Basil Miller, World-Wide Missions, undated, pages 65-85 and 118. And Pandita Ramabai, A Great Life In Indian Lessons by Helen S. Dyer, Pickering & Inglis, circa 1922, pages 66 and 99.
7. Good News in Bad Times by J. Edwin Orr, Zondervan Publishing House, 1953, page 219.

Chapter Twelve
1. Korean Church and Christian Book, History of the Korean Church and Review of 95 Different Christian Books, 2005 Frankfurter Buchmesses (Frankfurt Book Fair), Christian Council of Korea, 2005, pages 2, 11 and 49.
2. The Korean Pentecost & The Sufferings Which Followed by William Blair and Bruce Hunt, The Banner of Truth Trust, 1977, pages 52 and 61-66.
3. When the Spirit's Fire Swept Korea by Jonathan Goforth, Zondervan Publishing House 1943, Timothy Conjurske 1994, pages 7 and 16.
4. The Korean Pentecost & The Sufferings Which Followed by William Blair and Bruce Hunt, The Banner of Truth Trust, 1977, pages 67-72.
5. When the Spirit's Fire Swept Korea by Jonathan Goforth, Zondervan Publishing House 1943, Timothy Conjurske 1994, page 9.
6. The Korean Pentecost & The Sufferings Which Followed by William Blair and Bruce Hunt, The Banner of Truth Trust, 1977, pages 72-74.
7. www.sarang.org.
8. www.sarang.org.
9. www.english.sarang.org/again_1907.asp.
10. When the Spirit's Fire Swept Korea by Jonathan Goforth, Zondervan Publishing House 1943, Timothy Conjurske 1994, pages 12-13.
11. www.byfaith.co.uk/paulkorea.htm.
12. Various facts translated by a friend from Korean websites.
13. www.pust.kr.

Chapter Thirteen
1. Mighty Moments by Lionel B. Fletcher, Religious Tract Society, undated, circa 1931, pages 75-84 and 92-94.

2. www.ReesHowells.co.uk and *Rees Howells Intercessor* by Norman Grubb, Lutterworth Press, 1952, pages 159-166.
3. *Can Africa Be won* by W. J. W. Roome, A. &. C. Black, LTD, 1927, pages 7-8, 42, 82 and 160.
4. *The Revival We Need* by Oswald J. Smith, Marshall, Morgan & Scott, 1940, pages 105-109. And *Always Abounding, An Intimate Sketch of Oswald J. Smith of Toronto by* J. Edwin Orr, Marshall, Morgan & Scott, 1948, pages 68-72.
5. *Always Abounding – An intimate Sketch of Oswald J. Smith of Toronto*, by J. Edwin Orr, Marshall, Morgan & Scott, LTD, 1940, 1948, page 68.

Chapter Fourteen
1. *The Revival We Need* by Oswald J. Smith, Marshall, Morgan & Scott, 1940, pages 109-112. *An Intimate Sketch of Oswald J. Smith of Toronto by* J. Edwin Orr, Marshall, Morgan & Scott, 1948, pages, 14 and 72-75.
2. *The Shantung Revival* by Mary K. Crawford, The China Baptist Publication Society, 1933, pages 7-8.
3 *The Shantung Revival* by Mary K. Crawford, The China Baptist Publication Society, 1933, pages 34-35.
4. *Thirsting For God* by Eva Stuart Watt, Marshall, Morgan & Scott, Ltd., 1936, pages 145-150.
5. *The Promise Is To You! 10,000 Miles of Miracle to Palestine* by J. Edwin Orr, Marshall, Morgan & Scott, LTD, 1935, pages 109-113.

Chapter Fifteen
1. *This Is The Victory 10,000 Miles of Miracle in America* by J. Edwin Orr, Marshall, Morgan & Scott, LTD, 1936, pages 100-101 and 110.
2. *All Your Need 10,000 Miles of Miracle Through Australia and New Zealand* by J. Edwin Orr, Marshall, Morgan & Scott, LTD, undated, circa 1936, pages 15-17.
3. *Travelling Light – Bishop Oliver Allison of the Sudan Remembers*, published privately, 1983, pages 28-31.
4. *Revival An Enquiry* by Max Warren, SCM Press LTD, 1954, pages 50 and 52 and *Travelling Light – Bishop Oliver Allison of the Sudan Remembers*, published privately, 1983, page vii.
5. *A Pilgrim Church's Progress* by Oliver C. Allison, The Highway Press, 1966, p.41.
6. Ibid. pages 40-41.
7. *Travelling Light – Bishop Oliver Allison of the Sudan Remembers*, published privately, 1983, page 30.

Chapter Sixteen
1. *The Great Revival in Buenos Aires* by Louie W. Stokes, 1954.
2. www.jesus.org.uk/ja/mag_talkingto_silvoso.shtml.
3. *Revival Fires and Awakenings* by Mathew Backholer, ByFaith Media, 2006, pages 101-103. A revised and updated edition (2010) is now available.
4. www.maf.org/history#1950
5. Hevukhu Achumi Sema, unpublished report, cited in *From Head-Hunters To Church Planters* by Paul Hattaway, Piquant Editions Ltd, 2006, page 79.
6. *A Brief Account of the Nagaland Revivals and the Formation of Nagaland Christian Revival Church* by Neihulie Angami, NCRC, 1987, cited in *From Head-Hunters To Church Planters* by Paul Hattaway, Piquant, 2006, page 92.
7. *From Darkness to Light* by A Yanang Konyak, Christian Literature Centre, 1986 and *From Head-Hunters To Church Planters, An Amazing Spiritual Awakening in Nagaland* by Paul Hattaway, Piquant Editions Ltd, 2006.
8. *The Growth of the Baptist Church in Chakhesang Naga Tribe*, Pasedena: Fuller Theological Seminary, thesis, 1978 by Dozi Phuveyi, cited in *From Head-Hunters To Church Planters* by Paul Hattaway, Piquant Editions Ltd, 2006, page 85.

9. *AsiaLink Magazine* cited in *CWR Today* magazine, issue 2 Apr-Jun 2006, pages 8-9.
10. Hevukhu Achumi Sema, unpublished report, cited in *From Head-Hunters To Church Planters* by Paul Hattaway, Piquant Editions Ltd, 2006, pages 85-86.

Chapter Seventeen
1. *Tales of an African Intercessor* by Michael Howard, Out of Africa Publishers, 1998, pages 23 and 43-47. The book is available from www.kalibu.org
2. *A Pastor From Egypt* by Naiim Atef, Call of Hope, 2003, page 88.
3. www.cswusa.com/Countries/Eritrea.htm
4. www.cswusa.com/Countries/Eritrea.htm
5.www.openheaven.com/forums/forum_posts.asp?TID=30125&PN=1&TPN=1
6. see www.ReleaseInternational.org
7. www.sowers.org/test-tibet.html

Chapter Eighteen
1. *The Bible in the World, Volume VII 1911*, British and Foreign Bible Society, 1911, page 92.
2. *Fire From The North* DVD, A Justice and Liberty production for UCB TV, 2005, disk 2, Voices from the North, programme 3.

Chapter Nineteen
1. *Spread the Fire* magazine, Toronto Airport Christian Fellowship, Issue 3, May, 2006, page 4.
2. *The 700 Club, Newsletter*, Sept. 2006 and Operation World, 21st Century Edition by Patrick Johnson and Jason Mandryk, WEC International, 2001, page 131.
3. My thanks to Barkos Warjri for corresponding with me. And shillongrevival.com
4. www.mnnonline.org/article/13606

Chapter Twenty
1. *When the Spirit's Fire Swept Korea* by Jonathan Goforth, Zondervan Publishing House 1943, Timothy Conjurske 1994, page 12.
2. *The 59 Revival* by Ian R. K. Paisley, Ravenhill Free Presbyterian Church, 1958, 1969, page 81.
3. *Every Man a Bible Student* by Joe. E. Church, Scripture Union and C.S.S.M., 1938, 1961, preface and page 77.
4. *Revolution in World Mission* by K. P. Yohannan, gfa books, 1986, 1996, page 83.

Chapter Twenty-one
1. *The Price And Power of Revival* by Duncan Campbell, Sterling Printing Co., 1957, page 32.
2. *How Revival Comes, The Two National Broadcasts* by Colin C. Kerr, Henry E. Walter, London, 1942, pages 22-23.
3. *Holy Spirit, I Hunger For You* by Claudio Freidzon, Creation House, 1997, p.129.

Chapter Twenty-two
1. *Floods On Dry Grounds* by Eva Stuart Watt, Marshall, Morgan & Scott Ltd., 1939, 1943, page 26.
2. *Spurgeon on Revival* edited by Robert Backhouse, Kingsway, 1996, pp.28-29.
3. *The 59 Revival* by Ian R. K. Paisley, Ravenhill Free Presbyterian Church, 1958, 1969, pages 194 and 196.
4. *Revival Man, The Jock Troup Story* by George Mitchel, Christian Focus, 2002, pages 216-217.
5. *Sinners in the Hands of an Angry God*, Jonathan Edwards, Whitaker House, 1997, page 21.

6. *Floods On Dry Grounds* by Eva Stuart Watt, Marshall, Morgan & Scott Ltd., 1939, 1943, pages 119-120.

Chapter Twenty-three
1. *The Lewis Awakening 1949-1953* by Duncan Campbell, The Faith Mission, 1954, pages 15-16.
2. *How Revival Comes, The Two National Broadcasts* by Colin C. Kerr, Henry E. Walter, London, 1942, pages 16-17.
3. *Can God - ? 10,000 Miles of Miracle in Britain* by J. Edwin Orr, Marshall, Morgan & Scott, LTD, 1934, page 121.

Chapter Twenty-four
1. *Can We Pray For Revival?* - Brian H. Edwards, Evangelical Press, 2001, p. 201.
2. *Cataracts Of Revival* by G. J. Morgan, Marshall, Morgan & Scott, undated, p.82.
3. *The Bible in the World, Volume VII 1911*, British and Foreign Bible Society, 1911, page 87.
4. *Why Revival Tarries* by Leonard Ravenhill, Bethany House, a division of Baker Publishing Group, 1959, pages 59-60 and (extracts) page 152.
5. *Can God - ? 10,000 Miles of Miracle in Britain* by J. Edwin Orr, Marshall, Morgan & Scott, LTD, 1934, page 121.
6. *This Is The Victory 10,000 Miles of Miracle in America* by J. Edwin Orr, Marshall, Morgan & Scott, LTD, 1936, pages 127-128.
7. *All Your Need 10,000 Miles of Miracle Through Australia and New Zealand* by J. Edwin Orr, Marshall, Morgan & Scott, LTD, undated circa 1936, page 123.
8. *Prayer: Key to Revival* by Paul Y Cho with R. Witney Manzano, Word Publishing, 1984, page 158.

Chapter Twenty-five
1. *Narrative of Remarkable Conversion and Revival Incidents – Great Awakening of 1857-'8* by William C. Conant, Derby & Jackson, 1859, pages 282-283.
2. *A Box of Delights* – J. John & Mark Stibbe, Monarch Books, 2004, page 199.
3. *Where Lions Feed*, teaching tape from Brownsville Assembly of God.
4. *Charisma Reports The Brownsville Revival* by Marcia Ford, Creation House, 1997, (extracts), pages 120 and 124-125.
5. *Pandita Ramabai, India's Christian Pilgrim* by Basil Miller, World-wide Missions, undated, page 90.
6. Ibid. page 87 and *Pandita Ramabai, A Great Life in Indian Missions*, Helen S. Dyer, Pickering and Inglis, circa 1922, pages 103-104.
7. *Nine O'Clock in the Morning* by Dennis J. Bennett, Logos International, 1970, page 205.

Appendices B-E
1. *Thirsting For God* by Eva Stuart Watt, Marshall, Morgan & Scott, Ltd., 1936, pages 72 and 83.
2. *Word in Action* – Bible Society Magazine, winter 08, pages 7-8.
3. *A Light Shines in Central Asia, A Journey into the Tibetan Buddhist World* by Thomas Hale, William Carey Library, 2000, chapter 2.
4. *CWR Today* Issue 08 – Oct-Dec 2007, page 8.
5. www.christiantoday.com/news/middleeast/christian.revival.in.baghdad.as.iraqis.find.comfort.in.faith/419.htm.
6. www.assistnews.net/Stories/s06060123.htm.
7. *Times of Refreshing* by C. L Thomson, 1877, on CDR, page 52.

Appendix F
1. *Candidates in Waiting – A Manual of Home Preparation for Foreign Missionary Work* by Georgina A. Gollock, Church Missionary Society, 1892, 1898, page 88.

2. *The Life and Discoveries of David Livingstone – The Pictorial Edition* by J. Ewing Ritchie – Volume I, James Sangster and Co., c.1876, pages 427 and 429.
3. *India Awakening* by Sherwood Eddy, Missionary Education Movement, 1911, page 85.
4. Ibid. pages 99-100.
5. Ibid. page 98.
6. *A South India Diary* by J. E. Lessie Newbigin, SCM Press Ltd, 1951, pages 99-100 and 102-103.
7. Ibid. pages 88, 91-92.
8. *Revolution in World Missions* by K. P. Yohannan, GFA Books, 1986, 2004, pages 120-121.
9. *Batak Miracle, The Story of Damai, son of Sumatra* by Elizabeth Goldsmith, Overseas Missionary Fellowship, 1967, pages vii, 29, 32, 49, 53, 55 and 58 and *God Can Be Trusted* by Elizabeth Goldsmith, OM Publishing, 1984, 1993, pages 192-198.
10. *Batak Miracle, The Story of Damai, son of Sumatra* by Elizabeth Goldsmith, Overseas Missionary Fellowship, 1967, page vii.

Appendix G-H
1. *India Awakening* by Sherwood Eddy, Missionary Education Movement, 1911, pages 12-14, 98, 104, 123, 127 and 136.
2. Ibid. pages 10, 141, 143, 146 and 148-150.

End Quote
1. J. Taylor Smith – Everbody's Bishop by Maurice Whitlow, The Lutterworth Press, 1938, pages 33 and 37.

www.ByFaith.co.uk

www.RevivalNow.co.uk

www.MissionsNow.co.uk

www.GloryNow.co.uk - www.RevivalFire.co.uk

www.AwakeNow.co.uk - www.ReesHowells.co.uk

www.ProphecyNow.co.uk - www.ByFaithBooks.co.uk

www.ByFaithTV.co.uk - www.ByFaithDVDs.co.uk

www.ByFaithMedia.co.uk

www.UKPRAY.co.uk

www.GoPray.co.uk

www.xfaith.co.uk

ByFaith Books and DVDs

Revival Fires and Awakenings – *Thirty-Six Visitations of the Holy Spirit, A Call to Holiness, Prayer and Intercession for the Nations*, by Mathew Backholer. Whilst each revival is different, the author reveals the common characteristics and recurring experiences that come to the fore during four centuries of revivals and awakenings. The heaven-sent blessing of conversions, physical phenomena and deliverance, alongside teaching on prayer and intercession. Featuring 36 accounts of revivals and awakenings in eighteen countries from six continents. 2009 edition – Twenty-Two chapters.

Understanding Revival and *Addressing the Issues it Provokes* by Mathew Backholer. Revival is an amazing outpouring of the Holy Spirit but history records that many who have prayed for revival have rejected it when it came because they misunderstood the workings of the Holy Spirit and only wanted God to bless the Church on their terms. During times of heavenly visitations, there are Divine paradoxes and in the midst of God's dynamic, the devil will come to infiltrate and imitate so let us understand revival so that we do not reject it when He comes or bring the work of God into disrepute. 2009 edition – Thirty-one chapters.

Great Christian Revivals on DVD is an inspirational and uplifting account of some of the greatest revivals in church history. Filmed in England, Wales and Scotland and drawing upon archive information, the stories of the Welsh Revival (1904-1905), the Hebridean Revival (1949-1952) and the Evangelical Revival (1739-1791) are brought to life in this moving documentary. Using computer animation, historic photos and depictions, the events of the past are weaved into the present, as the old and new are blended together to bring these stories to life. 2009 – 72 minutes.

Revival Fire – *150 Years of Revivals* – *Spiritual Awakenings and Moves of the Holy Spirit* by Mathew Backholer documents in detail twelve revivals from ten countries on five continents. In every account, there are valuable lessons that can be learnt, alongside educational and inspiring conclusions that can be drawn from each historical account. 2010 edition – Fourteen chapters.

How to Plan, Prepare and Successfully Complete your Short-term Mission by Mathew Backholer is for volunteers, churches, independent STM teams and mission organisations. It is the ultimate guide to missions. Essential for individuals, leaders, teams or those planning a Christian gap year. It is the why, where and when of STMs. From his many adventures in over thirty-five nations, Mathew reveals how to plan well, avoid the pitfalls and successfully complete your STM! 2010 – Forty-eight chapters.

ByFaith – World Mission DVD is a cutting edge and compelling reality TV documentary that shows the real experience of a backpacking style Christian short-term mission in Asia, Europe and North Africa. With no scripts, no safety net and no easy way out, Paul and Mathew Backholer shoot through fourteen nations, in an 85-minute real-life documentary, which was filmed over three years. *ByFaith – World Mission* is perfect for an evening of global adventure and is the very best of ByFaith TV – season one. 2008.

How Christianity Made the Modern World by Paul Backholer. Christianity is the greatest reforming force that the world has ever known, yet its legacy is seldom comprehended. But now using personal observations from his research in over thirty-five nations, the author brings this legacy alive by revealing how Christianity helped create the path that led to Western liberty and laid the foundations of the modern world. 2009 – Thirty-seven chapters.

The Exodus Evidence In Pictures – The Bible's Exodus: The Hunt for Ancient Israel in Egypt, the Red Sea, the Exodus Route and Mount Sinai by Paul Backholer. The search for archaeological data to validate the biblical account of Joseph, Moses and the Hebrew Exodus from ancient Egypt. 2010, 100+ colour photos.

ByFaith – In Search of the Exodus on DVD. A three-thousand year old mystery will come alive as the epic tale of the biblical exodus will be tested and tried on the walls of Egyptian tombs and temples. Mathew and Paul Backholer search through ancient relics to find the evidence for the biblical exodus account. 2010.

Mission Preparation Training by Mathew Backholer covers 29 topics in 35 lessons. The book will aid the reader to discern the voice of God, find His will and direction and how to implement and prepare for the call on their life as part of the Great Commission. Covering the various aspects and approaches which can be used in evangelism, practical discipleship and how Christians can enter into the fullness of God, by being set free and delivered from past bondages and afflictions; (in practical hands-on ministry) being made whole in body, soul and spirit, whilst being built up in the most holy faith. Also beneficial for everyday discipleship.

www.ByFaithBooks.co.uk – www.ByFaithDVDs.co.uk

Lightning Source UK Ltd.
Milton Keynes UK
20 May 2010

154476UK00002B/1/P